USING PYTHON FOR ADVANCED EXCEL AUTOMATION

Hayden Van Der Post

Reactive Publishing

CONTENTS

PREFACE

Welcome to a transformative journey where the mundane meets the magnificent—where your spreadsheets become dynamic powerhouses fueled by the versatility of Python. Whether you've been wrestling with repetitive Excel tasks, seeking ways to boost productivity, or dreaming of harnessing data to drive strategic decisions, this book promises to be the catalyst for your next big leap.

Imagine this: you're sitting in your office or home workspace, surrounded by mountains of data in Excel files, yet you're still stuck manually crunching numbers and formatting reports. Now, picture a world where a few lines of code not only automate these tasks but also unlock insights hidden deep within your data. This guide is your passport to that world—a place where Python's power converges with Excel's familiarity to redefine what's possible in automation.

Using Python for Advanced Excel Automation: A Comprehensive Guide is designed with you in mind—whether you are a business analyst, a finance professional, a data enthusiast, or an IT specialist looking to merge technical skills with everyday operational needs. You don't need to be a seasoned programmer or an Excel wizard to benefit from this book. We start with the basics, gradually building your skill set until you're well-versed in advanced data manipulation, report generation, dashboard creation, and beyond.

In this book, you'll discover how Python can revolutionize the way you interact with Excel. Each chapter is meticulously structured to guide you through setting up your Python environment, automating mundane tasks, integrating with powerful libraries like Pandas, OpenPyXL, and XlsxWriter, and even bridging the gap between Python and Excel VBA. You'll learn not only to solve immediate challenges but also to envision innovative processes that will forever change your approach to data work. From crafting robust, error-proof scripts to designing aesthetically pleasing dashboards and advanced reports, you'll find real-world examples and thoughtful case studies that review both successes and lessons learned along the way.

But beyond technical proficiency, this book is about mindset—a call to embrace automation as a means to reclaim your time and ignite creativity. The skills you acquire here are not merely tools; they are investments in your professional growth and personal empowerment. By freeing yourself from repetitive tasks, you can focus on analysis, strategy, and the higher-impact decisions that drive success in any organization.

Every chapter is designed to be both a learning opportunity and a practical guide. We will walk you through essential topics like setting up your environment, ensuring data security, integrating databases, and much more, always with the aim of demystifying advanced concepts and providing step-by-step instructions that lead to tangible results. Whether you are just starting or looking to refine your existing skills, you will find this journey both engaging and rewarding.

As you embark on this adventure, remember that every script you write is a step toward a more efficient, creative, and insightful way of working. Let this book be the spark that ignites your passion for innovation—a bridge to a future where tedious tasks are eliminated, and your potential is fully unleashed.

Here's to your journey in mastering the art of Excel automation with Python—may every page inspire a breakthrough that transforms not just your work, but your entire professional outlook.

Welcome to a new era of productivity. Enjoy the ride!

INTRODUCTION

I n the world of data management and analysis, automation is revolutionizing traditional workflows. The combination of Python and Excel offers a unique opportunity to enhance both efficiency and accuracy, transforming repetitive tasks into manageable processes and enabling insightful analyses. This book, "Using Python for Advanced Excel Automation," serves as your comprehensive guide to leveraging this powerful partnership.

Consider the countless hours often spent on manual data entry, report generation, and complex calculations within Excel. Now, envision automating these processes with Python —a programming language celebrated for its versatility and seamless integration. This way, you can reduce those hours to mere minutes, allowing you to concentrate on strategic decision-making instead of mundane tasks.

The advantages of automation go beyond simply accelerating workflows. They pave the way for deeper insights through advanced data manipulation techniques that traditional Excel functions may not support effectively. With Python libraries like Pandas and OpenPyXL, you'll gain access to sophisticated functionalities that significantly enhance your Excel capabilities. Armed with these tools, you'll be well-equipped to handle large datasets, conduct intricate analyses, and present findings in visually engaging formats.

Many professionals have already embraced this shift. Take Sarah, for instance, a financial analyst who faced intense pressure to deliver accurate quarterly reports on tight deadlines. By integrating Python into her workflow, she automated the extraction of data from various sources and streamlined her reporting process. What once took days now required only hours, allowing her to increase accuracy while providing insightful analyses that impressed her stakeholders.

As you embark on this journey, you'll find actionable steps designed not just to introduce you to Python but also to deepen your understanding of how it can be seamlessly integrated with Excel. Each chapter builds upon the last, ensuring a cohesive learning experience that gradually expands your skill set without overwhelming you.

This book is crafted for anyone eager to boost productivity through automation—whether you're an experienced finance professional or an aspiring analyst looking to enter the field. The content caters to various skill levels and backgrounds while emphasizing practical applications over theoretical jargon.

As we explore the capabilities of Python for automating Excel tasks together, you'll find that this journey is about more than just acquiring new skills; it's also about shifting mindsets. Embracing technology often requires overcoming resistance—both personally and within work environments where established practices are deeply rooted. However, with determination and effective strategies for demonstrating the value of automation, you'll not only adapt but thrive in this evolving landscape.

Your commitment to mastering these skills will distinguish you in your field—empowering you not just as an employee but as an innovator capable of driving change within your organization. While challenges may arise along the way, remember that each obstacle presents an opportunity for growth.

Welcome aboard! Prepare for a transformative experience where each page brings you closer to mastering Python-powered Excel automation—a journey filled with opportunities for both professional mastery and fulfillment. Let's dive into this realm where efficiency meets insight and discover how automation can unlock new possibilities for you.

- **Purpose of the book**

Automation in data management is more than just a trend; it represents a critical evolution for professionals navigating the complexities of today's business landscape. This book, "Using Python for Advanced Excel Automation," is designed to equip you with the tools, knowledge, and confidence to harness Python's capabilities and streamline your Excel workflows effectively.

Consider the routine task of compiling data from multiple spreadsheets. This often requires meticulous attention and can be incredibly time-consuming. By automating this process, you can not only relieve yourself of this burden but also reduce the risk of human error. We will guide you through using Python libraries like Pandas and OpenPyXL to transform these tedious tasks into efficient operations that significantly boost your productivity.

The benefits of this automation extend beyond mere time savings. Learning to integrate Python with Excel unlocks advanced data manipulation techniques that surpass Excel's standalone capabilities. For example, filtering and aggregating large datasets becomes seamless when executed through Python scripts, leading to deeper insights that can inform strategic decisions and drive positive business outcomes.

Throughout this book, real-world examples will illustrate how professionals have successfully implemented these techniques. Take Mark, a marketing analyst who struggled to analyze customer feedback from diverse sources. By automating his data aggregation process with Python scripts within Excel, he transformed scattered insights into cohesive reports that guided his team's marketing strategies —ultimately saving time and enhancing clarity in their presentations.

Each chapter builds on the previous one, gradually guiding you from foundational concepts to more advanced topics —from reading complex datasets to automating report generation. This structured approach ensures that you develop a solid understanding before tackling sophisticated applications, allowing you to connect ideas naturally without feeling overwhelmed.

What sets this guide apart is its focus on practical insights tailored for professionals across various industries. Whether you're an experienced finance expert or just starting your career in data analysis, you will find relevant applications for your field. The hands-on exercises provided will enable you to practice and refine your skills in real-world scenarios.

Adopting new technologies can sometimes provoke apprehension; many professionals face resistance when trying to introduce automation within their teams or organizations. This book addresses those concerns directly by equipping you with strategies to demonstrate the value of automation to colleagues who may be hesitant about change. By fostering thoughtful engagement and showcasing tangible benefits, you can create an environment where innovation thrives rather than stagnates.

In the end, your journey through this book is about more than mastering technical skills; it's about cultivating a mindset geared towards continuous improvement and adaptability in an ever-evolving workplace landscape. Each chapter serves as a stepping stone toward positioning yourself as an innovator —someone who effectively leverages technology to enhance efficiency and drive results.

As we embark on this exploration together, prepare yourself for transformative insights that will arm you with the practical tools essential for success in today's fast-paced business world. Your commitment to learning will not only elevate your own capabilities but also positively influence those around you.

The path ahead is filled with opportunities for growth and innovation; embrace it wholeheartedly as we delve deep into leveraging Python for advanced Excel automation!

- **Who this book is for**

Understanding who can benefit from "Using Python for Advanced Excel Automation" is essential for maximizing the value this book offers. This guide isn't just for programmers or data scientists; it's designed for professionals across various sectors who aim to enhance their productivity and efficiency through automation.

If you're an analyst in finance, marketing, or operations, your role likely involves sifting through data and generating reports. You may spend hours managing spreadsheets, gathering information from multiple sources, and ensuring accuracy. The repetitive nature of these tasks can be draining, but this book provides practical methods to automate such processes, freeing up your time for more strategic activities. Imagine transforming a multi-step reporting process into a one-click operation—this is where Python becomes invaluable.

Project managers will also find immense value in these pages. As you juggle numerous tasks and coordinate with different teams, automating project tracking and reporting can significantly streamline workflows. By utilizing Python to pull real-time data from Excel, you can provide updates without constant manual input, allowing you to respond swiftly to changes and make informed decisions based on up-to-date information.

Educators and trainers involved in teaching or developing course materials will discover this book to be an essential resource as well. Automating grading processes or compiling feedback from students using Excel can enhance your teaching effectiveness, saving time that could be better spent on student engagement. The skills acquired from this guide can fundamentally reshape how educational data is handled.

Even if you're just starting your career in data analysis, the content here will equip you with foundational skills that are highly sought after in today's job market. You'll learn not only how to manipulate and analyze data but also how to present it effectively using automation tools that set you apart from your peers. Developing proficiency in integrating Python with Excel will give you a competitive edge when applying for roles that demand both analytical skills and technical know-how.

Team leaders aiming to drive efficiency within their departments will find actionable insights throughout this guide. You'll learn how to introduce automation gradually within your team—showing colleagues the benefits firsthand can foster an environment of innovation. Sharing success stories of early adopters within your organization reinforces the value of embracing new technologies.

This book emphasizes hands-on practice as well; each chapter includes real-world scenarios that reflect challenges professionals face daily. You won't merely read about concepts —you'll engage with them through exercises designed to reinforce learning and ensure mastery of the material.

To illustrate the impact of these techniques, consider Sarah, a human resources manager tasked with processing employee data for performance reviews. By leveraging Python scripts alongside Excel functionalities she learned in this book, Sarah automated her report generation process from weeks down to mere hours. This not only improved her accuracy but also significantly enhanced her ability to provide timely feedback —a crucial factor in employee satisfaction and retention.

The practical approach ensures that regardless of your current level of technical expertise—whether novice or experienced— you'll find insights tailored specifically for you. By consistently applying these skills, you'll cultivate a deeper understanding of both Excel and Python while enhancing your ability to tackle complex datasets efficiently.

As we delve deeper into automation techniques, remember that each section builds upon foundational concepts introduced in earlier chapters. This structure ensures that readers develop confidence as they navigate more advanced topics without feeling lost or overwhelmed.

In the end, the goal of this book is clear: to empower professionals across industries with tools that not only lead to individual success but also foster teamwork and collaborative innovation within organizations. Embrace the journey ahead; each step you take brings you closer to mastering the art of automation through Python and Excel!

- **Overview of Python and Excel**

Python and Excel form a powerful partnership that opens up a world of possibilities for automating routine tasks and boosting productivity. By understanding how these two tools work together, you can transform your approach to data management, streamline workflows, and ultimately achieve better results.

At the heart of this collaboration is Python, a versatile programming language celebrated for its simplicity and readability. This accessibility makes it an excellent choice not just for experienced developers, but also for professionals who may not have a deep technical background. With a rich ecosystem of libraries tailored for data manipulation—like

Pandas and OpenPyXL—Python enables users to efficiently process and analyze large datasets. Its capability to automate complex operations means you can tackle repetitive tasks in Excel programmatically, freeing you from the drudgery of manual input.

Excel, in contrast, is a robust spreadsheet application widely used across industries for data organization, analysis, and visualization. Its prevalence in business settings makes it indispensable for many professionals. However, as data volumes increase and reporting demands rise, relying solely on Excel's built-in features can become unwieldy. Integrating Python addresses these challenges by allowing users to harness the strengths of both platforms, thus simplifying processes that would otherwise require significant effort.

Consider how Python can enhance your Excel experience. Take this example, instead of spending hours manually updating weekly sales reports, a Python script can automatically gather data from various sources—such as databases or online APIs—aggregate the information, perform necessary calculations, and generate an updated Excel file ready for distribution. This not only saves time but also minimizes the risk of human error during reporting.

Additionally, combining Python with Excel enables advanced analytical capabilities that go beyond traditional spreadsheet functions. You can implement machine learning algorithms or conduct sophisticated statistical analyses directly from Python scripts and then write the results back into Excel for further examination or presentation. This synergy not only enhances individual productivity but also fosters collaboration within teams by providing standardized methods for data handling.

To illustrate this point, let's say you need to analyze customer feedback collected through surveys stored in an Excel sheet. Using Python's Pandas library can greatly simplify this task.

After importing your data into a DataFrame with just a few lines of code, you can easily perform sentiment analysis to assess overall customer satisfaction levels.

Here's how you could set up this analysis:

```python
import pandas as pd
from textblob import TextBlob

\#\# Load the feedback data from an Excel file
df = pd.read_excel('customer_feedback.xlsx')

\#\# Define a function to analyze sentiment
def analyze_sentiment(feedback):
    return TextBlob(feedback).sentiment.polarity

\#\# Apply sentiment analysis to the feedback column
df['Sentiment'] = df['Feedback'].apply(analyze_sentiment)

\#\# Save the results back to Excel
df.to_excel('feedback_analysis.xlsx', index=False)
```

In this example, we read customer feedback from an Excel file, analyze each entry's sentiment using TextBlob—a natural language processing library—and write the enriched data back into a new Excel file. Such automation provides valuable insights without the manual effort typically involved in qualitative analysis.

The true advantage of integrating Python with Excel lies not only in increased efficiency; it encourages a complete rethinking of how you approach challenges. Each time you implement automation, you're not just saving time; you're empowering yourself to focus on strategic decisions rather than routine tasks.

As you explore this guide, you'll learn how to leverage the powerful synergy between Python and Excel in various contexts—ranging from advanced reporting techniques to real-time data manipulation. Each chapter will provide practical examples that showcase the transformative impact of this partnership across different industries and job functions.

By embracing these tools, you'll acquire skills that are increasingly valuable in today's job market—skills that allow for greater adaptability in addressing challenges and innovating processes within your organization. Mastering the integration of Python with Excel positions you as a leader capable of driving meaningful change in your workplace.

- **Benefits of Python in Excel automation**

Combining Python and Excel creates a powerful toolkit that significantly enhances your ability to automate tasks and analyze data with precision. This synergy allows professionals to streamline workflows and elevate the quality of their outputs in ways that manual processes simply cannot match.

A key advantage of using Python alongside Excel is the remarkable efficiency it brings to data handling. When working with large datasets, relying solely on Excel can become cumbersome and time-consuming. In contrast, Python, equipped with robust libraries like Pandas, enables efficient data manipulation. With just a few lines of code, you can filter, group, and aggregate data, significantly reducing the time spent on repetitive tasks and allowing you to focus on analysis and decision-making.

Take this example, consider managing a financial portfolio where tracking asset performance is essential. Rather than manually updating an Excel spreadsheet each day, you can use Python to automate the process of pulling market data from APIs or databases. A straightforward script could retrieve the latest stock prices, calculate daily returns, and update your Excel file without any manual effort. This not only accelerates the process but also ensures your data remains current and accurate.

Here's an example of how this automation can be accomplished:

```python
import pandas as pd

import requests


\#\# Function to fetch stock prices from a hypothetical API

def fetch_stock_data(ticker):

response    =    requests.get(f'https://api.example.com/stocks/ticker')

return response.json()['latest_price']


\#\# List of stock tickers

stocks = ['AAPL', 'MSFT', 'GOOGL']


\#\# Create an empty DataFrame

stock_data = pd.DataFrame(columns=['Ticker', 'Price'])
```

\#\# Fetch prices for each stock

for stock in stocks:

price = fetch_stock_data(stock)

stock_data = stock_data.append('Ticker': stock, 'Price': price, ignore_index=True)

\#\# Save the data into an Excel file

stock_data.to_excel('stock_prices.xlsx', index=False)

` ` `

In this script, the latest prices for selected stocks are retrieved from an API and populated into an Excel sheet. Such automation not only saves valuable hours each week but also minimizes errors that can arise from manual data entry.

And, Python's analytical capabilities extend far beyond basic calculations available in Excel. For predictive modeling or complex statistical analyses, libraries like Scikit-learn or Statsmodels can be seamlessly integrated with your Excel data. Once your analysis is complete, you can easily export the results back into Excel for reporting or visualization purposes.

For example, if you're interested in forecasting sales based on historical trends stored in an Excel sheet, you can read this data into Python using Pandas, apply a linear regression model with Scikit-learn, and write the forecasted values back into your original workbook:

` ` `python

import pandas as pd

from sklearn.linear_model import LinearRegression

```
\#\# Load sales data from an Excel file
df = pd.read_excel('sales_data.xlsx')

\#\# Prepare features (independent variable) and target (dependent variable)
X = df[['Month']].values.reshape(-1, 1) \# Months as feature
y = df['Sales'].values \# Sales figures

\#\# Create a linear regression model
model = LinearRegression()
model.fit(X, y)

\#\# Predict future sales (e.g., for months 13-15)
future_months = [[13], [14], [15]]
predictions = model.predict(future_months)

\#\# Write predictions back to Excel
prediction_df = pd.DataFrame(predictions, columns=['Predicted Sales'])
prediction_df.to_excel('sales_forecast.xlsx', index=False)
` ` `
```

This method not only enhances forecasting accuracy but also enables a visual representation of predicted sales trends when plotted in Excel.

Integrating Python with Excel encourages a shift towards

data-driven decision-making. It transforms automation from a mere tool for efficiency into a pathway for innovation and improved business intelligence. Each step toward mastery opens new possibilities—changing how you engage with data and positioning you as a forward-thinking professional ready to tackle evolving challenges.

Throughout this guide, you will learn how to implement advanced automation strategies tailored to your unique workflows. The actionable insights provided will empower you to create innovative solutions that enhance productivity and place you at the forefront of your industry's technological evolution.

- **Structure of the book**

This book is carefully structured to guide you on your journey to mastering Python for Excel automation, ensuring that each concept builds upon the previous one. Each chapter unfolds systematically, transitioning from fundamental principles to advanced techniques, making the material both digestible and practical.

We begin with the foundational concepts of Python and Excel, introducing essential libraries that enable automation. The early chapters focus on setting up practical tools—installing necessary software, understanding basic Python syntax relevant to Excel tasks, and familiarizing yourself with different Excel file types. This groundwork is vital as it equips you with the skills needed for effective data manipulation as we progress into more complex topics.

As you advance, you'll delve into sophisticated data manipulation techniques using Pandas. Here, we focus on efficiently handling large datasets while applying various methods for cleaning and transforming data. Practical examples will demonstrate how to filter, sort, and aggregate data seamlessly, showcasing not just functionality but also how these techniques can solve real-world challenges you may encounter in your work.

Next, we turn our attention to scripting with OpenPyXL and XlsxWriter. These chapters provide hands-on experience in creating new workbooks, programmatically writing data, formatting cells, and even generating charts directly through Python scripts. Detailed walkthroughs will help you replicate these tasks easily. Take this example, automating report generation by pulling data from multiple sources will become a straightforward process rather than a daunting task.

Integration is another key focus of our exploration. We discuss how Python can enhance existing VBA (Visual Basic for Applications) workflows, allowing you to leverage both technologies for greater productivity. You'll learn to call Python scripts from within Excel and pass data seamlessly between the two environments. Real-world scenarios will illustrate this synergy; whether it's automating routine data updates or enhancing existing VBA macros with Python's robust libraries, the potential for increased efficiency is significant.

The discussion broadens to include database connectivity and web scraping techniques. Connecting Python to SQL databases or extracting data from web pages can greatly enhance your reporting capabilities. We'll provide scripts that enable you to retrieve and manipulate external data sources before incorporating them into your Excel environment for analysis or reporting.

Data visualization is another critical aspect of effective automation. In dedicated sections, we explore how to utilize libraries like Matplotlib and Seaborn alongside Excel's native functionalities to create compelling visual representations of your insights. Understanding best practices in visualization ensures that your findings are not only accurate but also engaging for stakeholders.

As you navigate through the complexities of reporting and

dashboard creation, you'll discover actionable strategies for designing comprehensive reports that incorporate advanced formatting techniques and interactivity—all facilitated by Python automation. This enhances the user experience while solidifying your reputation as a professional adept at leveraging technology for greater impact.

In the latter chapters, we address optimization strategies necessary for handling larger datasets or more complex processes efficiently. We identify common performance bottlenecks alongside solutions like batch processing and parallel processing techniques, ensuring your scripts run smoothly without sacrificing accuracy or detail.

Finally, we emphasize the importance of error handling and security considerations in automation projects. Through case studies illustrating both successful implementations and potential pitfalls encountered along the way, you'll gain invaluable insights into building robust systems while maintaining compliance with security standards.

The book culminates in practical case studies showcasing diverse applications of Python-Excel integration across various industries—from finance to healthcare—helping you understand where these principles can be applied in real-world scenarios. Each case study reinforces concepts learned throughout the book while highlighting their relevance in professional settings.

With this structured approach, you'll not only master technical skills but also cultivate a mindset geared toward innovation and continuous improvement in your data management practices. Prepare yourself for a transformative journey as you harness the power of Python within Excel; each chapter is designed to empower you with knowledge that leads directly to increased efficiency and effectiveness in your work life.

- **How to get the most out of this book**

To maximize your experience with "Using Python for Advanced Excel Automation," it's essential to fully engage with the material. Start by adopting a hands-on approach: rather than just reading, actively interact with the content. As you come across code snippets and practical examples, replicate them in your own Python environment. This not only reinforces your understanding but also gives you the opportunity to experiment with modifications that cater to your specific needs.

The book is structured in a way that each chapter builds upon the concepts introduced earlier, making it crucial to thoroughly understand foundational topics before progressing to more complex ones. For example, when exploring data manipulation techniques using Pandas, ensure you're comfortable with basic operations like reading and writing data before diving into advanced cleaning or aggregation methods. This depth of understanding helps you grasp the "why" and "how" behind each technique rather than merely following instructions.

As you explore libraries such as OpenPyXL and XlsxWriter, don't hesitate to go beyond the provided examples. If an example shows how to write data into cells, think about other formats or styles that could be beneficial for your use case. Experimenting with these options will deepen your understanding of how Python interacts with Excel and open up new avenues for automation.

Throughout your journey, keep a coding journal. Documenting the challenges you face and the solutions you find serves as a valuable reference for future projects. If a particular script resolves a recurring issue in your workflow, make a note of its function and any adjustments you've made. This practice not only solidifies your learning but also creates a personalized resource to revisit as needed.

Collaboration can also greatly enhance your learning

experience. Engaging with peers or online communities focused on Python and Excel can provide additional insights and support as you tackle complex topics. Discussing challenges or sharing successes fosters an environment where ideas thrive and solutions emerge collectively.

When applying the concepts from this book to real-world projects, start small. Tackle one automation task at a time to avoid feeling overwhelmed by multiple objectives. Take this example, if you've learned how to automate report generation, concentrate on successfully implementing that before moving on to more intricate tasks like creating interactive dashboards or integrating databases.

Maintain your curiosity about how Python capabilities intersect with Excel functionalities. Explore documentation beyond what's covered in this book; both Python's library references and Excel's help resources offer valuable insights into advanced features that can further enhance your automation efforts.

Consider undertaking mini-projects inspired by the case studies presented throughout the guide as you progress through each chapter. Whether it's creating an automated financial report similar to those discussed or designing a dashboard based on earlier data visualizations, these projects allow you to apply your skills practically while demonstrating the impact of what you've learned.

Finally, make it a habit to reflect regularly on your progress. This journey is not just about mastering technical skills; it's about transforming your approach to data management and analysis within Excel. By continuously assessing where you've been and where you're headed, you'll cultivate an innovative mindset that is essential for success in today's data-driven world.

By adopting this proactive approach to "Using Python for Advanced Excel Automation," you're positioning yourself not just to learn but to excel—becoming adept at harnessing technology's full potential in your professional sphere. The path ahead is filled with possibilities; embrace each step with enthusiasm as you develop newfound skills that will undoubtedly enhance your efficiency and effectiveness in your work life.

- **Prerequisites and assumptions**

To fully engage with "Using Python for Advanced Excel Automation," it's important to consider a few key prerequisites that will pave the way for your success. A fundamental understanding of Python programming is essential. Familiarity with core concepts such as variables, loops, functions, and data types will help you navigate more complex automation tasks. If you're unsure about these basics, resources like Codecademy or freeCodeCamp offer interactive lessons that can help build your confidence.

Once you have a grasp of Python fundamentals, the next step is to set up an environment where you can effectively run Python scripts. This usually involves configuring a local development environment using tools like Anaconda or installing Python directly from python.org. Both options allow you to create virtual environments, making it easier to manage dependencies without cluttering your system's global Python installation. This organized approach simplifies the management of libraries such as Pandas and OpenPyXL, which are central to our exploration of automation.

Equipping yourself with the necessary libraries is another important aspect of preparation. As you begin this journey, make sure to install key packages such as Pandas for data manipulation, OpenPyXL for working directly with Excel files, and XlsxWriter for advanced formatting capabilities. You can easily install these packages using pip—Python's package installer—by executing commands like pip install pandas openpyxl xlsxwriter in your command prompt or terminal.

Being comfortable with installing and importing libraries will save you time and reduce troubleshooting later on.

In addition to technical skills and setup, adopting a mindset geared toward experimentation will enhance your learning experience. Programming often involves troubleshooting and iterative improvements, so expect that not everything will work perfectly on the first try. As you work through examples in each chapter, think about how they might be applied in your own contexts or data scenarios. Embrace curiosity and creativity; for instance, if an example demonstrates creating a pivot table, consider how similar principles could be applied to different datasets you encounter.

A solid understanding of Excel itself is equally vital. Familiarize yourself with basic Excel functions—such as VLOOKUP, IF statements, and conditional formatting—and explore how these features can be automated using Python scripts. Knowing what Excel is capable of will help set realistic expectations for automation and identify tasks that could benefit from enhancement.

As we delve deeper into automation techniques later in the book, understanding how Python interacts with various Excel file formats (like .xlsx and .xlsm) will also prove valuable. Recognizing these distinctions will ensure smoother manipulation of files when implementing automated solutions.

In addition to technical prerequisites, cultivating problem-solving skills will significantly benefit your journey through this material. Approach challenges systematically by breaking them down into smaller components rather than tackling complex issues all at once. This method allows you to address errors without feeling overwhelmed.

Finally, keep an open mind about learning from others in the community. Engage with online forums such as Stack Overflow or dedicated Discord groups focused on Python and Excel automation; sharing experiences can enhance your understanding while offering fresh perspectives on overcoming obstacles.

By establishing these foundational prerequisites before diving into the rich content of this guide, you'll create an environment conducive to mastering Python and Excel automation—a skill set that can boost both your productivity and professional trajectory in increasingly data-driven fields. With this groundwork laid, you're now ready to transform your interactions with data through innovative automation solutions tailored specifically to your needs.

CHAPTER 1: GETTING STARTED WITH PYTHON AND EXCEL

Setting up your Python environment

To fully harness the power of Python for Excel automation, the first step is to create a well-organized Python environment. This foundation is essential for a smooth automation journey, as it allows you to explore and implement complex tasks with ease.

Start by downloading and installing Python from python.org if you haven't already done so. It's best to choose the latest stable release to ensure compatibility with essential libraries for your projects. During the installation, make sure to select the option that adds Python to your system's PATH. This step is crucial, as it enables you to run Python commands from any terminal or command prompt.

Once Python is installed, consider using Anaconda as an alternative method. Anaconda simplifies package management and deployment, making it particularly useful for data science applications. It comes pre-installed with many necessary libraries like NumPy and Pandas, which can save you time during setup. To get started, download the installer from the Anaconda website and follow the prompts; its user-friendly interface makes creating virtual environments straightforward.

Setting up virtual environments is not just a good practice; it effectively isolates project dependencies. For example, if you're working on two projects that require different library versions, virtual environments prevent conflicts between them. You can create a new environment in Anaconda Prompt or your terminal with the command conda create --name myenv python=3.x, where "myenv" can be any name you choose.

After establishing your environment, it's important to install several key libraries essential for Excel automation. The three most significant packages are Pandas, which excels in data manipulation; OpenPyXL, which allows you to read and write Excel files; and XlsxWriter, which provides advanced formatting capabilities. Installing these libraries is easy—just activate your environment and run:

```bash
pip install pandas openpyxl xlsxwriter
```

While this command sets up the necessary tools, understanding how each library interacts with Excel will enhance your ability to implement effective solutions later on. Take this example, Pandas is great for efficiently handling large datasets, while OpenPyXL gives you detailed control over Excel file formats.

As you set up these tools, consider how they relate to real-world scenarios where you'll apply automation techniques. For example, if you frequently generate monthly sales reports, automating data extraction and formatting with these libraries could save you significant time. Visualizing potential applications can spark creativity and foster problem-solving strategies as you progress through your learning.

Additionally, becoming comfortable with basic command-line operations will significantly streamline your workflow. Familiarize yourself with navigating directories and executing scripts in your terminal or command prompt. Mastering these fundamental skills will help prevent technical hurdles from disrupting your learning experience or slowing down productivity.

Alongside these technical preparations, cultivating a mindset geared toward experimentation is vital in programming. Embrace mistakes as valuable learning opportunities. Take this example, if an automated report generation script doesn't produce the expected results at first glance, use this chance to troubleshoot systematically—check for syntax errors or review your data inputs until clarity emerges.

It's also important to understand how Python interacts with different Excel formats such as .xlsx and .xlsm. Recognizing these distinctions will streamline file manipulation when implementing automated solutions later on.

Lastly, actively engaging with communities focused on Python and Excel automation—such as GitHub repositories or dedicated forums—can be invaluable. These platforms are excellent resources for troubleshooting common issues or discovering innovative applications of the techniques covered in this guide.

By laying a solid groundwork in establishing an effective Python environment while embracing a spirit of exploration and continuous learning, you're positioning yourself not just to automate tasks but also to innovate within your workflows. This structured approach will empower you to leverage technology in ways that enhance both efficiency and creativity throughout your career journey.

Installing necessary libraries (e.g., Pandas, OpenPyXL,

XlsxWriter)

Setting up your Python environment is just the starting point of your journey into Excel automation. To enhance your productivity, it's essential to install a few key libraries that will enable you to read, write, and manipulate Excel files with ease, setting the stage for more complex automation tasks in the future.

The first libraries you should consider are Pandas, OpenPyXL, and XlsxWriter. Each of these libraries plays a unique role that complements the others. Pandas is a powerful tool for data manipulation, capable of handling large datasets efficiently and simplifying the process of data analysis. OpenPyXL specializes in reading and writing Excel files, allowing you to work with existing spreadsheets or create new ones from scratch. On the other hand, XlsxWriter provides extensive formatting options, enabling you to design visually appealing reports that effectively convey information.

To get started with these libraries, open your terminal or Anaconda Prompt. If you're using Anaconda, you may already have some of these libraries pre-installed. For those using pip with standard Python installations, simply run the following command:

```bash
pip install pandas openpyxl xlsxwriter
```

This command installs all three libraries at once, saving you time and effort. Once installed, take a moment to explore each library's documentation; understanding their functionalities will empower you to apply them effectively in various scenarios.

Consider a situation where you're tasked with generating a monthly sales report. With Pandas, you can quickly import sales data from CSV files or databases and perform calculations

—such as summing totals or averaging figures—without getting bogged down in complex Excel formulas. Once the data is processed, OpenPyXL can be employed to write it back into an Excel file while ensuring everything is formatted correctly. Then, XlsxWriter can enhance your report further by adding charts or conditional formatting to highlight key metrics.

As you become more familiar with these libraries, practicing on sample datasets can greatly improve your learning experience. You might start by creating a simple script that uses OpenPyXL to read an Excel file and print its contents:

```python
import openpyxl

\#\# Load the workbook
workbook = openpyxl.load_workbook('sales_data.xlsx')

\#\# Select a worksheet
sheet = workbook.active

\#\# Print each row's values
for row in sheet.iter_rows(values_only=True):

print(row)
```

This straightforward script will help you understand how data is organized within an Excel file and prepare you for more advanced operations later on.

Another important aspect of working with these libraries is error handling. When automating tasks that involve multiple steps—such as reading from one file and writing into another

—issues may arise if something isn't formatted correctly or if expected data types aren't met. Implementing basic error handling can save you hours of frustration:

```python
try:

workbook = openpyxl.load_workbook('sales_data.xlsx')

except FileNotFoundError:

print("The specified file was not found.")
```

Such proactive measures will make your scripts more resilient as they grow in complexity.

Finally, don't underestimate the value of community engagement. Online forums like Stack Overflow and GitHub discussions offer invaluable insights from other users who have faced similar challenges. By participating in these communities, you'll not only find solutions but also share your own experiences—creating a cycle of knowledge sharing that benefits everyone involved.

By strategically installing these essential libraries and focusing on practical examples and real-world applications, you're laying a strong foundation for effective Excel automation using Python. This groundwork will be instrumental as you transition into more advanced techniques on your automation journey.

Understanding Python basics relevant to Excel

Understanding the basics of Python is essential for effectively utilizing its capabilities in Excel automation. Although Python's syntax may initially appear daunting, mastering a few fundamental concepts will enable you to interact effortlessly with Excel files. This foundation paves the way for tackling more complex tasks as you advance.

Begin by familiarizing yourself with Python's data types and structures, which are the backbone of any programming endeavor. Variables in Python can store various types of data, such as integers, floats, strings, and booleans. For example, if you want to represent sales figures in your Excel reports, you might define a variable like this:

```python
sales_total = 15000.75
```

This straightforward line establishes a floating-point number that can be utilized in calculations or reporting tasks later on. Additionally, getting comfortable with lists and dictionaries will greatly enhance your ability to manage data effectively. Lists allow you to group multiple items together, while dictionaries enable you to link keys with values—making them ideal for organizing datasets logically.

Here's how you might implement a list and dictionary in a practical scenario:

```python
sales_data = [15000.75, 23000.50, 18000.00] \# List of sales figures

monthly_sales =

January": 15000.75,

February": 23000.50,

March": 18000.00

  \# Dictionary mapping months to sales figures
```

In this context, lists and dictionaries offer flexible ways to handle your data before it interacts with Excel files.

Next, control flow structures like loops and conditional statements are crucial for executing tasks repeatedly or making decisions based on data conditions. Take this example, if you want to summarize monthly sales only when they exceed a certain threshold, you could use an if statement:

```python
for month, amount in monthly_sales.items():

if amount > 20000:

print(f"Sales in month exceeded target: \(amount:.2f")
```

This loop evaluates each month's sales against the target and prints relevant information when conditions are met.

Functions also play a vital role in structuring your code into reusable blocks. When automating tasks with Python, breaking down your script into functions can enhance both clarity and efficiency. For example:

```python
def calculate_average(sales):

return sum(sales) / len(sales)


average_sales = calculate_average(sales_data)

print(f"Average Sales: \)average_sales:.2f")
```

This function calculates the average of your sales figures—a common requirement for data analysis in reports.

Another important aspect is string manipulation, which is essential when working with text data in Excel files. Whether formatting headers or concatenating strings for improved readability, mastering these techniques will prove beneficial:

```python
header = "Monthly Sales Report

formatted_header = header.upper()

print(formatted_header)
```

Utilizing string methods like .upper() can significantly enhance the presentation quality of your reports.

Error handling is equally critical as it ensures your scripts run smoothly even when unexpected situations arise. By implementing try-except blocks, you can manage exceptions gracefully without crashing:

```python
try:

result = calculate_average(sales_data)

except ZeroDivisionError:

print("Sales data is empty; cannot calculate average.")
```

This simple approach to error handling safeguards against potential pitfalls, allowing you to maintain control over execution flow.

By understanding how these basic concepts interconnect, you'll be empowered as you start automating tasks within Excel using Python. It's not just about writing code; it's about applying it effectively in real-world scenarios—whether generating reports or performing complex analyses.

The path ahead offers rich opportunities for innovation and efficiency as you apply these foundational skills toward automating your Excel processes. Embrace this chance not only to learn Python but also to transform how you engage with data across your projects.

Introduction to Excel file types and compatibility

Excel is a powerful tool, and understanding its various file types and compatibility options can greatly enhance your automation efforts with Python. Excel primarily supports several file formats, each with unique features and limitations. Familiarity with these formats is essential for effective data manipulation and seamless integration between Python scripts and Excel workbooks.

The most commonly used format is the XLSX file, which serves as the default for newer versions of Excel. This format supports a wide range of features, including charts, pivot tables, and advanced formulas. When automating tasks in Python, libraries such as OpenPyXL or XlsxWriter make it easy to read from or write to XLSX files. For example, OpenPyXL allows you to access cell values, dynamically update them based on your analysis, and even create complex formatting directly within your Python scripts.

In contrast, the older XLS format may still be encountered in legacy systems or archived documents. While it provides similar functionalities to XLSX, it does not support newer Excel features and has a lower row limit—65,536 rows compared to over a million in XLSX. If your automation tasks involve interacting with legacy systems or files generated by older software versions, knowing how to handle both formats becomes crucial. The xlrd library in Python can effectively read from XLS files while also enabling you to convert them into more modern formats.

Another format that frequently comes into play is CSV (Comma-Separated Values). Unlike Excel's native formats, CSV files are plain text files that store tabular data without any formatting or complex features. Their simplicity and compatibility across various platforms make them a popular choice for data exchange. When working with CSV files in Python, the Pandas library excels; its read_csv function can quickly load large datasets into DataFrames for further analysis or manipulation. However, it's important to remember that saving back to CSV from Pandas or another library may result in the loss of specific Excel features like formulas or formatting since these are not supported in this basic text format.

Integrating these various formats into your workflow requires careful consideration of how data flows between them. Take this example, if you're pulling data from an external source —such as a database—and then exporting it to Excel for reporting purposes, using CSV as an intermediary step can be efficient. You might begin by exporting your database query results as a CSV file before reading that file back into a DataFrame for processing through Pandas. Finally, you can write the cleaned and manipulated data back into an Excel workbook.

Beyond merely knowing about different formats is understanding their implications for compatibility across various versions of Excel itself. Features available in one version may not be supported in another—especially when dealing with functions introduced in Office 365 or newer iterations of the software. Therefore, it's wise to test your automated solutions across different environments where they will be deployed.

This landscape of file types underscores the importance of flexibility and adaptability in your automation strategies. Effectively leveraging each format ensures that your solutions remain robust amid changes in software environments or organizational practices.

With this foundational understanding of file types and their compatibility considerations in Excel automation processes using Python, you're now better equipped to tackle real-world scenarios where selecting the right tool for each task is essential. This knowledge paves the way for deeper exploration into specific libraries designed to enhance your interaction with these various file types while streamlining task automation efficiently.

Basic operations with Excel using Python

Python's integration with Excel significantly boosts productivity and enhances the depth of your data analysis. By automating tasks in Excel, you can save countless hours that would otherwise be spent on manual data entry and manipulation. Once you become familiar with the various file formats and compatibility issues in Excel, you can effectively apply that knowledge to execute basic operations.

To get started, consider using OpenPyXL, one of the most popular libraries for interacting with Excel files, to read and write data. Take this example, if you have an Excel file containing sales data, you can automate the process of extracting this information into a Python script. Here's a simple example:

```python
import openpyxl

\#\# Load an existing workbook
workbook = openpyxl.load_workbook('sales_data.xlsx')

\#\# Select a specific sheet
sheet = workbook['Sales']

\#\# Read data from a specific cell
sales_value = sheet['B2'].value
```

```python
print(f'Sales Value: sales_value')
```

\#\# Write data to another cell

```python
sheet['C2'] = sales_value * 1.1 \# Increase sales value by 10%

workbook.save('updated_sales_data.xlsx')
```
` ` `

In this script, you open a workbook named sales_data.xlsx, retrieve the value from cell B2, increase it by 10%, and save the result to a new file. This example demonstrates how Python can streamline tasks that would otherwise be tedious and time-consuming.

Once you're comfortable with reading and writing data, you can enhance your reports by formatting cells programmatically with OpenPyXL. Proper formatting not only improves readability but also highlights critical data points. Here's how to apply basic formatting:

` ` `python

```python
from openpyxl.styles import Font
```

\#\# Set font style for headers

```python
header_font = Font(bold=True, color='FF0000')  \# Red bold font
```

\#\# Apply formatting to header row

```python
for cell in sheet[1]:  \# Assuming the first row contains headers
    cell.font = header_font
```

\#\# Save changes

workbook.save('formatted_sales_data.xlsx')

` ` `

This snippet formats all cells in the first row with bold red text, making the headers stand out in your reports.

After mastering data reading and writing, you can leverage Python to perform calculations directly within your script using Excel data. For example, if you want to calculate totals or averages from a range of cells, Python's capabilities combined with OpenPyXL facilitate these operations seamlessly.

Here's an example of calculating total sales across a range of rows:

```python
total_sales = 0
```

\#\# Assume sales are in column B starting from row 2

```
for row in range(2, sheet.max_row + 1):

total_sales += sheet[f'Brow'].value


print(f'Total Sales: total_sales')
```

` ` `

This loop iterates over each row in column B, accumulating the sales values into total_sales. The simplicity of this operation highlights how Python can eliminate repetitive calculations.

It's also crucial to handle errors effectively during automation. Anticipating issues such as missing values or incorrect data types helps safeguard your processes. Consider the following code:

```python
try:
```

```
for row in range(2, sheet.max_row + 1):

if isinstance(sheet[f'Brow'].value, (int, float)):

total_sales += sheet[f'Brow'].value

except Exception as e:

print(f'An error occurred: e')
```
` ` `

In this code, each value is checked for numeric type before being added to total_sales, preventing type errors that could disrupt your script's execution.

While these automation tasks improve efficiency, it's essential to adhere to best practices regarding organization and documentation within your code. Clear comments that explain the purpose of functions and critical sections will assist anyone who revisits or maintains the script later.

To further enhance your automation experience with Python and Excel, consider integrating libraries like Pandas for more robust data manipulation. Take this example, you can read data directly into a Pandas DataFrame from an Excel file:

` ` `python
```
import pandas as pd


df = pd.read_excel('sales_data.xlsx', sheet_name='Sales')

total_sales = df['Sales'].sum()

print(f'Total Sales (Pandas): total_sales')
```
` ` `

Using Pandas simplifies many operations, allowing for complex manipulations with fewer lines of code and enhancing clarity while performing advanced analyses.

Embracing these fundamental operations equips you with essential skills and opens doors to tackling more complex automation tasks in the future. This foundational capability is vital as you explore Python's extensive libraries and tools to transform your daily interactions with Excel files.

First script: Reading Excel files

Reading Excel files is a crucial step in automating your workflow with Python. By leveraging the right tools, you can efficiently extract, manipulate, and analyze data. One such tool, OpenPyXL, enables straightforward interaction with Excel files.

To begin reading an Excel file, you'll first need to load the workbook. Take this example, imagine you have a file named sales_data.xlsx that contains essential sales figures for your analysis. The initial task is to load this workbook and access the relevant sheet where your data is located. Here's how to do that:

```python
import openpyxl

\#\# Load an existing workbook
workbook = openpyxl.load_workbook('sales_data.xlsx')

\#\# Select the sheet named 'Sales'
sheet = workbook['Sales']
```

Now that you have access to the desired sheet, you can read data from specific cells. If you want to retrieve the sales value from cell B2, for example, you can do so with the following code:

```python
\#\# Read data from a specific cell
sales_value = sheet['B2'].value
print(f'Sales Value: sales_value')
```

This line of code fetches the value from cell B2 and prints it. If you decide to update this value, modifying the contents of any cell is easy, and you can save your changes with just a few additional lines:

```python
\#\# Increase sales value by 10%
sheet['C2'] = sales_value * 1.1


\#\# Save changes to a new file
workbook.save('updated_sales_data.xlsx')
```

In this snippet, the sales value is increased by 10% and written to cell C2 before saving the updated file as updated_sales_data.xlsx. Such simple modifications highlight how Python can significantly reduce manual effort.

Once you're comfortable with basic read and write operations, you can enhance your data presentation through formatting. Take this example, highlighting header rows can improve visibility:

```python
from openpyxl.styles import Font


\#\# Define font style for headers
```

```python
header_font = Font(bold=True, color='FF0000')  \# Bold red font
```

```python
\#\# Apply formatting to header row (assumed to be the first row)
for cell in sheet[1]:
    cell.font = header_font
```

```python
\#\# Save changes after formatting
workbook.save('formatted_sales_data.xlsx')
```
` ` `

This code modifies the font style of all cells in the first row to bold red, clearly indicating where the headers are located.

As you progress beyond simple modifications, you might want to perform calculations directly within your Python script using data pulled from Excel. For example, calculating total sales from a column is straightforward. If your sales figures are listed in column B starting from row 2, you can accomplish this with:

` ` `python

```python
total_sales = 0
```

```python
\#\# Sum sales values from column B
for row in range(2, sheet.max_row + 1):
    total_sales += sheet[f'Brow'].value
```

```python
print(f'Total Sales: total_sales')
```

` ` `

This loop iterates through each row of column B, summing up all sales values into total_sales. Automating such calculations not only saves time but also reduces errors associated with manual entry.

Error handling is another critical aspect when reading data from Excel. You may encounter non-numeric values or empty cells that could disrupt your calculations. To ensure your script remains robust against such issues, consider this approach:

` ` `python

try:

for row in range(2, sheet.max_row + 1):

if isinstance(sheet[f'Brow'].value, (int, float)):

total_sales += sheet[f'Brow'].value

except Exception as e:

print(f'An error occurred: e')

` ` `

By checking whether each value is numeric before adding it to total_sales, you prevent potential errors during execution. This practice enhances overall reliability and safeguards your calculations.

Documentation is essential for writing effective scripts. Clear comments explaining your code help both others and your future self understand what each part does at a glance. Consider incorporating comments throughout your script where necessary.

To take automation a step further, integrating libraries like Pandas provides advanced capabilities for data manipulation. Reading data directly into a Pandas DataFrame simplifies many operations:

```python
import pandas as pd

\#\# Load Excel file into a DataFrame
df = pd.read_excel('sales_data.xlsx', sheet_name='Sales')

\#\# Calculate total sales using Pandas
total_sales = df['Sales'].sum()
print(f'Total Sales (Pandas): total_sales')
```

Pandas offers powerful tools for data analysis with fewer lines of code compared to standard Python approaches, making complex manipulations much more manageable.

Mastering these basic operations equips you with essential skills for effectively automating processes with Python and Excel. With these tools at your disposal, you're well on your way to optimizing workflows and enhancing productivity through automation. As you gain confidence in reading and manipulating Excel files, you'll find yourself ready to tackle more complex tasks that will transform how you work with data even further.

Common file handling errors and troubleshooting

Handling files in Python, particularly when working with Excel, can be quite straightforward. However, it's common to encounter a variety of errors that warrant attention. By understanding these pitfalls and knowing how to troubleshoot them, you can significantly enhance your automation journey and save valuable time.

One prevalent issue involves file paths. If your script cannot locate the specified Excel file, it will raise a FileNotFoundError. This typically occurs due to an incorrect file path or if the file does not exist in the expected directory. To address this, make sure to provide the full path to your file or adjust the current working directory in your script. Here's a brief example:

```python
import os

\#\# Change working directory to where your Excel files are located
os.chdir('/path/to/your/excel/files')


\#\# Attempt to load workbook
try:
workbook = openpyxl.load_workbook('sales_data.xlsx')
except FileNotFoundError:
print("The specified file was not found. Please check the path.")
```

This simple check allows for more graceful error handling and guides users in correcting their paths.

Another frequent error occurs when attempting to access a sheet name that doesn't exist within the workbook. If you try referencing a sheet by a misspelled or altered name, a KeyError will be triggered. To prevent this from happening, it's beneficial to list all available sheets beforehand:

```python
\#\# List all sheet names in the workbook
print(workbook.sheetnames)
```

\#\# Select a sheet with validation

sheet_name = 'Sales'

if sheet_name in workbook.sheetnames:

sheet = workbook[sheet_name]

else:

print(f"The sheet 'sheet_name' does not exist.")

` ` `

This technique helps avoid unexpected failures and provides clear feedback on potential issues.

When dealing with cell data, type mismatches can also lead to complications during calculations. Take this example, if you attempt arithmetic operations on text values instead of numbers, Python will raise a TypeError. To mitigate this, implement type checks before performing calculations:

` ` `python

\#\# Initialize total sales

total_sales = 0

\#\# Loop through rows while ensuring proper type checks

for row in range(2, sheet.max_row + 1):

cell_value = sheet[f'Brow'].value

if isinstance(cell_value, (int, float)):

total_sales += cell_value

else:

print(f"Non-numeric value found at Brow: cell_value")

```
```

This method captures problematic values without halting your script and informs you of any data quality issues that require attention.

Empty cells can present additional challenges when reading data. You may encounter instances where a row is completely blank or contains missing values. By implementing checks for empty cells, you can keep your processes running smoothly:

```python
for row in range(2, sheet.max_row + 1):

cell_value = sheet[f'Brow'].value

if cell_value is None:

print(f"Empty cell found at Brow. Skipping...")

continue \# Skip empty cells

total_sales += cell_value
```

This proactive strategy prevents errors and ensures that only valid data contributes to your calculations.

Beyond these specific troubleshooting techniques, maintaining robust documentation throughout your code is vital. Clear comments elucidate your logic and decision-making process for both yourself and others who may read your code later. For example:

```python
\#\# Initialize total sales variable

total_sales = 0  \# This will hold the sum of all valid sales figures
```

\#\# Loop through each row in the Sales column starting from row 2

for row in range(2, sheet.max_row + 1):

...

` ` `

By documenting your intent clearly within your script, you can easily track down logic errors when things don't work as expected.

As you gain experience handling errors while reading from and manipulating Excel files with Python, you'll find resilience and adaptability become second nature. Effective troubleshooting not only streamlines your workflows but also boosts your confidence as you tackle increasingly complex automation tasks.

Engaging with these common challenges equips you with essential skills for robust Excel automation using Python. With practice, every obstacle presents an opportunity for growth and learning. As you advance on this journey, remember that each resolved error enhances not only your technical proficiency but also strengthens your problem-solving abilities—a crucial asset in today's data-driven landscape.

CHAPTER 2:
ADVANCED DATA
MANIPULATION

Reading large datasets efficiently

Efficiently reading large datasets is an essential skill for anyone working with Python and Excel. As organizations increasingly rely on data-driven decision-making, the ability to manage substantial information sets can distinguish you in a competitive landscape. While Excel is a powerful tool, it does have limitations, particularly when processing extensive datasets. This is where Python becomes an invaluable partner, offering enhanced capabilities for data management and manipulation.

When tackling large datasets, the first step is determining how to import the data into your Python environment. Libraries such as Pandas provide specialized functions designed for efficient data loading. Instead of reading the entire dataset into memory at once—which can lead to performance issues or crashes—Pandas allows for chunked loading. This method is especially beneficial when working with sizable Excel files.

Here's a practical example of how to read a large Excel file in chunks using Pandas:

```python
import pandas as pd

\#\# Specify the path to your Excel file
file_path = 'large_dataset.xlsx'

\#\# Create an empty list to hold processed data
data_chunks = []

\#\# Read the Excel file in chunks of 1000 rows
for chunk in pd.read_excel(file_path, chunksize=1000):
\#\# Perform any necessary data cleaning or transformation here
cleaned_chunk = chunk.dropna()  \# For example, drop rows with missing values
data_chunks.append(cleaned_chunk)

\#\# Concatenate all cleaned chunks into a single DataFrame
final_data = pd.concat(data_chunks)
```

This approach allows you to work with manageable portions of your dataset at any given time, thus reducing memory consumption and improving processing speed.

Once your data is loaded efficiently, the next task often involves filtering and querying it effectively. Pandas excels in this area through its powerful DataFrame operations. Take this example, if you're interested in analyzing sales figures above a certain threshold, you can utilize boolean indexing:

```python
\#\# Assuming 'sales' is a column in your DataFrame

high_sales = final_data[final_data['sales'] > 5000]
```

This line filters your DataFrame to include only rows where sales exceed 5,000, allowing you to conduct further analysis without altering the original dataset.

Grouping your data for summarization is another crucial step when handling large datasets. Grouping enables you to perform calculations such as sums or averages based on categories—essential for generating insightful reports.

```python
\#\# Group by 'region' and calculate total sales per region

sales_by_region = final_data.groupby('region')['sales'].sum().reset_index()
```

This code snippet groups your dataset by region and computes total sales for each area, providing a clear picture of performance across different markets.

However, managing large datasets isn't solely about efficiency; it's also vital to maintain accuracy and integrity within your data. When working with substantial records, implementing checks to ensure analysis quality becomes essential. For example, verifying that no unexpected values exist within critical columns can prevent erroneous conclusions.

You might integrate validation steps into your workflow:

```python
```

\#\# Check for any negative sales figures

if (final_data['sales'] < 0).any():

print("Warning: Negative sales values detected.")

` ` `

Incorporating proactive checks not only bolsters the reliability of your findings but also showcases diligence in data handling —a quality highly valued across industries.

As you deepen your expertise, you'll discover more sophisticated techniques for effectively reading and manipulating large datasets. Take this example, merging datasets from multiple sources becomes increasingly vital; after all, data rarely originates from a single source in today's interconnected world. Merging allows you to combine disparate datasets into a cohesive structure that enhances analytical insight.

For example:

` ` `python

\#\# Assuming we have another DataFrame 'additional_info'

merged_data = pd.merge(final_data, additional_info, on='id', how='left')

` ` `

In this scenario, 'id' serves as the common key between two datasets. The merged result enriches your analysis while maintaining the original dataset's structure.

In the end, mastering the art of efficiently reading large datasets transcends mere tool usage; it involves cultivating a mindset oriented toward continuous improvement and learning. Each dataset presents unique challenges; overcoming these hurdles fosters resilience and adaptability. Embrace this journey as an opportunity not only for technical growth but also for enhancing problem-solving skills—an invaluable asset in any professional context.

Whether you're preparing quarterly reports or analyzing market trends, having robust methods for handling large volumes of data will significantly empower you in your role. As you continue on this path of automation and efficiency using Python with Excel, remember that each new technique learned adds another tool to your arsenal—one that can drastically enhance both productivity and insight generation within any organization.

Working with DataFrames in Pandas

Working with DataFrames in Pandas is a vital skill that can significantly enhance your data manipulation capabilities. After importing large datasets, harnessing the powerful DataFrame structure allows for advanced data analysis and transformations, streamlining your workflow.

Essentially of Pandas is the DataFrame, a two-dimensional, size-mutable, potentially heterogeneous tabular data structure with labeled axes (rows and columns). This flexibility makes it exceptionally useful for organizing and analyzing structured data. For example, once you've imported a dataset of sales figures, the first step is often to convert this data into a DataFrame for easier manipulation. Here's how to initiate this process:

``` python

import pandas as pd


\#\# Reading an Excel file into a DataFrame

df = pd.read_excel('sales_data.xlsx')
```

This command imports the data from the specified Excel file into a Pandas DataFrame named df. With your data in this format, accessing specific rows or columns becomes straightforward. You can easily view the first five entries of your dataset by calling:

```python
print(df.head())
```

This initial inspection helps you familiarize yourself with both the structure and content of your data.

As you navigate through the extensive features of Pandas, understanding how to efficiently perform operations on DataFrames is essential. One common operation is selecting specific columns. If you're interested only in analyzing sales amounts and regions, you can filter your DataFrame like this:

```python
sales_region_df = df[['region', 'sales']]
```

This creates a new DataFrame containing just the region and sales columns, allowing you to focus on relevant data without altering the original dataset.

Handling missing values is another crucial aspect of working with DataFrames. Datasets often contain NaN (Not a Number) entries that can skew analysis results if not addressed properly. To manage this issue, you might use:

```python
\#\# Drop rows with any NaN values
cleaned_df = df.dropna()
```

Alternatively, if you prefer to fill missing values with zeros—suitable in certain contexts—you can use:

```python
```

```python
filled_df = df.fillna(0)
```

Both methods are important depending on your analysis needs: dropping rows may be appropriate when you have sufficient data points left, while filling could be better when zero represents an acceptable default.

Filtering data based on specific conditions opens up opportunities for targeted insights. Take this example, if you want to analyze sales exceeding 10,000, boolean indexing provides a concise way to filter:

```python
high_sales = df[df['sales'] > 10000]
```

This line generates a new DataFrame containing only those records where sales exceed 10,000, allowing you to concentrate your analysis on top-performing entries.

Another powerful feature of Pandas is grouping data for summarization. If you're tasked with determining average sales by region, you can achieve this with grouping:

```python
average_sales_by_region = df.groupby('region')['sales'].mean().reset_index()
```

This command groups your original DataFrame by the region column and calculates the mean sales for each region. The use of reset_index() ensures that the result remains tidy, making it suitable for further analysis or reporting.

The versatility of DataFrames also extends to merging datasets—a common necessity when dealing with related information across multiple files or sources. To merge two datasets based on a common key column (for example, customer_id), you would use:

```python
merged_df = pd.merge(df1, df2, on='customer_id')
```

This creates a new DataFrame that combines rows from both original datasets where the customer_id matches, enriching your analysis with additional context or attributes.

Another noteworthy feature is the ability to apply functions across rows or columns within a DataFrame—known as vectorized operations. This approach optimizes performance significantly compared to traditional looping methods. For example, if you want to calculate total revenue by multiplying price and quantity sold across all rows efficiently, you can do so like this:

```python
df['total_revenue'] = df['price'] * df['quantity']
```

This method allows calculations to be applied simultaneously across all relevant entries without cumbersome iteration.

```python
import matplotlib.pyplot as plt
```

\#\# Plotting average sales by region

```
plt.bar(average_sales_by_region['region'],
average_sales_by_region['sales'])
```

```
plt.xlabel('Region')
```

```
plt.ylabel('Average Sales')
```

```
plt.title('Average Sales by Region')
```

```
plt.show()
```
` ` `

By combining these techniques—importing datasets into DataFrames, filtering and cleaning data, summarizing insights through grouping and merging—you establish a strong foundation for further exploration of advanced analytical techniques.

Mastering Pandas' capabilities not only simplifies complex tasks but also builds confidence in handling diverse datasets effectively. As every dataset presents its own nuances and challenges, being adaptable and open to learning enhances both technical skills and analytical reasoning—essential qualities for any professional setting focused on data-driven decisions.

Data cleaning techniques

Data cleaning is the cornerstone of any successful data analysis project. After working with DataFrames in Pandas, the next logical step is to ensure your datasets are ready for analysis. Clean data not only leads to reliable insights but also supports informed decision-making, while messy data can obscure patterns and result in erroneous conclusions. As such, developing a solid understanding of various data cleaning techniques is essential.

One common challenge in datasets is the presence of missing or null values. These gaps can occur due to incomplete data entry or errors during data collection, and ignoring them can significantly skew your results. To address this issue effectively, you need strategies for inspecting and treating missing values.

To quickly assess the extent of missing values in your DataFrame, you can use the following code:

` ` `python

\#\# Checking for missing values

missing_values = df.isnull().sum()

print(missing_values)

``` ` `` ```

This command counts the NaN entries in each column, helping you identify which areas need attention. Depending on the context of your analysis, you can choose from several approaches to handle these missing values:

1. Dropping Rows: If the number of missing entries is small relative to your dataset size, you might consider dropping those rows:

``` `` `python```

cleaned_df = df.dropna()

``` ` `` ```

1. Filling Missing Values: In some instances, it makes more sense to fill these gaps with appropriate substitutes—such as replacing NaNs with the median or mean value of that column:

``` `` `python```

df['column_name'].fillna(df['column_name'].mean(), inplace=True)

``` ` `` ```

The choice between dropping and filling depends on your specific analysis needs; each method carries implications for how your results will be interpreted.

In addition to handling missing values, ensuring consistent formatting across your dataset is crucial for effective analysis. Variations in date formats, inconsistent text capitalization, or differing numerical formats can introduce errors when aggregating or comparing data. For example, if you're dealing
```

with a date column that contains formats like "MM/DD/YYYY" and "DD-MM-YYYY," standardizing these entries is essential:

```python
\#\# Converting dates to a standard format
df['date_column'] = pd.to_datetime(df['date_column'])
```

This approach converts all date entries into a uniform datetime object, making further analysis simpler.

Textual inconsistencies also warrant attention—especially with categorical variables such as product names or regions. Take this example, having "New York," "new york," and "NEW YORK" represented differently in your dataset could lead to confusion. A straightforward way to normalize text entries is by using string methods:

```python
df['city'] = df['city'].str.lower().str.strip()
```

This line ensures that all city names are converted to lowercase and that any leading or trailing spaces are removed, promoting consistency throughout the dataset.

Another important aspect of data cleaning involves identifying outliers—values that deviate significantly from the rest of your dataset. Outliers can distort statistical analyses and lead to misleading interpretations if not addressed properly. One effective method for detecting outliers is by using the interquartile range (IQR):

```python
Q1 = df['sales'].quantile(0.25)

Q3 = df['sales'].quantile(0.75)

IQR = Q3 - Q1
```

\#\# Identifying outliers

outliers = df[(df['sales'] < (Q1 - 1.5 * IQR)) | (df['sales'] > (Q3 + 1.5 * IQR))]
```

This snippet helps identify sales entries that fall outside the expected range based on IQR criteria.

Additionally, converting categorical variables into numerical representations through one-hot encoding allows for more sophisticated analyses without sacrificing data integrity:

```python

df_encoded = pd.get_dummies(df[['region']], drop_first=True)
```

By creating dummy variables for categorical features while avoiding issues related to multicollinearity, you enhance your dataset's readiness for advanced modeling.

Finally, consider implementing validation techniques at this stage of your workflow; confirming that no logical inconsistencies exist will improve overall data quality. For example, you might check whether sales figures contain negative values where they shouldn't:

```python

if (df['sales'] < 0).any():

print("Warning: Negative sales values detected!")
```

Through systematic cleaning efforts—addressing missing values, normalizing formats, detecting outliers, and encoding categories—you lay a strong foundation for insightful analysis and reporting.
```

Filtering and sorting data

Filtering and sorting data are foundational operations that empower you to extract meaningful insights from your datasets. Once you've cleaned your data, the next step typically involves isolating specific subsets or organizing it in a way that highlights trends and patterns. Mastering DataFrame manipulation is key to enhancing your analytical capabilities significantly.

Filtering enables you to isolate rows in a DataFrame based on specific conditions, which is invaluable when you want to analyze only a portion of your data—such as sales figures for a particular region or within a specific date range. For example, if you want to focus on sales records from the year 2023, you can use the following code:

```python
\#\# Filtering for sales data in 2023

filtered_sales = df[df['date_column'].dt.year == 2023]
```

This command extracts all rows where the date_column falls within 2023, resulting in a DataFrame that contains only the relevant entries. Such filtering techniques allow you to narrow down your dataset to precisely what you need for analysis.

And, you can combine multiple filters using logical operators. Take this example, if you're interested in analyzing sales data specifically from New York in 2023, adding another condition becomes straightforward:

```python
filtered_ny_sales = df[(df['date_column'].dt.year == 2023) & (df['city'] == 'new york')]
```

In this case, the & operator effectively combines both

conditions. Just remember to enclose each condition within parentheses when using multiple criteria.

Sorting data is equally essential, as it allows for quick visual assessments of trends and performance metrics over time or across categories. You can sort your DataFrame based on one or more columns. Take this example, if you're interested in viewing your sales figures from highest to lowest for the year 2023, you might write:

```python
sorted_sales = filtered_sales.sort_values(by='sales', ascending=False)
```

This line sorts the filtered DataFrame by the sales column in descending order, clearly highlighting which transactions contributed most significantly during that period.

Sorting isn't limited to a single column; you can easily sort by multiple columns as well. For example, if you'd like to prioritize sales figures while also sorting city names alphabetically within each sales group:

```python
sorted_sales_multi = filtered_sales.sort_values(by=['sales', 'city'], ascending=[False, True])
```

In this scenario, primary sorting occurs on sales, while secondary sorting arranges cities in alphabetical order.

Often in data analysis, you'll need more than just raw numbers; summaries such as averages or totals across specific groups become essential. This is where grouping comes into play. With Pandas, grouping allows for seamless aggregation of your data. Consider calculating average sales per city for your filtered dataset:

```python
average_sales_per_city      =      filtered_sales.groupby('city')
['sales'].mean().reset_index()
```

This command groups your filtered dataset by city and computes the average sales for each group, providing insights into which regions perform best financially.

Additionally, chaining filtering and grouping operations together can enhance efficiency. After filtering and grouping, if you want to sort these averages from highest to lowest:

```python
top_average_sales                                         =
average_sales_per_city.sort_values(by='sales',
ascending=False)
```

Chaining operations improves code readability and reduces clutter from intermediate variables in your workspace.

As you explore filtering and sorting techniques with Pandas further, don't overlook the visualization tools available within Python libraries like Matplotlib or Seaborn. Visualizing sorted or filtered data can reveal insights that raw numbers may obscure. Take this example, creating a simple bar plot of top-performing cities based on average sales can be accomplished with:

```python
import matplotlib.pyplot as plt


plt.figure(figsize=(10, 6))

plt.bar(top_average_sales['city'], top_average_sales['sales'])
```

```
plt.title('Average Sales Per City')

plt.xlabel('City')

plt.ylabel('Average Sales')

plt.xticks(rotation=45)

plt.show()
```
` ` `

This visualization translates numerical insights into an easily digestible format—enabling stakeholders to grasp trends quickly and efficiently.

With a solid understanding of filtering and sorting techniques, along with aggregation methods like grouping, you're now equipped with essential tools for deeper analysis and informed decision-making. These skills not only streamline your workflow but also enhance clarity in presentations—making it easier for colleagues or stakeholders to comprehend complex datasets at a glance.

As complex queries become second nature through practice and repetition, you'll find yourself approaching Excel automation projects with greater confidence and agility—an essential skill set as you continue exploring Python's capabilities within Excel environments.

Grouping and aggregating data

Grouping and aggregating data allows you to distill extensive datasets into meaningful summaries, which in turn facilitates informed decision-making. While filtering and sorting help isolate specific records or arrange data for visual clarity, grouping takes your analysis a step further by enabling the computation of statistics across various segments of your data. This deeper analysis can unlock insights that significantly influence strategy and operations.

Consider the example of analyzing sales data for a large retail chain. Simply knowing total sales figures isn't enough; understanding how those sales break down across different regions, product categories, or time periods provides actionable intelligence. With Pandas, the process of grouping data becomes both intuitive and powerful.

Imagine you have already filtered your dataset to include only transactions from 2023. To analyze the performance of different product categories within that year, you can group the data accordingly:

```python
\#\# Grouping sales by product category and summing totals

category_sales = filtered_sales.groupby('product_category')['sales'].sum().reset_index()
```

In this example, the groupby function creates a new DataFrame where each row represents a distinct product category. The sum() function aggregates the sales figures for each category, allowing you to identify which products are driving revenue.

To gain even deeper insights, you may want to calculate not just totals but also averages and counts. You can extend our previous example to include multiple aggregations using the agg() method:

```python
\#\# Aggregating multiple statistics

aggregated_data = filtered_sales.groupby('product_category').agg(

total_sales=('sales', 'sum'),

average_sales=('sales', 'mean'),
```

```
transaction_count=('sales', 'count')

).reset_index()
```

This command returns a DataFrame that includes total sales, average sales per transaction, and the number of transactions for each product category. Such comprehensive metrics allow you to evaluate performance from various angles.

Next, consider more complex scenarios where you want to analyze sales trends over time within each product category. By introducing additional grouping criteria—such as month or quarter—you can achieve greater granularity:

```python
\#\# Grouping by month and product category

monthly_category_sales                    =
filtered_sales.groupby([filtered_sales['date_column'].dt.to_peri
od("M"), 'product_category'])['sales'].sum().unstack().fillna(0)
```

In this code snippet, the sales data is grouped by both month and product category. The unstack() method reshapes the resulting DataFrame so that each column represents a product category with rows corresponding to months, allowing for quick comparisons across categories over time.

Aggregation extends beyond simple sums or averages; it can also include more sophisticated statistical measures like medians or standard deviations:

```python
\#\# Advanced aggregation including median and standard deviation

advanced_aggregates       =       filtered_sales.groupby('city')
['sales'].agg(['mean', 'median', 'std']).reset_index()
```

```
` ` `
```

This command generates a DataFrame containing not only mean sales but also median values and standard deviations per city, providing a clearer picture of variability in your data.

```python
import matplotlib.pyplot as plt

plt.figure(figsize=(10, 6))

plt.bar(aggregated_data['product_category'],
aggregated_data['total_sales'])

plt.title('Total Sales by Product Category in 2023')

plt.xlabel('Product Category')

plt.ylabel('Total Sales')

plt.xticks(rotation=45)

plt.show()
` ` `
```

This straightforward yet effective visualization enables stakeholders to quickly grasp which categories are performing well compared to others.

And, consider combining filtering and grouping operations into one streamlined process. If you're interested in assessing only high-performing cities after grouping:

```python
high_performers                              =
advanced_aggregates[advanced_aggregates['mean']         >
threshold_value]
` ` `
```

This line filters down to cities where average sales exceed a specified threshold—ideal for identifying key markets.

Mastering these grouping and aggregation techniques will transform how you interact with data in Excel through Python. As these processes become second nature, your analytical proficiency will flourish. Your newfound capability not only empowers individual analysis but also enhances collaborative efforts with teams that rely on clear interpretations of complex datasets.

With these skills at your disposal, you'll be well-equipped to tackle more intricate analytical challenges and deliver insights that inform strategic initiatives—an essential part of your journey in mastering Python's application in Excel automation.

Handling dates and times

Handling dates and times in data analysis is often an overlooked yet essential aspect that can significantly enhance your insights. As you transition from grouping and aggregating data, mastering the manipulation of temporal data opens a world of possibilities. Time-based analysis enables you to uncover trends, seasonal patterns, and shifts in behavior over time. In the context of Excel automation with Python, effectively leveraging date and time transforms raw data into actionable intelligence.

To begin, it's crucial to understand how dates are represented in your datasets. In Pandas, dates can be treated as datetime objects, which provide powerful functionalities for manipulation. When working with Excel files, dates may appear in various formats that require conversion for effective analysis. The pd.to_datetime() function is invaluable for this task:

```python
\#\# Converting a column to datetime

sales_data['date_column']                                    =
```

```
pd.to_datetime(sales_data['date_column'])
```
` ` `

This line ensures your date column is recognized as datetime objects, allowing you to perform time series operations smoothly. After conversion, you can extract specific components such as year, month, or day for further analysis:

` ` `python

\#\# Extracting year and month from the date column

```
sales_data['year'] = sales_data['date_column'].dt.year

sales_data['month'] = sales_data['date_column'].dt.month
```
` ` `

These new columns serve as powerful filters for grouping your data more meaningfully. Take this example, if you want to analyze monthly sales performance, you can efficiently aggregate your data by month:

` ` `python

\#\# Grouping by year and month

```
monthly_sales = sales_data.groupby(['year', 'month'])
['sales'].sum().reset_index()
```
` ` `

This aggregation allows you to visualize monthly sales trends, making it easier to detect patterns or anomalies over specific periods.

Beyond basic operations, handling time intervals can yield deeper insights. For example, if you're interested in analyzing the number of transactions within specific time frames—such as weekly or quarterly—Pandas offers convenient methods for resampling time series data:

` ` `python

\#\# Resampling sales data on a weekly basis

```python
weekly_sales = sales_data.resample('W', on='date_column')
['sales'].sum().reset_index()
```

The resample() method groups the sales data into weekly buckets, which is especially beneficial when dealing with large datasets where granularity matters for trend analysis.

Consider a scenario where you need to assess quarterly performance while accommodating varying fiscal quarters instead of sticking to calendar quarters. You can create custom date ranges using the pd.date_range() function combined with logical conditions to filter your data accordingly:

```python
\#\# Filtering sales in Q1 of 2023 (January - March)

q1_sales = sales_data[(sales_data['date_column'] >= '2023-01-01') & (sales_data['date_column'] < '2023-04-01')]
```

This precision allows for analyses that align with specific business needs or reporting periods.

Another important aspect of date handling is calculating differences between dates—whether assessing customer retention periods or tracking product lifecycles. You can compute the difference between two datetime objects directly:

```python
\#\# Calculating the number of days between two dates

sales_data['days_since_purchase'] = (pd.Timestamp.now() - sales_data['date_column']).dt.days
```

With this new column, you can identify customers who haven't made a purchase in over 30 days and potentially target them with tailored marketing campaigns.

Additionally, visualizing time-based data is crucial for conveying insights effectively. Time series plots can illustrate trends clearly. Using Matplotlib, you can easily plot monthly sales over time:

```python
import matplotlib.pyplot as plt

plt.figure(figsize=(12, 6))

plt.plot(monthly_sales['date'], monthly_sales['sales'])

plt.title('Monthly Sales Trends')

plt.xlabel('Month')

plt.ylabel('Total Sales')

plt.xticks(rotation=45)

plt.grid()

plt.show()
```

This visualization provides stakeholders with immediate clarity on how sales have evolved over the months—a vital component for strategic planning.

As you become more adept at managing dates and times within your datasets, remember that these skills will greatly enhance your analytical capabilities. The ability to dissect temporal trends empowers not only individual analyses but also collaborative efforts across teams reliant on comprehensive reports and forecasts.

Incorporating these techniques into your workflow will elevate your proficiency in Python's integration with Excel automation. Armed with practical examples and an understanding of how date manipulation impacts analysis, you're now well-positioned to derive meaningful insights from temporal data, paving the way for improved decision-making and strategic initiatives within your organization.

Merging and joining datasets

Merging and joining datasets is an essential skill that enriches your analysis and provides deeper insights. Building on your understanding of handling dates and times, it's crucial to learn how to effectively combine different data sources. These sources often contain valuable information that, when integrated, can lead to powerful outcomes.

Take this example, consider two datasets: one containing customer information and another detailing their purchase history. To analyze customer behavior effectively, you would merge these datasets using a common identifier like customer_id. Here's how it's done:

```python
import pandas as pd

\#\# Sample data frames
customers = pd.DataFrame(
'customer_id': [1, 2, 3],
'name': ['Alice', 'Bob', 'Charlie']
)

purchases = pd.DataFrame(
'purchase_id': [101, 102, 103],
'customer_id': [1, 2, 1],
'amount': [250.00, 150.00, 100.00]
```

)

\#\# Merging datasets on customer_id

merged_data = pd.merge(customers, purchases, on='customer_id', how='inner')

``` `

This code snippet combines the two data frames into one that includes customer names alongside their corresponding purchase amounts. The how parameter specifies the type of join; in this case, an inner join retains only entries with matching keys in both datasets.

However, you might encounter situations where not every record in one dataset has a counterpart in another. In such cases, outer joins can be beneficial as they retain all records from both sides while filling in missing values:

``` `python

\#\# Performing an outer join

merged_data_outer = pd.merge(customers, purchases, on='customer_id', how='outer')

``` `

This approach provides a comprehensive view of all customers and their purchases—even if some customers have no recorded transactions.

Once you've successfully merged your datasets, it's often necessary to clean up any resulting anomalies or missing values to ensure data integrity for accurate analysis. For example:

``` `python

\#\# Filling NaN values after merging

merged_data_outer.fillna('amount': 0, inplace=True)
` ` `

By replacing NaN values with zero for amounts where no purchases were made, you maintain the usability of your dataset while preserving essential structural information.

In addition to merging based on specific keys with merge(), you may sometimes need to concatenate data frames when stacking similar datasets either vertically or horizontally. The concat() function is designed for this purpose:

` ` `python

\#\# Concatenating two data frames vertically

combined_sales = pd.concat([sales_data_2022, sales_data_2023], ignore_index=True)
` ` `

This method is particularly useful when aggregating yearly sales reports into one cohesive dataset for comprehensive analysis across multiple years.

To further enhance your analytical capabilities when merging complex datasets—such as those that include hierarchical relationships—you might employ techniques like multi-indexing or additional parameters within your merge commands:

` ` `python

\#\# Merging with multiple keys

complex_merge = pd.merge(orders_df, products_df,

left_on=['product_id', 'order_date'],

right_on=['id', 'date'],

how='left')

\` \` \`

In this example, we're merging based on both product ID and order date—ensuring that our combined dataset retains relevant temporal context alongside product details.

Another important aspect of merging datasets is its impact on performance—especially when dealing with large volumes of data. Monitoring for unnecessary duplicates or heavy computations during joins can save processing time and resources. Managing this efficiently is crucial when navigating expansive databases typically encountered in business settings.

Incorporating these practical methods into your workflow will not only streamline your analysis but also provide clarity and depth in reports generated through Excel automation using Python tools. As you continue to build foundational skills in seamlessly merging datasets within Python's ecosystem —and reflecting those insights back into Excel—you'll find yourself increasingly adept at navigating complex analytical landscapes where informed decisions are vital for success.

Pivot tables with Pandas

Pivot tables are one of Excel's most powerful features, providing a dynamic way to summarize and analyze large datasets. In the world of data manipulation with Python, the Pandas library brings this capability to life in a seamless and intuitive manner. By enabling the creation of pivot tables, Pandas not only enhances data analysis but also fosters a more programmatic approach to summarizing data, paving the way for greater automation and efficiency.

At the heart of creating a pivot table in Pandas is the pivot_table() function. This function allows you to clearly specify your data source, index, columns, and aggregation functions. Take this example, consider a DataFrame containing sales data that includes information about various transactions:

```python
import pandas as pd

data =
'Product': ['A', 'B', 'A', 'C', 'B', 'C'],
'Region': ['North', 'South', 'South', 'North', 'North', 'South'],
'Sales': [100, 150, 200, 300, 250, 100]


df = pd.DataFrame(data)
```

With this DataFrame in hand, creating a pivot table that summarizes total sales by product and region is straightforward. The following code accomplishes this:

```python
pivot_table = df.pivot_table(values='Sales', index='Product', columns='Region', aggfunc='sum')
print(pivot_table)
```

The output presents a structured view of total sales per product across different regions:

```
Region North South
Product
A 100 200
B 250 150
```

C 300 100

` ` `

This example demonstrates how quickly insights can be generated from your data using Pandas. The flexibility of the aggfunc parameter is worth noting; while we used sum in this case, it can also accommodate functions like mean, count, or even user-defined functions for tailored aggregations.

As you explore further, you'll find advanced features within the pivot table functionality that enhance your analytical capabilities. For example, you might want to apply multiple aggregation functions simultaneously or fill missing values for improved readability in reports. This can be easily achieved by passing a list of functions to the aggfunc parameter:

` ` `python

pivot_table_multi = df.pivot_table(values='Sales', index='Product', columns='Region',

aggfunc=[np.sum, np.mean])

print(pivot_table_multi)

` ` `

This generates a multi-level pivot table displaying both sum and average sales figures side by side. Now you can assess not only total sales but also average sales per transaction—an essential metric for evaluating performance.

When working with larger datasets or more complex scenarios, managing NaN values becomes crucial. Pandas provides an effective way to handle these using the fill_value argument within pivot_table(). This guarantees that your summary tables remain informative even when certain combinations of categories are missing from the dataset:

` ` `python

pivot_table_filled = df.pivot_table(values='Sales',

```
index='Product', columns='Region',

aggfunc='sum', fill_value=0)

print(pivot_table_filled)
```
```

By utilizing this technique, any missing entries in your pivot table will be replaced with zeroes instead of NaN values, making your reports clearer and more actionable.

Integrating pivot tables into your Python workflow not only enhances efficiency but also unlocks deeper analytical possibilities. As you become more comfortable with these tools, think about how they can be woven into your regular reporting processes. Automating weekly or monthly reports with scripts that generate updated pivot tables can save time while ensuring accuracy.

One of the remarkable aspects of using Pandas for pivot tables is its scalability. Whether you're dealing with hundreds or thousands of rows of data, the principles remain consistent. You can easily adapt your approach as datasets grow or shift focus—be it analyzing customer purchases over time or aggregating performance metrics across various departments.

Pandas empowers you to manipulate data flexibly and dynamically without being restricted by manual processes often found in Excel. Your journey into automating data analysis through Python continues as you embrace these functionalities and apply them in real-world scenarios, driving impactful decisions based on clear insights derived from your data.

**Exporting cleaned data to Excel**

Exporting cleaned data to Excel is a crucial step in the workflow of any data analyst or business intelligence professional. After manipulating and organizing datasets in Python, the ability to output them to an Excel file facilitates
```

easier sharing, collaboration, and further analysis in a familiar environment. Libraries like Pandas streamline this process, offering various options for customizing exported files.

Once you have a cleaned DataFrame—perhaps after filtering out outliers or aggregating data—you can effortlessly export it using the to_excel() method from Pandas. Take this example, consider our earlier sales DataFrame. After performing the necessary cleaning operations, you might want to export it into an Excel workbook:

```python
import pandas as pd

\#\# Sample cleaned DataFrame.

data =

'Product': ['A', 'B', 'A', 'C', 'B', 'C'],

'Region': ['North', 'South', 'South', 'North', 'North', 'South'],

'Sales': [100, 150, 200, 300, 250, 100]


df = pd.DataFrame(data)

\#\# Exporting the cleaned DataFrame to Excel

df.to_excel('cleaned_sales_data.xlsx', index=False)
```

By setting index=False, you ensure that Pandas does not write row indices into your Excel file. This is important for maintaining a clean output without unnecessary index columns cluttering your spreadsheet.

To enhance the usability of your exported file further, you can utilize additional parameters in to_excel(). For example, specifying a particular sheet name adds clarity:

```python
df.to_excel('cleaned_sales_data.xlsx', sheet_name='SalesData', index=False)
```

When working with multiple DataFrames that need to be exported within the same Excel workbook, the ExcelWriter class becomes invaluable. This functionality allows you to create multiple sheets efficiently. Here's how you can achieve this:

```python
with pd.ExcelWriter('multi_sheet_report.xlsx') as writer:

df.to_excel(writer, sheet_name='SalesData', index=False)

\#\# Assume df2 is another cleaned DataFrame

df2.to_excel(writer, sheet_name='SummaryData', index=False)
```

This approach consolidates all relevant information into one cohesive document, improving accessibility for stakeholders who may not be familiar with Python or coding.

For those needing additional formatting features in their exported sheets—such as adjusting column widths or applying styles—Pandas integrates well with libraries like XlsxWriter. The following example illustrates how to format columns in your exported Excel file:

```python
with pd.ExcelWriter('styled_sales_data.xlsx', engine='xlsxwriter') as writer:
```

HAYDEN VAN DER POST

```
df.to_excel(writer, sheet_name='SalesData', index=False)

\#\# Accessing the workbook and worksheet
workbook = writer.book
worksheet = writer.sheets['SalesData']

\#\# Setting column widths for better readability
worksheet.set_column('A:A', 20) \# Width for Product column
worksheet.set_column('B:B', 15) \# Width for Region column
worksheet.set_column('C:C', 10) \# Width for Sales column

\#\# Adding cell formats (optional)
format1 = workbook.add_format('num_format': '\#,\#\#0') \# Format for sales numbers

worksheet.set_column('C:C', None, format1) \# Apply format to Sales column
` ` `
```

By employing such techniques, you not only export data but also enhance its presentation quality. This guarantees that stakeholders receive information that is both visually appealing and easy to interpret.

When handling larger datasets or ensuring consistency across exports from various sources, it's essential to maintain attention to detail regarding data types and integrity. Verify that numerical values remain correctly formatted without unintended alterations during export processes.

Incorporating automation into your exporting routine can significantly boost efficiency. You might create a scheduled

82

task or script that automatically exports fresh data daily or weekly by encapsulating these commands within functions tailored to your specific needs.

In the end, exporting cleaned data transcends merely outputting numbers into an Excel file; it involves preserving clarity and utility while ensuring seamless access and understanding among all users involved in data-driven decision-making. As you integrate these tools and techniques into your workflow, sharing insights will become not only more straightforward but also far more impactful in guiding strategies and actions within your organization.

Automating repetitive tasks

Automating repetitive tasks in Excel can greatly enhance your productivity while minimizing the risk of human error. Imagine having Python handle tedious data manipulations, routine reporting, or even complex calculations—tasks that often consume hours of your valuable time. In today's fast-paced business environment, this level of automation is not merely a luxury; it has become a necessity.

Take, for example, the process of generating weekly sales reports. Typically, this involves pulling data, cleaning it up, and formatting it for presentation. Instead of manually repeating these steps each week, you could create a script that accomplishes all these tasks in one go. By using the Pandas library, you can easily load your data from an Excel file, apply necessary transformations, and save the results back to an organized format.

Here's a simple way to set up such a script:

```python
import pandas as pd


\#\# Load sales data from Excel
```

```
df = pd.read_excel('weekly_sales.xlsx')
```

\#\# Data cleaning: removing duplicates

```
df.drop_duplicates(inplace=True)
```

\#\# Data transformation: calculating total sales per product

```
total_sales = df.groupby('Product')['Sales'].sum().reset_index()
```

\#\# Export the cleaned and transformed data

```
total_sales.to_excel('weekly_total_sales.xlsx', index=False)
```
` ` `

This script automates the entire workflow—from loading the data to cleaning it and exporting it in a structured format. You can run this script weekly with a simple command or even integrate it into a task scheduler to automate the timing.

Automation goes beyond just executing scripts; it also encompasses error handling and notifications. Incorporating logging mechanisms into your scripts can help track successes and failures. By utilizing Python's built-in logging library, you can keep records of what happens during each run:

` ` `python

```
import logging
```

\#\# Configure logging

```
logging.basicConfig(filename='automation.log',
level=logging.INFO)
```

```python
try:

\#\# Your automation code here

df.to_excel('weekly_total_sales.xlsx', index=False)

logging.info('Export successful: weekly_total_sales.xlsx')

except Exception as e:

logging.error(f'Error occurred: e')

` ` `
```

By capturing events in logs, you gain visibility into potential issues without needing to monitor every execution actively. This proactive approach ensures that if something goes wrong—like a missing file or incorrect data types—you'll be alerted immediately rather than discovering the problem after someone has encountered faulty reports.

You can further streamline your automation by scheduling scripts using tools like Windows Task Scheduler or cron jobs on Unix-based systems. This setup eliminates the need for manual initiation altogether; Python will execute according to your defined schedule without requiring further intervention.

Additionally, consider implementing automated email notifications to share results directly with stakeholders. Take this example, after generating reports or conducting analyses, you can automatically send an email with the results attached, ensuring everyone is informed without any extra effort on your part:

```python
` ` `python

import smtplib

from email.mime.multipart import MIMEMultipart

from email.mime.application import MIMEApplication
```

```
def send_email(file_path):
msg = MIMEMultipart()
msg['Subject'] = 'Weekly Sales Report'
msg['From'] = 'your_email@example.com'
msg['To'] = 'recipient@example.com'

with open(file_path, "rb") as attachment:
```

Part = Mimeapplication(Attachment.read(), Name=File_path)

```
part['Content-Disposition']                =                f'attachment;
filename="file_path"'
msg.attach(part)

with smtplib.SMTP('smtp.example.com', 587) as server:
server.starttls()
server.login('your_email@example.com', 'your_password')
server.send_message(msg)

send_email('weekly_total_sales.xlsx')
```
` ` `

This integration not only saves time but also ensures that critical information reaches those who need it promptly.

Lastly, think about utilizing templates for the reports generated by Python. By creating standard formats in

Excel that align with your organization's expectations, you can maintain consistency while allowing for necessary automation adjustments. Automating tasks does not mean sacrificing quality or personalization; rather, it enhances both.

The ability to automate repetitive tasks fundamentally transforms how professionals engage with their work processes. As you implement these strategies into your routine, you'll find yourself not only saving time but also freeing up mental space to focus on higher-value activities —those requiring critical thinking and strategic decision-making rather than mere number-crunching.

Embrace this shift towards automation and let Python handle the heavy lifting, allowing you to steer your projects toward greater insights and innovations.

CHAPTER 3: SCRIPTING EXCEL WITH OPENPYXL

Introduction to OpenPyXL

OpenPyXL is an essential library in Python for Excel automation, allowing users to effortlessly read, write, and manipulate Excel files. This tool is particularly valuable for those looking to harness Python's computational strength alongside Excel's user-friendly interface. The ability to interact programmatically with Excel opens up numerous opportunities for automating tasks that would otherwise be tedious and time-consuming.

To get started with OpenPyXL, you'll first need to install it. If you haven't already done so, you can easily install the library via pip:

```bash
pip install openpyxl
```

Once the installation is complete, you can begin creating your first workbook. Here's a simple example of how to create a new

Excel file and populate it with data:

```python
from openpyxl import Workbook

\#\# Create a new workbook and select the active worksheet
wb = Workbook()
ws = wb.active

\#\# Add data to cells
ws['A1'] = 'Product'
ws['B1'] = 'Sales'

\#\# Populate data rows
products = ['Apples', 'Oranges', 'Bananas']
sales = [1000, 1500, 2000]

for i in range(len(products)):
    ws[f'Ai + 2'] = products[i]
    ws[f'Bi + 2'] = sales[i]

\#\# Save the workbook
wb.save('sales_data.xlsx')
```

In this example, we created a new workbook named sales_data.xlsx, which contains product names alongside their corresponding sales figures. The use of f-strings for cell addressing makes it easy to dynamically populate data.

Beyond basic data entry, OpenPyXL enables more complex manipulations. Take this example, you can format cells to enhance readability or highlight key figures. Here's how to make the header row bold:

```python
from openpyxl.styles import Font

\#\# Applying styles

header_font = Font(bold=True)

for cell in ws["1:1"]: \# Apply to the first row (header)

cell.font = header_font


\#\# Save changes again

wb.save('sales_data_formatted.xlsx')
```

With this code snippet, we've emphasized the header row by applying bold formatting. OpenPyXL offers a wide range of styling options; you can adjust colors, modify alignment, and even apply borders to cells.

Another powerful feature of OpenPyXL is its ability to integrate formulas directly into your worksheets. This allows you to utilize Excel's built-in functions without leaving your Python environment. For example:

```python
\#\# Adding a formula to calculate total sales in cell B5

ws['B5'] = '=SUM(B2:B4)'
```

```python
\#\# Save workbook with formula included

wb.save('sales_data_with_formula.xlsx')
```

This addition ensures that the sum of sales is calculated automatically whenever the workbook is opened or refreshed in Excel.

As you explore OpenPyXL's capabilities further, you'll uncover features such as creating charts, managing multiple sheets within a single workbook, and working with images—tools that significantly enhance your automation potential. Take this example:

```python
from openpyxl.chart import BarChart, Reference

\#\# Create a bar chart for sales data

chart = BarChart()

data = Reference(ws,

min_col=2,

min_row=1,

max_col=2,

max_row=4)

categories = Reference(ws,

min_col=1,

min_row=2,

max_row=4)
```

```
chart.add_data(data)

chart.set_categories(categories)

chart.title = "Sales by Product

ws.add_chart(chart, "D2")


\#\# Save workbook with chart added

wb.save('sales_data_with_chart.xlsx')
` ` `
```

This snippet illustrates how straightforward it is to incorporate visual elements like charts into your Excel file using OpenPyXL. By automatically integrating visual data representations into your reports, you not only enhance their impact but also improve usability.

OpenPyXL goes beyond facilitating basic tasks; it empowers users to create sophisticated automated workflows tailored to their specific needs. As professionals increasingly seek efficiency through automation tools like Python and libraries such as OpenPyXL, embracing these technologies will undoubtedly provide a competitive edge in any field.

Through this exploration of OpenPyXL's capabilities, you've begun to see how Python can revolutionize traditional spreadsheet tasks into streamlined processes. Each discussed functionality builds upon the last—demonstrating that mastering these tools lays the groundwork for achieving comprehensive automation in your projects.

Creating new workbooks and sheets programmatically

Creating new workbooks and sheets programmatically with OpenPyXL opens the door to automating Excel tasks with both precision and efficiency. This functionality enables you to generate spreadsheets from scratch and customize them to meet specific requirements, ultimately streamlining your data management processes.

To start creating a new workbook, instantiate a Workbook object. By default, this action opens a blank workbook featuring a single sheet. Here's how to get started:

```python
from openpyxl import Workbook


\#\# Create a new workbook

workbook = Workbook()


\#\# Access the active sheet

sheet = workbook.active


\#\# Rename the default sheet

sheet.title = "Sales Report
```

In this example, we create an instance of Workbook, access its active sheet, and rename it for clarity. This lays the groundwork for further data manipulation.

You can also add multiple sheets to your workbook as needed, allowing for different datasets or analyses relevant to your project. Here's how to create additional sheets:

```python
\#\# Create additional sheets

workbook.create_sheet(title="Inventory")

workbook.create_sheet(title="Expenses")
```

```
```

By using create_sheet, you've expanded your workbook to include sections for inventory and expenses, which aids in organized data management.

Filling these sheets with data is straightforward. Take this example, let's populate the "Sales Report" sheet with some sample sales data:

```python
\#\# Populate the Sales Report sheet

sales_data = [

["Product", "Sales"],

["Apples", 1000],

["Oranges", 1500],

["Bananas", 2000]

]


for row in sales_data:

sheet.append(row)
```

The append method simplifies this process by automatically finding the next available row in the specified sheet and inserting the provided values.

Once your sheets are populated, saving your work is crucial. You can easily save your newly created workbook by specifying a filename:

```python
\#\# Save the workbook
```

```
workbook.save("sales_report.xlsx")
```

This command finalizes your work, creating an Excel file named sales_report.xlsx that contains all your entered data.

Beyond basic creation and population, OpenPyXL offers advanced features that enhance user experience. Take this example, formatting headers for improved visibility in reports can be easily accomplished using styles from OpenPyXL's styles module:

```python
from openpyxl.styles import Font


\#\# Apply bold font to header row

for cell in sheet["1:1"]: \# This targets the first row (header)

cell.font = Font(bold=True)
```

In this snippet, we loop through each cell in the header row and apply bold formatting using the Font class from OpenPyXL's styling tools.

The ability to manipulate existing sheets adds another layer of versatility. You may need to adjust or delete specific sheets based on changing project requirements:

```python
\#\# Delete an unnecessary sheet if needed

if "Inventory" in workbook.sheetnames:

std = workbook["Inventory"]

workbook.remove(std)
```

This code checks for the existence of an "Inventory" sheet before removing it from the workbook—an efficient way to manage content dynamically.

Additionally, OpenPyXL supports integrating functions directly into cells, enabling calculations right within Excel without manual intervention after creation:

```python
\#\# Adding a formula for total sales calculation in a designated cell

sheet["B6"] = "=SUM(B2:B5)
```

When this workbook is opened in Excel, it will automatically compute the total of sales entries, showcasing how Python simplifies both automation and calculation tasks.

As you explore these capabilities, consider their application in real-world scenarios—whether compiling reports or organizing extensive datasets across multiple sheets. Programmatically generating workbooks saves time while enhancing accuracy.

With these foundational skills—creating workbooks, adding and formatting sheets—you are well on your way toward mastering advanced Excel automation using Python. Each function not only simplifies traditional tasks but also empowers you to innovate within your workflows. As these capabilities become second nature, you'll find yourself equipped to tackle increasingly complex projects with confidence and ease.

Writing data to Excel cells

After creating a workbook and adding sheets, the next step is to write meaningful data into those cells. OpenPyXL offers several methods for inputting data, providing flexibility to suit your needs. The simplest approach is to assign values directly to specific cells or use lists to populate rows.

For example, if you want to record sales data in your "Sales Report" sheet, you might structure your data like this:

```python
\#\# Prepare sales data

sales_data = [

["Product", "Sales"],

["Apples", 1200],

["Oranges", 1600],

["Bananas", 2100]

]
```

To efficiently input this list into the Excel sheet, you can use a loop that iteratively appends each row of sales data, allowing for dynamic population of the spreadsheet:

```python
\#\# Populate the Sales Report sheet with sales_data

for row in sales_data:

sheet.append(row)
```

This method minimizes errors and enables bulk entry, saving both time and effort.

In addition to simple entries, formatting your data can significantly enhance readability and impact. Take this example, if you want to highlight headers or specific values, OpenPyXL provides tools for changing font styles and background colors:

```python
from openpyxl.styles import Font, PatternFill
```

\#\# Apply bold font and background color for header row

header_fill = PatternFill(start_color="FFFF00", end_color="FFFF00", fill_type="solid")

for cell in sheet["1:1"]: \# Targeting the first row (header)

cell.font = Font(bold=True)

cell.fill = header_fill

```
```

In this snippet, we not only bold the headers but also apply a yellow background using PatternFill. Such formatting enhances the overall aesthetics of your report while making critical information stand out.

When dealing with numerical data, embedding formulas directly into Excel cells can significantly boost functionality. For example, if you want to calculate total sales dynamically within Excel instead of beforehand in Python:

```python
```

\#\# Adding a formula for total sales calculation in a designated cell

sheet["B6"] = "=SUM(B2:B5)

```
```

This command instructs Excel to sum all values from cells B2 to B5 once the file is opened—an efficient way to keep calculations updated automatically.

If you need to modify existing content or replace specific cells with new values—perhaps adjusting a forecast—OpenPyXL allows for straightforward changes:

```python
\#\# Update sales figure for Oranges

sheet["B3"] = 1700  \# Changing Oranges' sales from 1600 to 1700
```

This direct assignment method helps maintain control over your datasets, ensuring accuracy as adjustments are made.

However, efficient management of sheets is just as important as manipulating data. The ability to remove or rename sheets contributes significantly to keeping your workbook organized:

```python
\#\# Rename an existing sheet for clarity

sheet.title = "Updated Sales Report
```

As businesses evolve and projects shift focus, maintaining clarity within spreadsheets becomes essential.

The potential for automation extends beyond these basics; consider how you might build upon these foundations by integrating external datasets or applying conditional formatting based on relevant thresholds for your organization's goals.

By utilizing these techniques, you can transform spreadsheets into dynamic dashboards that respond fluidly as conditions change. Leveraging Python's capabilities alongside Excel's rich features positions you for success in streamlining workflows and enhancing decision-making processes.

With practice in writing data efficiently and effectively managing sheets with OpenPyXL, you'll be well-prepared not only for basic automation but also for tackling more complex tasks as you explore deeper integration between Python and

Excel. Embrace these tools; they are essential steps toward achieving excellence in automation.

Formatting cells and ranges

Formatting cells and ranges in Excel with OpenPyXL is a vital skill that enhances both the visual appeal and clarity of your spreadsheets. Effective formatting can elevate a basic report into a polished, professional document that conveys information more clearly. As you become proficient in formatting techniques, you'll notice a significant improvement in the user experience for anyone interacting with your data.

A fundamental aspect of cell formatting involves adjusting font styles. By modifying attributes such as boldness, italics, or size, you can establish a hierarchy of information that naturally guides the reader's eye. Take this example, to emphasize header rows or key figures, applying bold formatting can be particularly effective:

```python
from openpyxl.styles import Font


\#\# Set header font style

header_font = Font(bold=True)

for cell in sheet["1:1"]:  \# Targeting the first row (header)

cell.font = header_font

```

In this code snippet, all cells in the first row are set to bold, making it easier for readers to quickly identify important information.

Color is another essential element in making data stand out. Utilizing background colors to highlight specific cells or ranges can draw attention where it's needed most. For example, if you want to highlight profit margins that exceed a certain threshold, consider this approach:

```python
from openpyxl.styles import PatternFill


\#\# Highlight profits greater than 2000

highlight_fill = PatternFill(start_color="FFCCCB", end_color="FFCCCB", fill_type="solid")

for row in range(2, sheet.max_row + 1):

if sheet.cell(row=row, column=3).value > 2000: \# Assuming profits are in column C

sheet.cell(row=row, column=3).fill = highlight_fill
```

Here, any profit exceeding 2000 is highlighted with a light red background, drawing immediate attention to high performers within your dataset.

In addition to color and font adjustments, applying number formats is crucial for financial reports. Ensuring numbers are displayed as currency enhances clarity significantly:

```python
from openpyxl.styles import NumberFormat


\#\# Apply currency format to sales figures

for row in range(2, sheet.max_row + 1):

sheet.cell(row=row, column=2).number_format = '\#,\# \#0.00' \# Assuming sales figures are in column B
```

This simple addition formats sales figures with commas and two decimal places—making it easier for stakeholders to interpret financial data at a glance.

Beyond aesthetics and clarity, managing cell borders can further improve organization within your spreadsheet. Borders help delineate different categories or groups of data:

```python
from openpyxl.styles import Border, Side

\#\# Define border style
thin_border = Border(left=Side(style='thin'),
right=Side(style='thin'),
top=Side(style='thin'),
bottom=Side(style='thin'))

\#\# Apply border to header row and data range
for cell in sheet["1:1"]:
cell.border = thin_border

for row in range(2, sheet.max_row + 1):
for cell in sheet[row]:
cell.border = thin_border
```

By adding thin borders around both the header and data cells, you create visual separation that enhances readability and organization throughout your report.

Conditional formatting takes your capabilities even further by allowing dynamic styling based on specific criteria. Take this example, if you need to flag any values below an acceptable threshold automatically, OpenPyXL's built-in conditional formatting features make this straightforward:

``` python

from openpyxl.formatting.rule import CellIsRule


\#\# Apply conditional formatting for values less than 1000

sheet.conditional_formatting.add('B2:B10',
CellIsRule(operator='lessThan',         formula=['1000'],
stopIfTrue=True,

fill=PatternFill(start_color="FF9999",    end_color="FF9999",
fill_type="solid")))

```

With this line of code, any sales figure below 1000 will automatically receive a light pink background whenever the spreadsheet is opened or recalculated.

As you delve into these techniques and integrate them into your workflows, remember that effective formatting extends beyond mere appearance; it enhances communication through improved clarity and accessibility of information. Each adjustment not only beautifies but also elevates the utility of your spreadsheets.

By mastering these tools, you can create dynamic reports that resonate with their intended audience while ensuring critical insights remain prominent. With practice and creativity, you'll unlock new dimensions of functionality within your automated processes using Python and Excel seamlessly together.

Using Excel formulas in Python scripts

Integrating Excel formulas into Python scripts allows you

to leverage Excel's powerful computational features while enjoying Python's versatility and automation capabilities. This combination can greatly enhance data analysis tasks and improve workflow efficiency. As you explore this topic, you'll learn how to use Excel formulas within your Python scripts to perform calculations, manipulate data, and extract insights directly from your spreadsheets.

A key library that enables this integration is OpenPyXL, which provides the tools to read and write Excel files seamlessly. With OpenPyXL, you can dynamically embed Excel formulas in your spreadsheets, making them responsive to changes in your data. Take this example, imagine you want to calculate total sales for a specific period directly within your Python script:

```python
from openpyxl import Workbook

\#\# Create a new workbook and select the active worksheet
wb = Workbook()
sheet = wb.active

\#\# Sample data: Sales figures for the first quarter
sales_data = [1000, 1500, 2000]
for index, value in enumerate(sales_data, start=1):
sheet.cell(row=index, column=1).value = value

\#\# Adding a formula to calculate total sales
sheet.cell(row=len(sales_data) + 1, column=1).value = '=SUM(A1:A3)'
```

```python
\#\# Save the workbook

wb.save('sales_report.xlsx')
` ` `
```

In this example, the sales figures are entered into the first column, and the formula =SUM(A1:A3) automatically calculates the total sales. When you open the resulting Excel file, it will display the computed total based on any updates made to the individual sales entries.

Going beyond simple calculations, consider scenarios that involve conditional logic or more complex formulas requiring references to multiple cells. For example, if you want to assess whether quarterly sales have exceeded a target amount and display an appropriate message, you can add:

```python
` ` `python
\#\# Set target sales

target_sales = 4000


\#\# Adding formula for conditional message

sheet.cell(row=len(sales_data) + 2, column=1).value = f'=IF(SUM(A1:A3)>target_sales,"Target Met","Target Not Met")'
` ` `
```

This line utilizes an IF statement to check if the total sales surpass a specified target, returning either "Target Met" or "Target Not Met." This formula dynamically evaluates based on the existing data whenever it is recalculated in Excel.

One of the major advantages of embedding Excel formulas is their automatic updates in response to data changes. In environments where sales figures fluctuate frequently, using embedded formulas allows stakeholders to view real-time results without needing to rerun Python scripts or manually adjust calculations.

```python
\#\# Assuming additional sales data in the next column

additional_sales_data = [2000, 2500, 3000]

for index, value in enumerate(additional_sales_data, start=1):

sheet.cell(row=index, column=2).value = value


\#\# Adding an array formula for average calculation

sheet.cell(row=len(sales_data) + 4, column=2).value = '=AVERAGE(A1:B3)'
```

This example demonstrates how to calculate the average of two columns of sales data using the AVERAGE function, highlighting the versatility and power of formulas when working with multi-column datasets.

And, Excel's ability to create dynamic charts complements these scripting techniques beautifully. To visually represent your data alongside the calculations automatically generated by your Python scripts, integrating charting functions is essential. After inserting your data and formulas into the workbook, you could add:

```python
from openpyxl.chart import BarChart, Reference


\#\# Create a bar chart for visual representation of sales data

chart = BarChart()

data = Reference(sheet,
```

```
min_col=1,

min_row=1,

max_col=2,

max_row=len(sales_data))

chart.add_data(data, titles_from_data=True)

chart.title = "Quarterly Sales Comparison

sheet.add_chart(chart, "D5")


\#\# Save changes to workbook

wb.save('sales_report_with_chart.xlsx')
` ` `
```

This code generates a bar chart comparing two sets of sales figures side by side. Such visualizations not only enhance reports but also provide stakeholders with quick insights into performance trends at a glance.

By incorporating Excel formulas directly within Python scripts, you create a powerful synergy that boosts productivity. Each embedded formula acts as a live calculator that responds instantly as data changes—providing immediate feedback and analysis without manual intervention.

As you integrate these techniques into your automation workflows, remember that creativity is essential. Experiment with different types of formulas—such as lookup functions or financial models—to discover how they can further enrich your analyses and reporting processes. The more effectively you combine Python's programming capabilities with Excel's formulaic strength, the more impactful your automated solutions will be in delivering valuable insights quickly and efficiently.

Managing Excel charts with OpenPyXL

To begin with, it's important to familiarize yourself with the various chart types supported by OpenPyXL. Popular options include bar charts, line charts, pie charts, and scatter plots—each offering unique advantages for illustrating different aspects of your data. Take this example, bar charts are particularly effective for comparing quantities across categories, while line charts excel at showcasing trends over time.

Let's dive into creating a simple bar chart using OpenPyXL. Imagine you have sales data for four quarters and wish to visualize it effectively. The following code snippet demonstrates how to set up your Excel workbook with the relevant data and insert a bar chart.

```python
from openpyxl import Workbook

from openpyxl.chart import BarChart, Reference


\#\# Create a new workbook and select the active worksheet

wb = Workbook()

sheet = wb.active


\#\# Sample sales data

data = [

["Quarter", "Sales"],

["Q1", 15000],

["Q2", 20000],
```

```
    ["Q3", 25000],
    ["Q4", 30000]
]

\#\# Populate the worksheet with data
for row in data:
    sheet.append(row)

\#\# Define the range for the chart data
chart_data = Reference(sheet,
min_col=2,
min_row=1,
max_col=2,
max_row=len(data))

\#\# Create a BarChart instance
chart = BarChart()
chart.add_data(chart_data, titles_from_data=True)
chart.title = "Sales Performance by Quarter
chart.x_axis.title = "Quarters
chart.y_axis.title = "Sales (\()

\#\# Add the chart to the worksheet
sheet.add_chart(chart, "E5")
```

\#\# Save the workbook

wb.save('sales_performance_chart.xlsx')

``` ` `` `

In this example, we start by creating a workbook and inputting our sales data. We then specify which cells contain the data we want to visualize using Reference. After creating the BarChart object and populating it with our reference data, we define the chart's title and axis labels before adding it to the worksheet.

Once your basic chart is created, customization becomes crucial for making your visuals more engaging and informative. OpenPyXL allows you to adjust styles such as colors, fonts, and borders to enhance readability. For example:

``` ` `` `python

\#\# Customize chart appearance

chart.style = 13 \# Change style to one of OpenPyXL's pre-defined styles

chart.legend.position = 'r' \# Set legend position to right

``` ` `` `

These adjustments can significantly improve the appeal of your visualizations and facilitate quicker interpretation for stakeholders.

In addition to creating charts, managing existing ones is straightforward with OpenPyXL. You may need to update a chart's data source as new information becomes available or modify its design based on feedback. To do this efficiently:

1. Updating Data: Change the values directly in your worksheet cells.

2. Refreshing Charts: After updating values in cells
```

referenced by a chart, simply save your workbook; Excel will refresh the chart upon opening.

Understanding how multiple charts can interact within a single workbook can further enhance your reporting capabilities. By creating various charts that pull from different datasets, you can provide comprehensive insights at a glance.

For an advanced example, consider generating both a bar and a line chart for comparative analysis of two datasets—sales versus expenses over four quarters:

```python
from openpyxl.chart import LineChart


## Sample expense data (assumed in new column)
expense_data = [12000, 15000, 18000, 22000]
for index, value in enumerate(expense_data):
sheet.cell(row=index + 2, column=3).value = value


## Create a LineChart instance for expenses
line_chart = LineChart()
line_chart.title = "Expenses vs Sales
line_chart.x_axis.title = "Quarters
line_chart.y_axis.title = "Amount (\))


## Adding both datasets for comparison
data_expenses = Reference(sheet,
min_col=3,
min_row=1,
```

```
max_row=len(expense_data) + 1)

data_sales = Reference(sheet,

min_col=2,

min_row=1,

max_row=len(data))


line_chart.add_data(data_sales, titles_from_data=True)

line_chart.add_data(data_expenses, titles_from_data=True)


\#\# Positioning the line chart below the bar chart

sheet.add_chart(line_chart, "E20")


\#\# Save changes to workbook

wb.save('sales_vs_expenses_chart.xlsx')

` ` `
```

This snippet illustrates how easy it is to visually juxtapose two datasets within one Excel report—highlighting trends side by side for clearer analysis.

As you create these visual aids with Python and OpenPyXL, consider adding interactivity through hyperlinks or embedding dynamic elements like slicers if needed. While static charts provide significant insights on their own, enabling user interaction enhances their analytical experience.

By embracing these techniques, you not only empower yourself to produce sophisticated reports but also position yourself as an innovative contributor within any team or organization. With practice and creativity in managing

Excel charts through Python scripts via OpenPyXL, you'll gain confidence in crafting compelling visual narratives that resonate with stakeholders while advancing your professional expertise in automation.

Handling Excel styles and themes

Let's begin with cell formatting. OpenPyXL offers a robust set of tools for customizing fonts, fills, borders, and alignment. Take this example, if you want to make your sales data stand out, you could apply bold formatting to the headers and add background colors for clarity. Here's a code snippet that demonstrates these techniques:

```python
from openpyxl.styles import Font, Color, PatternFill


\#\# Sample styling for headers

header_font = Font(bold=True, color="FFFFFF")

header_fill = PatternFill(start_color="0072C6", end_color="0072C6", fill_type="solid")


\#\# Apply styles to header row

for cell in sheet["1:1"]: \# Assuming the first row contains headers

cell.font = header_font

cell.fill = header_fill
```

In this example, the headers are formatted in bold with a white font against a blue background. Such styling enhances readability and establishes a consistent visual identity across your reports.

Having covered cell-level styling, let's shift our focus to managing themes throughout entire worksheets. Themes dictate font styles, color schemes, and effects used across your workbook. This is especially useful when you want to maintain brand consistency in business reports or presentations.

Although OpenPyXL does not directly support complex Excel themes like those found in the Excel application itself, you can emulate a thematic approach by defining a consistent set of styles for various elements within your workbook. For example:

```python
\#\# Define a theme color palette

theme_colors =

header": "0072C6",

font": "FFFFFF",

data_fill": "E7F3FE


\#\# Apply data fill color to specific data range

data_fill = PatternFill(start_color=theme_colors["data_fill"], end_color=theme_colors["data_fill"], fill_type="solid")

for row in sheet.iter_rows(min_row=2): \# Skip header row

for cell in row:

cell.fill = data_fill \# Apply fill color to each data cell
```

This approach allows for cohesive design elements that can be reused throughout your workbook.

Next, let's discuss the importance of borders—an essential aspect of presenting data clearly. Borders help delineate sections of your worksheet or highlight critical figures. Here's how you can add borders to specific cells:

``` python
from openpyxl.styles import Border, Side


\#\# Define border style

thin_border            =            Border(left=Side(style='thin'), right=Side(style='thin'),

top=Side(style='thin'), bottom=Side(style='thin'))


\#\# Apply border to specific range (e.g., sales data)

for row in sheet.iter_rows(min_row=2, max_row=len(data) + 1,

min_col=1, max_col=len(data[0])):

for cell in row:

cell.border = thin_border  \# Apply border style to each cell in the range
``` 

By strategically applying borders around key areas like totals or averages, you draw attention where it matters most.

Now let's consider alignment—a subtle yet impactful aspect of styling that affects how information is visually presented. Take this example, centering column titles or right-aligning numerical data can greatly enhance clarity:

``` python
from openpyxl.styles import Alignment
```

\#\# Center align header titles

for cell in sheet["1:1"]:

cell.alignment = Alignment(horizontal='center')

\#\# Right align numerical values in sales column (assumed as column B)

for row in sheet.iter_rows(min_row=2):

row[1].alignment = Alignment(horizontal='right') \# Adjusting second column (index 1)

` ` `

Implementing these alignment adjustments not only improves aesthetics but also aids interpretation during presentations.

With these foundational styling techniques established, you might consider incorporating additional enhancements such as conditional formatting. While OpenPyXL provides basic options for this through methods like ConditionalFormatting, effectively using them requires thoughtful planning about which insights should be highlighted within your datasets.

Take this example, if you're tracking sales performance over time and wish to flag any quarters where sales fell below a certain threshold:

` ` `python

from openpyxl.formatting.rule import CellIsRule

\#\# Add conditional formatting rule for low sales values (assumed threshold)

sheet.conditional_formatting.add('B2:B5',

116

```
CellIsRule(operator='lessThan',          formula=['20000'],
stopIfTrue=True,

fill=PatternFill(start_color='FFCCCB',   end_color='FFCCCB',
fill_type='solid')))
```
` ` `

In this example, any sales value below (20,000 will be shaded red—providing an immediate visual cue that invites further investigation.

By now, you've seen that handling Excel styles and themes with OpenPyXL transcends mere aesthetics; it's about creating intuitive experiences that allow users to engage meaningfully with your data. Each formatting choice—from bold fonts and vibrant colors to precise alignments—works harmoniously to foster understanding and insight among stakeholders.

Embracing these styling capabilities empowers you not just to present raw numbers but also to narrate compelling stories through your Excel reports. As you continue honing these skills with practice and creativity at every opportunity, you'll find yourself well-equipped to produce documents that resonate powerfully in any business context.

CHAPTER 4:
AUTOMATING EXCEL
WITH XLSXWRITER

Overview of XlsxWriter library

T he XlsxWriter library is a powerful tool for automating Excel tasks, appealing to both novice and advanced users. Its versatility enables the creation of complex Excel files with ease, allowing users to focus more on data analysis rather than on tedious formatting tasks. As you explore XlsxWriter, you'll discover that it not only simplifies spreadsheet creation but also enhances their visual appeal through extensive customization and formatting options.

One of XlsxWriter's standout features is its ability to write data quickly and efficiently. The library supports various data types—numbers, strings, dates, and even formulas—with minimal effort. Take this example, when generating a simple sales report, you can output an entire dataset in just a few lines of code:

```python
import xlsxwriter
```

```
\#\# Create a new workbook and add a worksheet
workbook = xlsxwriter.Workbook('sales_report.xlsx')
worksheet = workbook.add_worksheet()

\#\# Sample sales data
data = [
['Product', 'Sales', 'Date'],
['Product A', 15000, '2023-01-01'],
['Product B', 20000, '2023-01-02'],
]

\#\# Write data to the worksheet
for row_num, row_data in enumerate(data):
worksheet.write_row(row_num, 0, row_data)

workbook.close()
```

In this example, you can see how effortlessly an entire table is generated, with each entry neatly placed in its corresponding row and column. This efficiency becomes invaluable when handling large datasets, where manual entry would be tedious and prone to errors.

Beyond simple data entry, XlsxWriter allows users to apply intricate formatting styles that can significantly enhance the readability of your spreadsheets. Take this example, if you want to make your sales figures stand out, the library enables you to format cells with specific colors and fonts seamlessly. Here's how you could highlight sales data in green for values exceeding a certain threshold:

```python
\#\# Create formats for highlighting

highlight_format = workbook.add_format('color': 'green', 'bold': True)


\#\# Apply formatting based on condition

for row_num in range(1, len(data)):

if data[row_num][1] > 15000: \# If sales exceed 15,000

worksheet.write(row_num, 1, data[row_num][1], highlight_format)
```

This code not only writes the sales figures but also highlights those above the defined threshold, providing visual cues that facilitate quick data analysis and informed decision-making.

Further enhancing your reports are XlsxWriter's capabilities related to charts within Excel. Charts can provide visual representations that make complex datasets more digestible. Integrating charts into your spreadsheets with XlsxWriter is straightforward. For example, if you wish to visualize sales trends over time, you can implement it as follows:

```python
\#\# Adding a chart

chart = workbook.add_chart('type': 'column')


\#\# Configure the series of the chart from the data
```

```
chart.add_series(
'name': 'Sales Data',
'categories': '=Sheet1!\)C\(2:\)C\(3',
'values': '=Sheet1!\)B\(2:\)B\(3',
)
```

\#\# Insert the chart into the worksheet

```
worksheet.insert_chart('E2', chart)
```

` ` `

This snippet creates a column chart based on your sales data, transforming your spreadsheet from a simple collection of numbers into a dynamic storytelling tool through visuals.

While creating visually appealing spreadsheets is essential, ensuring consistency across different files or sections within the same workbook is equally important. Creating templates with predefined formats can save significant time and maintain uniformity. By defining standard styles for headers, body text, and other elements at the beginning of your script, you can easily apply these styles across various worksheets without starting from scratch each time.

` ` `python

\#\# Define common formats at the start

```
header_format = workbook.add_format('bold': True, 'bg_color':
'\#F4CCCC')

cell_format = workbook.add_format('border': 1)
```

\#\# Use defined formats consistently throughout the workbook

```
worksheet.write('A1', 'Product', header_format)

worksheet.write('B1', 'Sales', header_format)

worksheet.write('A2', 'Product A', cell_format)

worksheet.write('B2', 15000, cell_format)
```
```

By establishing these templates early on, you enhance workflow efficiency while ensuring high-quality output across all documents.

With these features at your disposal—quick data writing, advanced formatting options, seamless chart creation, and effective templating—you are well-equipped to create robust Excel workbooks that meet various business needs. The XlsxWriter library not only boosts productivity but also elevates the professionalism of your reports.

As you continue to explore XlsxWriter's capabilities in your automation journey, remember that practice is key. Experimenting with different functionalities will deepen your understanding and expand your toolkit for future projects. The potential of this library is vast; embracing it will enable you to craft not just functional spreadsheets but also compelling narratives with your data—a skill that will undoubtedly set you apart in any professional arena.

**Writing data to Excel files**

Writing data to Excel files using Python opens up a world of possibilities, allowing you to automate tedious tasks and significantly enhance your productivity. Libraries like XlsxWriter and OpenPyXL make it easy to write data efficiently, whether you're creating simple tables or complex spreadsheets.

Let's begin with XlsxWriter, a powerful library designed for creating Excel files with advanced features. To get
```

started, ensure that XlsxWriter is installed in your Python environment by running the following command in your terminal:

```bash
pip install XlsxWriter
```

After installation, creating an Excel file is straightforward. Here's how to write some basic data into an Excel file:

```python
import xlsxwriter

\#\# Create a new Excel file and add a worksheet
workbook = xlsxwriter.Workbook('example.xlsx')
worksheet = workbook.add_worksheet()

\#\# Write some data headers
worksheet.write('A1', 'Name')
worksheet.write('B1', 'Age')
worksheet.write('C1', 'City')

\#\# Write some data
data = [
['Alice', 30, 'New York'],
['Bob', 25, 'Los Angeles'],
['Charlie', 35, 'Chicago'],
]
```

```
row = 1 \# Start from the second row (index 1)
for name, age, city in data:
worksheet.write(row, 0, name)  \# Column A
worksheet.write(row, 1, age)    \# Column B
worksheet.write(row, 2, city)   \# Column C
row += 1

\#\# Close the workbook
workbook.close()
` ` `
```

In this script, we create an Excel file named example.xlsx and populate it with names, ages, and cities. Each write method specifies the row and column indices for placing the data.

To enhance readability and visual appeal, you might consider formatting your data. XlsxWriter supports various formatting options that can elevate the presentation of your spreadsheets. Let's refine our previous example by adding some formatting:

```python
\#\# Creating a new workbook and adding a worksheet again
for demonstration.
workbook = xlsxwriter.Workbook('formatted_example.xlsx')
worksheet = workbook.add_worksheet()

\#\# Define formatting options
bold_format = workbook.add_format('bold': True)
```

```python
centered_format = workbook.add_format('align': 'center')

\#\# Write headers with formatting
worksheet.write('A1', 'Name', bold_format)
worksheet.write('B1', 'Age', bold_format)
worksheet.write('C1', 'City', bold_format)

\#\# Add some data with formatting
data = [
['Alice', 30, 'New York'],
['Bob', 25, 'Los Angeles'],
['Charlie', 35, 'Chicago'],
]

row = 1
for name, age, city in data:
worksheet.write(row, 0, name)
worksheet.write(row, 1, age)
worksheet.write(row, 2, city)
row += 1

\#\# Apply centered format to header rows
worksheet.set_row(0, None, centered_format)
```

\#\# Close the workbook

workbook.close()

` ` `

In this example, we introduce two formats: one for bold text in the headers and another for centering text. This level of customization ensures that your output is not only functional but also visually easy to interpret at a glance.

As you continue to explore these libraries for writing data into Excel files, keep in mind that handling larger datasets may require optimizing memory usage and processing time. Take this example, instead of writing row by row (which can slow down execution), consider collecting all your data first in a list or DataFrame before writing it in one batch.

For scenarios where speed is crucial—such as during quarterly reports or presentations—you might find it beneficial to utilize pandas alongside XlsxWriter. Here's how you can do this:

` ` `python

import pandas as pd

\#\# Sample DataFrame creation

data =

'Name': ['Alice', 'Bob', 'Charlie'],

'Age': [30, 25, 35],

'City': ['New York', 'Los Angeles', 'Chicago']

df = pd.DataFrame(data)

\#\# Write DataFrame to an Excel file using Pandas with XlsxWriter as the engine.

df.to_excel('pandas_example.xlsx', index=False)

```
` ` `
```

This approach simplifies writing large sets of structured data by leveraging pandas' built-in capabilities while still enjoying XlsxWriter's advantages for Excel-specific features.

Throughout these examples of writing to Excel files using Python libraries like XlsxWriter—and integrating with pandas for more complex datasets—you can see how automation greatly enhances efficiency in analysis-heavy environments. It reduces errors associated with manual entry and frees up valuable time for more strategic tasks.

The next time you find yourself manually transferring data into spreadsheets or struggling with outdated reporting methods... remember the power at your fingertips! Your journey into automation is just beginning—embrace it fully!

Creating and customizing Excel charts

Creating charts in Excel significantly enhances the visual representation of data, enabling deeper insights into trends and patterns. By leveraging Python libraries like XlsxWriter and OpenPyXL, you can automate the creation and customization of these charts, making your data easier to interpret and share effectively.

Let's begin with XlsxWriter to create a straightforward chart. Before we dive into the code, ensure that your data is well-structured. Here's an example dataset illustrating sales data across different months:

```python
import xlsxwriter
```

```
\#\# Create a new workbook and add a worksheet
workbook = xlsxwriter.Workbook('sales_data.xlsx')
worksheet = workbook.add_worksheet()

\#\# Sample sales data
months = ['January', 'February', 'March', 'April', 'May']
sales = [1000, 1500, 1200, 1700, 2000]

\#\# Write the months and sales data to the worksheet
worksheet.write_column('A1', months)
worksheet.write_column('B1', sales)

\#\# Create a chart object
chart = workbook.add_chart('type': 'column')

\#\# Configure the series of the chart from the worksheet data
chart.add_series(
'name': 'Sales',
'categories': '=Sheet1!\)A\(1:\)A\(5',
'values': '=Sheet1!\)B\(1:\)B\(5',
)

\#\# Insert the chart into the worksheet
```

```python
worksheet.insert_chart('D2', chart)
```

\#\# Close the workbook

```python
workbook.close()
```

` ` `

In this snippet, we start by writing our sales data into an Excel sheet. We then create a column chart using XlsxWriter by specifying "Sales" as the series name and linking it to our dataset's categories and values. Finally, we place the chart in a specified location on our sheet.

To elevate your reports further, consider customizing your charts. Take this example, you may want to alter the colors of your columns or add titles and labels for enhanced clarity. Here's how to enrich our previous example with some formatting:

` ` `python

```python
chart.set_title('name': 'Monthly Sales Data')

chart.set_x_axis('name': 'Months')

chart.set_y_axis('name': 'Sales in \)')

chart.set_style(11) \# Apply a predefined style for aesthetics


\#\# Further customization can include changing colors:
chart.add_series(

'name': 'Sales',

'categories': '=Sheet1!\(A\)1:\(A\)5',

'values': '=Sheet1!\(B\)1:\(B\)5',

'fill': 'color': '\#5ABA8E', \# Custom color for bars
```

)

```
` ` `
```

This additional customization not only ensures that your chart communicates information effectively but also presents it with style. The ability to adjust elements like titles and colors allows you to tailor presentations to align with branding or specific audience preferences.

Now let's explore OpenPyXL. If you're working with existing Excel files or require more complex manipulations beyond what XlsxWriter offers, here's how you can create charts using this library:

```python
` ` `python
from openpyxl import Workbook

from openpyxl.chart import BarChart, Reference


\#\# Create a new workbook and add a worksheet

wb = Workbook()

ws = wb.active


\#\# Sample sales data written directly into cells

ws.append(['Month', 'Sales'])

data = [

['January', 1000],

['February', 1500],

['March', 1200],

['April', 1700],
```

```
['May', 2000]
]

for row in data:
ws.append(row)

\#\# Define references for categories and values
categories = Reference(ws,
min_col=1,
min_row=2,
max_row=6)
values = Reference(ws,
min_col=2,
min_row=1,
max_row=6)

\#\# Create a bar chart
bar_chart = BarChart()
bar_chart.add_data(values)
bar_chart.set_categories(categories)
bar_chart.title = "Monthly Sales Data
bar_chart.x_axis.title = "Months
bar_chart.y_axis.title = "Sales in \(
```

\#\# Add bar chart to the worksheet

ws.add_chart(bar_chart, "D2")

\#\# Save the workbook

wb.save("openpyxl_sales_data.xlsx")

` ` `

In this OpenPyXL example, we append our sales data directly into cells before creating a BarChart object. By defining references for categories and values based on cell locations, we can efficiently set up our chart. Adding it to our worksheet is as simple as calling add_chart.

Both libraries have unique strengths tailored to different needs: XlsxWriter excels at creating new Excel files rich with features, while OpenPyXL is ideal for modifying existing files or working within complex structures.

Conditional formatting in Excel

Conditional formatting in Excel enhances clarity and insight by allowing users to highlight trends, identify key data points, and flag anomalies with ease. This feature transforms raw data into visually intuitive information, making it easier to analyze and act upon. When combined with Python, you can automate the application of these formatting rules, ensuring consistency across your datasets while saving valuable time.

Let's explore how to apply conditional formatting using the OpenPyXL library. To begin, it's essential that your data is well-organized. For this example, consider a dataset that tracks monthly sales figures across various regions. Here's a straightforward setup:

` ` `python

```python
from openpyxl import Workbook

from openpyxl.styles import PatternFill


\#\# Create a new workbook and add a worksheet

wb = Workbook()

ws = wb.active


\#\# Sample sales data

ws.append(['Region', 'Sales'])

data = [

['North', 5000],

['South', 7000],

['East', 3000],

['West', 10000]

]


for row in data:

ws.append(row)


\#\# Define fill colors for conditional formatting

high_sales_fill      =      PatternFill(start_color='FF0000',
end_color='FF0000', fill_type='solid')  \# Red for high sales

low_sales_fill      =      PatternFill(start_color='00FF00',
end_color='00FF00', fill_type='solid')  \# Green for low sales
```

```
\#\# Apply conditional formatting based on sales values

for row in range(2, len(data) + 2):  \# Start from the second row to skip header

if ws.cell(row=row, column=2).value > 6000:  \# Sales above 6000

ws.cell(row=row, column=2).fill = high_sales_fill

else:

ws.cell(row=row, column=2).fill = low_sales_fill


\#\# Save the workbook

wb.save('conditional_formatting_sales.xlsx')
```
` ` `

In this script, we start by creating a workbook and filling it with sample sales data. The crucial step involves defining PatternFill objects for different conditions—using red for high sales and green for low sales. The loop iterates through each row of the dataset, beginning from the second row to bypass headers. It evaluates the value in the "Sales" column and applies the corresponding fill color based on this assessment.

This approach not only enhances visual understanding but also enables stakeholders to quickly grasp performance metrics at a glance.

Next, we can explore XlsxWriter as another effective tool for implementing conditional formatting. In the example below, we apply conditional formatting directly while writing our data:

` ` `python

import xlsxwriter

```python
#\# Create a new workbook and add a worksheet
workbook                                    =
xlsxwriter.Workbook('conditional_formatting.xlsx')
worksheet = workbook.add_worksheet()

#\# Sample sales data
worksheet.write_row('A1', ['Region', 'Sales'])
data = [
['North', 5000],
['South', 7000],
['East', 3000],
['West', 10000]
]

row_number = 1
for region, sales in data:
worksheet.write(row_number, 0, region)
worksheet.write(row_number, 1, sales)
row_number += 1

#\# Define conditional formats using XlsxWriter's built-in features
high_sales_format     =     workbook.add_format('bg_color':
'\#FF0000')  \# Red background for high sales
```

```
low_sales_format    =    workbook.add_format('bg_color':
'\#00FF00')  \# Green background for low sales
```

\#\# Apply conditional formatting rules to the Sales column (B2:B5)

```
worksheet.conditional_format('B2:B5',

'type': 'cell',

'criteria': '>',

'value': 6000,

'format': high_sales_format,

)
```

```
worksheet.conditional_format('B2:B5',

'type': 'cell',

'criteria': '<=',

'value': 6000,

'format': low_sales_format,

)
```

\#\# Close the workbook

```
workbook.close()
```
` ` `

In this example using XlsxWriter, we create an Excel file with the same dataset but utilize its built-in conditional_format method. Here, we define two formats—one red and one green —based on specific criteria applied directly within Excel upon creation. This setup allows users to immediately see which regions are performing well and which ones are lagging behind as soon as they open their reports.

Implementing these automation techniques streamlines your workflow and ensures that your colleagues receive clear insights at every opportunity. As you incorporate these strategies into your reporting processes, consider how much more effective decision-making can be when stakeholders have immediate visual feedback rather than sifting through rows of numbers.

Looking ahead, you might want to explore more advanced scenarios where multiple conditions are applied simultaneously or leverage formulas within conditional formatting rules to manage complex datasets dynamically. This exciting avenue further amplifies Excel's potential when enhanced by Python!

Using advanced Excel formulas and functions

Leveraging advanced Excel formulas and functions can greatly enhance your ability to analyze data and extract meaningful insights. These formulas form the backbone of effective Excel-based analysis, allowing for seamless calculations, text manipulation, and logical evaluations. When you combine these capabilities with Python automation, the potential expands exponentially. You can create dynamic reports and interactive dashboards that adapt to your data in real time.

Let's explore how to harness some of Excel's powerful functions within a Python context. A prime example is the VLOOKUP function, which allows you to search for a value in one column and return a corresponding value from another column. This functionality is particularly useful for cross-referencing datasets. Here's how to implement VLOOKUP using the OpenPyXL library for automation.

Suppose you have two datasets: one with product details and another containing sales data. Your goal is to pull product names into the sales dataset based on product IDs. Below is a step-by-step implementation:

```python
from openpyxl import Workbook

\#\# Create a new workbook and add worksheets
wb = Workbook()
ws1 = wb.active
ws1.title = "Products
ws2 = wb.create_sheet(title="Sales")

\#\# Sample product data
products = [
['Product ID', 'Product Name'],
[101, 'Widget A'],
[102, 'Widget B'],
[103, 'Widget C']
]

for row in products:
ws1.append(row)

\#\# Sample sales data with product IDs
sales = [
['Sale ID', 'Product ID', 'Quantity'],
```

```
    [1, 101, 5],

    [2, 102, 3],

    [3, 103, 8],

    [4, 101, 2]

    ]


for row in sales:

ws2.append(row)


\#\# Adding VLOOKUP formula to the Sales sheet

for row in range(2, len(sales) + 2):

ws2[f'Drow'] = f'=VLOOKUP(Brow, Products!\)A\(2:\)B\(4, 2, FALSE)'


\#\# Save the workbook

wb.save('vlookup_sales.xlsx')
    ` ` `
```

In this script, we create two sheets: one for products and another for sales. The VLOOKUP formula is programmatically inserted into the Sales sheet by referencing the Products sheet. That's why, when you open the Sales sheet in Excel, it automatically populates the Product Name based on the Product ID.

The advantage of automating such tasks lies not only in speed but also in accuracy—ensuring that your reports are consistently updated with correct information without manual entry errors.

Next, consider the power of array formulas that can perform multiple calculations simultaneously. For example, the SUMIFS function calculates the sum of a range based on multiple criteria. Let's say you want to sum total sales based on both product type and region. Here's how to set that up using Python:

```python
\#\# Create a new workbook for sales analysis

wb_sales = Workbook()

ws_sales_analysis = wb_sales.active


\#\# Sample data for sales analysis

sales_data = [

['Region', 'Product Type', 'Sales Amount'],

['North', 'Widget A', 5000],

['South', 'Widget B', 7000],

['North', 'Widget C', 3000],

['South', 'Widget A', 10000],

]


for row in sales_data:

ws_sales_analysis.append(row)


\#\# Adding SUMIFS formula

ws_sales_analysis['E1'] = 'Total Sales Widget A North'

ws_sales_analysis['E2'] = '=SUMIFS(C2:C5, A2:A5, "North",
```

B2:B5, "Widget A")'

\#\# Save the analysis workbook

wb_sales.save('sales_analysis.xlsx')

` ` `

In this case, we create another workbook specifically for analyzing sales data by region and product type. The SUMIFS function calculates the total sales amount where both conditions—region being "North" and product type being "Widget A"—are met.

Utilizing these formulas through Python not only streamlines your workflow but also enhances your spreadsheets' analytical capabilities. By automating the application of advanced functions, you ensure that stakeholders have immediate access to insightful data without needing to configure formulas manually each time.

As you continue exploring advanced Excel features through Python automation, consider how you can use functions like INDEX, MATCH, or even complex nested formulas to uncover deeper insights within your datasets. The more proficient you become at integrating these tools into your workflows, the more efficient and impactful your reporting will be.

And, combining dynamic formulas with Python's data manipulation capabilities fosters innovation. You could develop scripts that adjust calculations based on varying inputs or automate entire reporting processes that update in real-time as new data becomes available. This agile reporting empowers organizations to make swift, informed decisions while adapting to evolving business landscapes.

The integration of advanced Excel functions within Python not only simplifies repetitive tasks but also opens doors for creativity and analytical depth—making it an invaluable skill set for any data-driven professional aiming to excel in today's fast-paced environment.

Inserting images and charts into Excel

Inserting images and charts into Excel can significantly enhance your data presentations, making them more engaging and easier to understand. Visual elements have the power to transform raw data into insights that are readily accessible, allowing stakeholders to grasp key points at a glance. By automating this process with Python, you not only eliminate manual tasks but also ensure consistency and save valuable time.

Let's begin by exploring how to insert images into an Excel workbook using the OpenPyXL library. Consider a sales report where you want to display product images alongside their respective sales data. Automating this task not only improves the visual appeal of your reports but also standardizes the way images are presented across various documents.

Here's a simple example of how to insert an image into an Excel file:

```python
from openpyxl import Workbook

from openpyxl.drawing.image import Image


\#\# Create a new workbook and add a worksheet

wb = Workbook()

ws = wb.active

ws.title = "Sales Report


\#\# Sample sales data
```

```
sales_data = [

['Product', 'Sales Amount'],

['Widget A', 5000],

['Widget B', 7000],

]


for row in sales_data:

ws.append(row)


\#\# Insert an image

img = Image('path_to_image/widget_a.png')

ws.add_image(img, 'C2') \# Position the image at cell C2


\#\# Save the workbook

wb.save('sales_report_with_images.xlsx')
```
` ` `

In this example, we create a straightforward sales report with product names and their corresponding sales amounts. The Image class from OpenPyXL allows us to load an image file, which we then add to the worksheet at a specified cell. The beauty of this approach lies in its simplicity; with just a few lines of code, you can significantly enhance the visual aspect of your reports.

Now, let's shift our focus to chart creation. Charts are vital for visualizing trends and patterns in your data, providing clarity that numbers alone often fail to convey. Using Python's XlsxWriter library, you can programmatically generate various types of charts—such as bar charts, line charts, or pie charts—tailored to your specific data needs.

Here's how to create a simple bar chart using XlsxWriter:

```python
import xlsxwriter

\#\# Create a new workbook and add a worksheet
workbook = xlsxwriter.Workbook('sales_chart.xlsx')
worksheet = workbook.add_worksheet()

\#\# Sample data for the chart
data = [
['Product', 'Sales'],
['Widget A', 5000],
['Widget B', 7000],
['Widget C', 3000],
]

\#\# Write the data to the worksheet
for row in data:
worksheet.write_row(*row)

\#\# Create a bar chart
chart = workbook.add_chart('type': 'bar')
```

```
\#\# Configure the series for the chart

chart.add_series(

'name': 'Sales',

'categories': '=Sheet1!\)A\(2:\)A\(4',

'values': '=Sheet1!\)B\(2:\)B\(4',

)


\#\# Insert the chart into the worksheet

worksheet.insert_chart('D2', chart)


\#\# Close the workbook

workbook.close()
```
` ` `

In this script, we define our sales data and write it to an Excel sheet. By using add_chart, we create a bar chart that references our sales data directly from the worksheet. This seamless integration allows for easy updates; if your underlying data changes, so will your chart when you reopen the workbook.

The efficiency gained through automation becomes particularly evident when considering scenarios where multiple reports require similar visual enhancements. Instead of manually adjusting each file or chart layout, you can develop robust scripts that standardize formatting and presentation styles across all your outputs.

As you incorporate these visual elements into your Excel reports via Python, think about how they can help tell compelling stories with your data. Whether highlighting monthly sales growth or comparing product performance across regions, well-placed images and thoughtfully designed charts can deliver powerful insights that resonate with your audience.

Additionally, experimenting with different types of visuals— such as scatter plots for trend analysis or pie charts for market share representation—can further enrich your presentations. The more diverse your visual toolkit becomes through automation, the better equipped you'll be to communicate complex information clearly and effectively.

This capability not only amplifies the impact of your reports but also positions you as an innovator within your organization—someone who understands how to translate data into actionable intelligence. As you continue mastering these techniques, consider their broader implications: how can enhanced reporting drive decision-making processes or lead to more strategic outcomes within your team or company?

By merging Python's automation capabilities with Excel's rich visualization options, you're not just working more efficiently; you're reshaping how decisions are made based on data insights. Embrace this synergy as you advance in mastering advanced Excel automation through Python.

Customizing Excel spreadsheets for reports

Customizing Excel spreadsheets for reports is an essential skill that can significantly enhance the clarity and professionalism of your presentations. By thoughtfully incorporating design elements into your reports, you create a more engaging experience for your audience, enabling them to quickly and effectively glean insights from the data. This customization transcends mere aesthetics; it focuses on making information both accessible and actionable.

To begin, let's explore formatting options that can elevate your spreadsheets. Consistent styling is crucial for maintaining readability and keeping your audience focused on the key information. Using Python's OpenPyXL library, you can automate the formatting of cells—including font styles, colors, and borders—streamlining the process. For example, if you want to highlight key figures in your report, you can programmatically apply bold formatting and background colors to those cells to attract attention.

Here's a simple example of how to implement basic formatting:

```python
from openpyxl import Workbook

from openpyxl.styles import Font, PatternFill


\#\# Create a new workbook and add a worksheet

wb = Workbook()

ws = wb.active

ws.title = "Monthly Sales Report


\#\# Sample sales data

data = [

['Product', 'Sales Amount'],

['Widget A', 5000],

['Widget B', 7000],

]


\#\# Write data to the worksheet and apply formatting

for row in data:
```

```
ws.append(row)

\#\# Apply bold font to headers
for cell in ws["1:1"]:
cell.font = Font(bold=True)

\#\# Highlight sales amount with a fill color
fill = PatternFill(start_color="FFFF00", end_color="FFFF00",
fill_type="solid")
for cell in ws["B2:B3"]:
cell.fill = fill

\#\# Save the workbook
wb.save('formatted_sales_report.xlsx')
```

In this example, we create a new workbook and populate it with sample sales data. We then use the Font class to bold the header cells and apply a yellow fill color to the sales amounts using PatternFill. These straightforward formatting techniques can greatly enhance your report's readability.

Moving beyond basic styling, consider using conditional formatting to automatically highlight trends or outliers. This feature allows certain cells to change appearance based on their values, making significant data points stand out without requiring manual adjustments.

OpenPyXL supports conditional formatting through its ConditionalFormatting class. Take this example, you can highlight sales amounts greater than)6,000 with the following code:

```python
from openpyxl.formatting.rule import CellIsRule

\#\# Create conditional formatting rule for sales greater than \(6000

rule = CellIsRule(operator='greaterThan', formula=['6000'], stopIfTrue=True,

fill=PatternFill(start_color="FF9999", end_color="FF9999", fill_type="solid"))

\#\# Apply rule to the sales amount column

ws.conditional_formatting.add('B2:B3', rule)

\#\# Save the workbook with conditional formatting applied

wb.save('conditional_formatted_sales_report.xlsx')
```

In this case, we add a conditional format that highlights any sale exceeding)6,000 with a red background. This makes it easy for anyone reviewing the report to quickly identify high-performing products.

Charts also play a critical role in effectively conveying your data narrative. Using XlsxWriter allows you not only to create charts but also to customize their appearance—titles, labels, and colors—ensuring they align with your overall report design.

Here's an example of how to customize chart elements:

```python
```

```python
import xlsxwriter

workbook = xlsxwriter.Workbook('custom_chart.xlsx')
worksheet = workbook.add_worksheet()

data = [
['Product', 'Sales'],
['Widget A', 5000],
['Widget B', 7000],
]

\#\# Write data to worksheet
for row in data:
worksheet.write_row(*row)

\#\# Create a bar chart with customizations
chart = workbook.add_chart('type': 'bar')
chart.set_title('name': 'Monthly Sales Performance')
chart.set_x_axis('name': 'Products')
chart.set_y_axis('name': 'Sales Amount')

chart.add_series(
'name': 'Sales',
'categories': '=Sheet1!\(A\)2:\(A\)3',
```

```
'values': '=Sheet1!\(B\)2:\(B\)3',
)


worksheet.insert_chart('D2', chart)


workbook.close()
` ` `
```

In this snippet, we define not only the chart type but also set titles for both axes and the overall chart title. Such customizations lend a professional appearance while providing essential context for viewers.

And, consider how these enhancements contribute functionally as well as aesthetically. The presentation of data can influence decision-making; well-customized reports facilitate quicker comprehension and instill confidence in stakeholders regarding your analysis.

In the end, effective reporting goes beyond merely presenting numbers; it's about weaving a narrative through those numbers. Each customization—whether through strategic cell styling or impactful visuals—serves as an opportunity to emphasize critical insights and foster meaningful discussions within your organization. Your ability to leverage Python for these tasks positions you as more than just an Excel user; it establishes you as an innovator in crafting data-driven narratives within your team or business context.

Handling Excel macros with Python

Integrating Excel macros with Python significantly enhances your automation capabilities. While macros have traditionally served as essential tools for automating repetitive tasks in Excel, the addition of Python provides unparalleled flexibility and control over more complex processes. This combination not only boosts efficiency but also broadens the range of possibilities for working with your data.

Macros, typically created using Visual Basic for Applications (VBA), can often feel cumbersome and limited in comparison to what Python offers. By harnessing Python, you can interact with Excel macros in a way that combines the best features of both languages. For example, while VBA excels at automating tasks within Excel, Python shines in managing file operations, manipulating data, and integrating with various data sources seamlessly.

To begin using Python with Excel macros, you'll need to install some essential libraries—most notably pywin32. This library enables Python to communicate with Excel through COM (Component Object Model), allowing you to execute existing macros or create new ones directly within your Python scripts.

Here's a simple step-by-step guide on how to call an existing Excel macro from Python:

1. **Install the Required Library:

First, ensure that you have pywin32 installed. You can easily do this using pip:

```bash
pip install pywin32
```

1. **Open the Excel Application and Workbook:

Use Python to launch Excel and open the workbook that contains your macro.

```python
import win32com.client


\#\# Launch Excel
```

```python
excel = win32com.client.Dispatch("Excel.Application")

excel.Visible = True \# Set to True if you want to see Excel


\#\# Open the workbook

workbook = excel.Workbooks.Open('C:\\path_to_your_file\
\macro_workbook.xlsm')
```
` ` `

1. **Run the Macro:**

Invoke a macro by its name using the Application.Run method.

```python
\#\# Run the macro named 'YourMacroName'

excel.Application.Run("YourMacroName")
```
` ` `

1. **Close the Workbook:**

After executing the macro, you may want to save changes and close the workbook.

```python
workbook.Save()

workbook.Close()

excel.Quit()
```
` ` `

This straightforward script not only illustrates how to run an existing macro but also highlights how Python acts as a powerful wrapper around your VBA functions, enabling more sophisticated workflows that can integrate additional data sources or processing steps.

Creating new macros through Python involves a bit more

complexity. For example, if you want to generate a new macro programmatically, you can write VBA code as a string within your Python script and then insert it into Excel. Here's how that might look:

```python
vba_code = ""

Sub NewMacro()

MsgBox "Hello from Python!

End Sub

"


\#\# Insert the VBA code into a module

excel.VBE.ActiveProject.VBComponents.Add(1).CodeModule.InsertLines(1, vba_code)


\#\# Now you can run this new macro

excel.Application.Run("NewMacro")
```

This method allows for dynamic creation or modification of macros based on specific conditions or input data, greatly enhancing your automation capabilities.

Error handling is another crucial aspect when working with both Python and Excel. Various issues—such as incorrect data types, missing references, or logic errors within VBA code —can lead to errors during macro execution. Implementing robust error handling in your Python scripts will help maintain resilience in your automation processes.

For example, you could use try-except blocks to handle exceptions effectively:

```python
try:

excel.Application.Run("YourMacroName")

except Exception as e:

print(f"An error occurred: e")

finally:

workbook.Close(SaveChanges=True)

excel.Quit()
```

This approach not only captures exceptions but also ensures that resources are properly cleaned up afterward.

As we consider the integration between Python and VBA macros, it's vital to think about future-proofing your work. As organizations evolve and adopt newer technologies and methodologies, converting VBA macros into scalable solutions with Python will ensure that your automation efforts remain relevant and effective.

By exploring this synergy further, you'll find that combining these two powerful tools can truly transform your workflows. You aren't just executing macros; you're crafting automated solutions that leverage advanced programming techniques for optimal results. This opens doors for innovation across various processes—from financial modeling to intricate reporting structures—empowering you to take charge of your data automation journey with confidence and creativity.

CHAPTER 5:
INTEGRATING PYTHON WITH EXCEL VBA

*Understanding VBA and its
role in Excel automation*

U nderstanding VBA and its role in Excel automation
is essential for anyone looking to enhance their skills
with Python. Visual Basic for Applications (VBA) has
long been a key tool for automating tasks in Excel, enabling
users to record simple macros or write complex scripts to
manipulate workbooks and worksheets. While VBA remains
a powerful option, its limitations become clear when dealing
with larger datasets or more complex tasks that require
advanced programming features. This is where Python comes
into play, offering a robust alternative that complements VBA's
strengths.

VBA is seamlessly integrated into the Excel ecosystem,
allowing for the automation of repetitive tasks with ease.
Users can create macros that handle everything from

formatting cells to performing calculations automatically. However, as projects grow in complexity, the rigid structure of VBA can become a constraint. Python's flexibility empowers you to overcome these challenges. For example, Python's extensive libraries enable you to manage data from multiple sources, conduct complex analyses, and interact with web APIs —capabilities that can be cumbersome or even impossible to achieve with pure VBA.

To effectively integrate Python into your Excel automation alongside VBA, it's crucial to understand how these two languages can communicate. This integration often begins with establishing a connection between Python and Excel using the pywin32 library. This library acts as a bridge between your Python scripts and Excel's COM interface, allowing for direct interaction.

A practical example of this integration involves opening an existing Excel workbook containing a macro written in VBA:

1. **Set Up Your Environment:

First, ensure pywin32 is installed:

```bash
pip install pywin32
```

1. **Open Your Workbook:

```python
import win32com.client


\#\# Launching Excel

excel = win32com.client.Dispatch("Excel.Application")

excel.Visible = True \# Set visibility for debugging purposes
```

```python
\#\# Opening your macro-enabled workbook
workbook = excel.Workbooks.Open('C:\\path_to_your_file\\macro_workbook.xlsm')
```

1. **Execute a Macro:

```python
\#\# Running an existing macro named 'MyMacro'
excel.Application.Run("MyMacro")
```

1. **Cleaning Up:

```python
\#\# Saving changes and closing
workbook.Save()
workbook.Close()
excel.Quit()
```

This example not only demonstrates how to execute a macro but also highlights how Python enhances automation capabilities by enabling batch processes and integrating additional data handling beyond what VBA can accomplish on its own.

If you wish to create new macros dynamically using Python, you can write a string of VBA code directly into your script and inject it into Excel like this:

```python
vba_code = ""
```

```
Sub HelloWorld()

MsgBox "Hello from your Python script!

End Sub

"
```

\#\# Adding the new macro to the active project

```
excel.VBE.ActiveProject.VBComponents.Add(1).CodeModule.InsertLines(1, vba_code)
```

\#\# Running the newly created macro

```
excel.Application.Run("HelloWorld")
```
` ` `

This level of dynamic functionality allows for significant adaptability within your automation processes—enabling you to tailor scripts based on real-time needs or data inputs.

Error handling is also crucial when working with both languages, ensuring your scripts are resilient against unexpected issues such as incorrect data formats or runtime exceptions within your macros. Implementing error handling mechanisms helps maintain operational stability:

` ` `python

```
try:

excel.Application.Run("YourMacroName")

except Exception as e:

print(f"An error occurred: e")

finally:
```

```
workbook.Close(SaveChanges=True)

excel.Quit()
` ` `
```

This example captures errors effectively while ensuring resources are cleaned up properly—an essential practice for maintaining system performance and preventing memory leaks.

As organizations increasingly adopt sophisticated technologies alongside Excel's capabilities, understanding both VBA and Python will position you favorably within any team environment. The strategic integration of these tools empowers you to build comprehensive automation solutions that evolve alongside changing business needs.

By combining the simplicity of VBA with the extensive power of Python, you can craft workflows that are not only efficient but also scalable and adaptable over time. This synergy significantly enhances your ability to make data-driven decisions across various departments—whether in finance, marketing analytics, or operational efficiency—driving innovation throughout your organization's processes.

Incorporating these insights into your work will elevate not only how you automate but also how you engage with complex datasets and derive meaningful outcomes from them. Embracing this dual-language approach could redefine what's possible within your own data landscape, leading to greater efficiency and innovation in every facet of your professional endeavors.

Comparing Python and VBA capabilities

When evaluating the capabilities of Python and VBA for Excel automation, it's important to appreciate the unique strengths each language offers. VBA, as a built-in language within Excel, allows for seamless interaction with Excel objects. This direct integration makes it easy for users to automate tasks without needing additional setup, which is particularly beneficial for quickly automating repetitive tasks. However, VBA can become limiting when faced with larger datasets or complex operations that require more advanced programming features.

In contrast, Python significantly broadens the scope of possibilities. With libraries like Pandas for data manipulation and OpenPyXL for file handling, Python equips users with powerful tools for sophisticated analyses and data management. While VBA is effective at managing simple loops and conditional statements, Python excels in dealing with intricate data structures and performing advanced calculations effortlessly.

To illustrate this difference, consider the task of analyzing a large sales dataset. With VBA, you might encounter constraints related to memory limits or performance as your dataset expands. Python, however, can process data in chunks, allowing for efficient handling of extensive datasets. For example, reading an Excel file containing sales data using Pandas is straightforward:

```python
import pandas as pd


\#\# Reading an Excel file

sales_data        =        pd.read_excel('C:\\path_to_your_file\
\sales_data.xlsx')


\#\# Displaying the first few rows

print(sales_data.head())
```

This approach grants immediate access to your data with

minimal setup. You can easily filter and analyze this dataset using Python's robust functionalities without being hindered by the limitations often associated with VBA.

Additionally, Python's error handling capabilities are more nuanced than those found in VBA. By using try-except blocks, you can manage exceptions effectively:

```python
try:
```

\#\# Attempting to read an Excel file

```python
sales_data = pd.read_excel('C:\\path_to_your_file\\missing_data.xlsx')
except FileNotFoundError:
print("The specified file was not found.")
```

This flexibility ensures that your scripts remain resilient even when unexpected issues arise.

And, integrating Python with Excel allows users to adopt modern programming practices such as modular coding and version control through systems like Git. In contrast, VBA's development environment lacks these features, which can complicate collaborative projects or team-based workflows.

To demonstrate a practical integration example between Python and Excel using pywin32, let's explore how to automate a report generation process:

1. Set up your environment by ensuring pywin32 is installed:

```bash
pip install pywin32
```

1. **Create a new report:
```python
import win32com.client

\#\# Starting the Excel application
excel = win32com.client.Dispatch("Excel.Application")
excel.Visible = True

\#\# Creating a new workbook
workbook = excel.Workbooks.Add()

\#\# Adding data to the first sheet
sheet = workbook.Sheets(1)
sheet.Cells(1, 1).Value = "Product
sheet.Cells(1, 2).Value = "Sales
```

1. **Insert data programmatically:
```python
products = ['Product A', 'Product B', 'Product C']
sales = [15000, 23000, 12000]

for i in range(len(products)):
sheet.Cells(i + 2, 1).Value = products[i]
sheet.Cells(i + 2, 2).Value = sales[i]
```

HAYDEN VAN DER POST

1. **Save the workbook:

```python
workbook.SaveAs('C:\\path_to_your_file\.xlsx')

workbook.Close()

excel.Quit()
```

This example illustrates how you can programmatically create an Excel report using Python while leveraging its capabilities beyond what VBA typically offers.

To wrap things up, the comparison between Python and VBA highlights that while both languages have their advantages in automating Excel tasks, they cater to different needs based on task complexity. VBA provides quick solutions within Excel's ecosystem but may struggle under demanding scenarios that require advanced programming techniques. Conversely, Python emerges as a versatile tool capable of efficiently managing extensive datasets while promoting collaboration through modern development practices.

By integrating both languages into your workflow, you enhance your automation capabilities and align yourself with organizations seeking innovative solutions to their data challenges. Leveraging the complementary strengths of Python and VBA empowers you to develop comprehensive automation strategies that drive efficiency across various functions—ultimately leading to improved decision-making processes within your organization.

Calling Python scripts from VBA

To fully leverage the combined strengths of Python and VBA, it's essential to understand how to call Python scripts directly from within VBA. This integration allows users to tap into Python's extensive libraries and advanced data processing capabilities while working within the familiar Excel environment. By merging these two powerful tools, you can create a hybrid approach that enhances efficiency and expands the functionality available for automating complex tasks.

Before diving into this integration, ensure your system is ready. Installing the pywin32 package is crucial, as it enables VBA to interact with Python scripts via COM (Component Object Model). Here's how to set it up:

1. **Install the pywin32 Library:

If you haven't installed it yet, open your command prompt or terminal and execute:

```bash
pip install pywin32
```

With the library installed, you can start calling your Python scripts from VBA. Let's walk through a basic example where a simple Python script processes data and returns results back to Excel.

Step 1: Create A Simple Python Script

Begin by creating a Python script named process_data.py. In this script, you'll define a function that performs calculations or manipulations on data:

```python
\#\# process_data.py
import pandas as pd


def calculate_sales_average(file_path):
```

```
\#\# Read Excel file

data = pd.read_excel(file_path)

\#\# Calculate average sales

average_sales = data['Sales'].mean()

return average_sales
```
` ` `

This function reads an Excel file containing sales data and computes the average sales figure.

Step 2: Write The Vba Code To Call The Python Script

Next, you'll need to write VBA code that interacts with this Python script. Open Excel and access the VBA editor by pressing Alt + F11. In the editor, create a new module and input the following code:

` ` `vba
```vba
Sub CallPythonScript()

Dim objShell As Object

Dim pythonScriptPath As String

Dim excelFilePath As String

Dim result As Variant


' Specify paths

pythonScriptPath = "C:\path_to_your_file\process_data.py

excelFilePath = "C:\path_to_your_file\sales_data.xlsx
```

```
' Create shell object
Set objShell = CreateObject("WScript.Shell")

' Call the Python script using the shell command
result = objShell.Exec("python """ & pythonScriptPath & """ """
& excelFilePath & """").StdOut.ReadAll()

' Output result back to Excel cell (for example, A1)
Range("A1").Value = result

' Clean up
Set objShell = Nothing
End Sub
```
` ` `

In this code snippet, you create a shell object that executes your Python script from within VBA. The output is captured and placed into an Excel cell.

Step 3: Run Your Macro

After entering your VBA code, return to Excel and run the macro CallPythonScript. Ensure that your sales data is formatted correctly in sales_data.xlsx, with a column labeled "Sales." When executed, your macro should display the calculated average sales in cell A1.

Handling Errors and Edge Cases

While integrating Python with VBA offers numerous

advantages, it's essential to consider error handling as well. If your script encounters issues—such as missing data or an incorrect file path—it could lead to unexpected results or crashes. To mitigate these risks, implement error handling in both your Python script and your VBA code.

In Python, wrap critical operations in try-except blocks:

```python
def calculate_sales_average(file_path):

try:

data = pd.read_excel(file_path)

average_sales = data['Sales'].mean()

return average_sales

except Exception as e:

return f"Error processing file: e
```

In your VBA code, check if the output contains an error message before placing it into an Excel cell:

```vba
If InStr(result, "Error") > 0 Then

MsgBox "There was an error: " & result

Else

Range("A1").Value = result

End If
```

The ability to call Python scripts from VBA not only boosts productivity but also allows users to access powerful data processing capabilities that are not available directly through

Excel alone. This hybrid approach enables professionals to streamline complex workflows and conduct more sophisticated analyses while maintaining ease of use within their existing frameworks.

As organizations increasingly seek innovative solutions for their automation challenges, mastering this integration places you at the forefront of technological advancement in Excel automation. Embrace this synergy between programming languages; it empowers you to significantly enhance your automation capabilities while fostering collaboration across departments.

Passing data between VBA and Python

To enable smooth data exchange between Python and VBA, it is essential to grasp the mechanics of effectively passing data back and forth. This interaction empowers you to leverage Python's computational strengths while taking advantage of Excel's robust front-end capabilities. By integrating these two environments, you can significantly enhance your workflows, allowing for more sophisticated data manipulation and reporting.

Imagine managing a dataset in Excel that requires complex calculations or transformations best suited for Python's extensive libraries. For example, if you have a large sales dataset in an Excel workbook needing advanced statistical analysis or machine learning models, you don't have to extract data manually or rely solely on Excel's built-in functions. Instead, you can seamlessly transfer the dataset to a Python script for processing and return the results to Excel for further use.

Passing Data from Excel to Python

The first step in this integration involves sending data from your Excel sheet to a Python script. This typically includes reading specific cell ranges or entire sheets based on your requirements.

Step 1: Prepare Your Data

Begin by ensuring that your Excel file contains relevant data. Take this example, let's say you have sales figures organized in columns A and B, where column A lists product names and column B contains sales numbers.

Step 2: Modify The Python Script

Next, adjust your Python script to accept input parameters for processing. Below is an example of how you might modify a script to accept values from Excel:

```python
\#\# process_data.py

import sys

import pandas as pd


def calculate_sales_average(sales_data):

try:

\#\# Convert input string back into DataFrame

data = pd.read_json(sales_data) \# Expecting JSON format

average_sales = data['Sales'].mean()

return average_sales

except Exception as e:

return f"Error processing data: e


if __name__ == "__main__":
```

```python
sales_data_json = sys.argv[1]    \# Get JSON string from command line argument

print(calculate_sales_average(sales_data_json))
```

` ` `

In this version of the script, it reads a JSON string representing your sales data.

Step 3: Prepare Vba To Send Data

Now, you'll need to write VBA code that gathers your sales data, converts it into JSON format, and then calls the Python script. Utilizing a library like VBA-JSON will make it easy to convert Excel ranges into JSON strings.

` ` ` vba

```vba
Sub PassDataToPython()

Dim objShell As Object

Dim pythonScriptPath As String

Dim jsonData As String

Dim i As Long

Dim lastRow As Long


' Specify paths

pythonScriptPath = "C:\path_to_your_file\process_data.py


' Create JSON array from Excel range

jsonData = "[
```

```vba
lastRow = Cells(Rows.Count, 1).End(xlUp).Row ' Assuming
data starts at row 1

For i = 2 To lastRow ' Skip header row

jsonData = jsonData & """Product""": """ & Cells(i, 1).Value & """,
""Sales""": " & Cells(i, 2).Value & ",

Next i

' Remove trailing comma and close JSON array

If Right(jsonData, 1) = "," Then jsonData = Left(jsonData,
Len(jsonData) - 1)

jsonData = jsonData & "]

' Create shell object to call Python script with JSON string as
argument

Set objShell = CreateObject("WScript.Shell")

result = objShell.Exec("python """ & pythonScriptPath & """ """
& jsonData & """").StdOut.ReadAll()

' Output result back to Excel cell (for example, A1)

Range("A1").Value = result

End Sub
```

` ` `

Handling Data Returned from Python

After executing the macro, the output from your Python script —such as the calculated average sales—will appear in cell A1 of your active worksheet. This integration not only automates repetitive tasks but also enhances accuracy in calculations that can be cumbersome when using traditional spreadsheet methods.

Ensuring Robustness Through Error Handling

Robustness is crucial when automating processes across different environments. By incorporating error-handling mechanisms within both your Python script and VBA code, you can ensure smooth operations even in the face of unexpected scenarios.

To enhance error handling in the previous VBA example, check if the output contains any error keywords before displaying it:

```vba
If InStr(result, "Error") > 0 Then

MsgBox "There was an error: " & result

Else

Range("A1").Value = result

End If
```

Facilitating data transfer between VBA and Python opens up new avenues for productivity, allowing users to harness powerful analytical capabilities within their familiar Excel environment. Mastering this integration positions you as an invaluable asset within any organization seeking innovative approaches to data management.

As automation increasingly shapes how professionals interact with their workspaces, embracing these technical skills will not only enhance your productivity but also cultivate a culture of efficiency across teams. Each interaction between these tools reinforces your ability to drive impactful changes while broadening your technical skill set in today's evolving landscape.

Use cases for Python and VBA integration

In the world of data automation, combining Python and VBA creates a powerful synergy that can significantly boost productivity. By understanding how to leverage both languages, professionals can harness their unique strengths, resulting in workflows that are not only efficient but also adaptable to various project requirements. Let's delve into some compelling use cases where this integration truly excels.

One of the most prominent applications is in financial modeling. Imagine a finance team responsible for generating weekly reports based on sales data from multiple sources. Here, VBA can automate the initial stages of report creation, such as pulling data from spreadsheets and performing preliminary calculations. However, for more complex analyses —like running predictive models or integrating external APIs for real-time financial metrics—Python becomes indispensable. By calling Python scripts directly from VBA, analysts can perform sophisticated calculations without the need to switch between platforms, thereby streamlining their workflow.

Take this example, consider a scenario where an analyst needs to retrieve real-time stock prices from a financial API and integrate that information into an existing Excel model. The initial retrieval of historical data could be managed by VBA through a simple button click that initiates the process. Once this foundational data is established, Python can be utilized to fetch real-time updates and apply machine learning algorithms for trend analysis. This seamless transition not only saves time but also enhances prediction accuracy by minimizing manual errors.

Another notable application is in reporting automation across various departments. A marketing team, for example, may rely on Excel to track campaign performance metrics. Integrating Python scripts can elevate their analysis significantly. By using VBA to trigger these scripts, the team can automatically generate visualizations based on dynamic datasets that refresh with each new reporting cycle. Instead of spending hours creating pivot tables or charts manually each month, a single command could initiate a series of Python functions that extract relevant insights and update Excel with visuals ready for presentation.

The healthcare sector offers yet another compelling use case for the integration of Python and VBA. Medical professionals often depend on Excel for tracking patient data and managing treatment plans. However, manually handling large datasets can lead to oversights and inefficiencies. An integrated solution could involve using VBA macros to facilitate user inputs while leveraging Python's robust libraries, such as Pandas, for deeper statistical analyses—like identifying trends in patient recovery rates or predicting outcomes based on treatment histories.

Imagine a scenario where patient data is collected over time in Excel spreadsheets but requires advanced statistical processing to uncover patterns in recovery times across different demographics. The initial data entry could be streamlined through user-friendly forms created with VBA. When it's time for analysis—perhaps comparing various treatment plans—a simple command would execute a Python script that performs complex statistical tests and outputs the findings back into Excel for easy review.

And, organizations frequently face challenges when consolidating disparate datasets from various departments into a coherent report. Effectively utilizing both technologies can alleviate this burden significantly. Take this example, you could set up a system where VBA collects sales figures from multiple regional teams across different workbooks and compiles them into one central file. Subsequently, Python could analyze this unified dataset—identifying outliers or generating forecasts based on historical trends—all without requiring manual intervention.

These examples highlight how integrating Python with VBA opens up numerous possibilities across industries by automating repetitive tasks while enhancing analytical capabilities beyond what either language could achieve independently. The seamless interplay between user-friendly interactions through Excel's interface and powerful computational processing via Python creates a versatile toolkit that empowers professionals to achieve more with less effort.

These use cases provide just a glimpse into how combining these two technologies can transform workflows within organizations. Each integration is unique and should be tailored to specific project needs and objectives. As you continue your journey in mastering these tools together, consider how your own processes might benefit from such powerful collaboration—and embrace the potential waiting at your fingertips through this dynamic duo.

Debugging VBA and Python collaboration

Debugging the collaboration between VBA and Python can often be challenging, but mastering this process is crucial for maximizing the potential of both languages in your Excel automation projects. As professionals increasingly integrate these two technologies, developing the ability to troubleshoot and refine their collaboration becomes an essential skill.

Imagine a scenario where you have a VBA macro designed to invoke a Python script for data analysis. If the macro doesn't execute as expected, the first step is to isolate the issue.

This usually entails verifying that the VBA code correctly references the Python environment and checks whether the paths to any required files are accurate. A helpful debugging strategy is to incorporate MsgBox statements within your VBA code. These alerts can confirm whether specific sections of the macro are functioning properly, enabling you to identify where things may be going awry.

For example, if your VBA script includes a line like Shell "python my_script.py", you might insert MsgBox "Script executed" immediately after it. If this message appears but no results are reflected in Excel, it indicates that the problem lies within the Python script itself. Conversely, if the message doesn't display at all, this suggests that an error occurred earlier in your macro.

Once you've verified that your VBA is correctly calling Python, turn your attention to troubleshooting the Python script. Start by running it independently in its native environment to ensure it operates without errors. Utilizing an IDE like PyCharm or even a simple command line can help confirm its functionality. If any exceptions arise—such as data type mismatches or missing libraries—address these issues before reintegrating it with your VBA code.

Take this example, consider a situation where your Python script attempts to read an Excel file using Pandas but encounters a FileNotFoundError. In this case, ensure that your script specifies the correct file path and confirms that all referenced files are present in that location. Additionally, implementing error handling in your Python code with try-except blocks allows you to catch exceptions gracefully and send informative error messages back into Excel via designated cells.

Another common issue occurs when transferring data between VBA and Python. If you're passing a range of values from Excel to your Python script and noticing discrepancies or unexpected results, examine how you're formatting that data within your VBA code prior to transmission. Are you accurately converting ranges into lists? Is there any mismatch in data types? Using intermediate variables to store values can clarify what is being passed through at each stage.

Let's consider a practical example: suppose you want to send an array of sales figures from an Excel sheet to Python for analysis. You could use something like:

```vba
Dim salesData As Variant

salesData = Application.Transpose(Range("A1:A10").Value)
```

This line captures values from cells A1 through A10 and transposes them into an array format suitable for passing into your Python script. Ensuring this step is executed flawlessly is vital; even minor oversights here can lead to incorrect analyses later on.

Also, logging emerges as an invaluable tool for debugging both languages simultaneously. In Python, consider utilizing logging features with the logging module instead of simple print statements for more precise control over output levels (info, warning, error). This approach helps track data flow through your scripts and pinpoint failure points when executing tasks initiated by VBA.

For example:

```python
import logging

logging.basicConfig(filename='debug.log',
level=logging.DEBUG)
```

```
def analyze_data(data):

try:

\#\# Analysis code here

logging.info('Data analysis completed successfully.')

except Exception as e:

logging.error(f'Error during analysis: e')
```
` ` `

Creating log files not only assists with troubleshooting but also allows for retrospective examination of processes —facilitating improvements in future iterations of your workflows.

As with any complex integration task, patience is essential when debugging interactions between VBA and Python. Iterative testing—making small adjustments and promptly checking results—often provides clearer insights than attempting to debug large segments of code at once.

By incorporating robust error handling into both your VBA macros and Python scripts, alongside strategic logging practices, you equip yourself with effective tools for troubleshooting and refining automated processes. This not only enhances immediate productivity but also contributes significantly to long-term efficiency gains in your Excel automation projects. Embrace these techniques; they will strengthen your skills and improve collaboration across teams reliant on these technologies.

Examples of VBA and Python working together

When exploring the integration of VBA and Python for automation tasks, practical examples play a crucial role in illustrating how these two programming environments can work together effectively. By harnessing their unique strengths, you can develop powerful workflows that not only save time but also enhance accuracy.

Consider a financial analyst tasked with automating the extraction and analysis of data from multiple Excel sheets. In this scenario, imagine a VBA macro that gathers sales figures from various worksheets within an Excel workbook and then passes this data to a Python script for advanced analysis.

Here's a simplified version of such a VBA macro:

```vba
Sub ExtractSalesData()
Dim ws As Worksheet
Dim salesData As Variant
Dim combinedData() As Variant
Dim counter As Integer

ReDim combinedData(1 To 100, 1 To 1) ' Adjust size as needed
counter = 1

For Each ws In ThisWorkbook.Worksheets
If ws.Name <> "Summary" Then ' Exclude summary sheet
salesData = ws.Range("A1:A10").Value ' Assuming data is in A1:A10
For i = LBound(salesData) To UBound(salesData)
combinedData(counter, 1) = salesData(i, 1)
counter = counter + 1
Next i
```

End If

Next ws

' Pass combined data to Python here

End Sub

```
```

In this code snippet, the ExtractSalesData subroutine compiles data from all worksheets except the "Summary" sheet into an array. The next step involves passing this combinedData array to your Python script for further processing, typically achieved through a command line call to the Python interpreter.

Take this example:

```vba
Shell "python analyze_sales.py " & Join(combinedData, ",")
```

This line executes the Python script while sending the sales data as command-line arguments. The corresponding analyze_sales.py script can then parse this input, performing various statistical analyses or generating visualizations.

Here's an example of how you might handle the incoming data in Python:

```python
import sys


def main():

\#\# Accept incoming sales data from command line arguments.
```

```python
try:

sales_data = list(map(float, sys.argv[1].split(','))) \# Convert to float and split by comma.

print("Analyzing sales data...")

\#\# Perform analysis (e.g., calculate total sales).

total_sales = sum(sales_data)

print(f"Total Sales: total_sales")


except ValueError as e:

print(f"Error processing input: e")


if __name__ == "__main__":

main()
```
` ` `

In this example, the Python script receives the comma-separated sales data as a single string from the VBA macro. It splits this string into a list of floats and computes the total sales while ensuring that any input format issues are caught and reported.

For larger datasets, consider using temporary files instead of command-line arguments to avoid limitations on argument length. Storing your combinedData in a CSV file is an effective strategy. The VBA macro could save the data like this:

```vba
Open "sales_data.csv" For Output As \#1

For i = LBound(combinedData) To UBound(combinedData)

Print \#1, combinedData(i, 1)
```

Next i

Close \#1

Shell "python analyze_sales.py

` ` `

Then in your Python script, you would replace command-line reading with file I/O:

` ` `python

import pandas as pd

def main():

\#\# Read CSV file containing sales data.

try:

sales_data = pd.read_csv('sales_data.csv', header=None)

total_sales = sales_data.sum().values[0]

print(f"Total Sales: total_sales")

except Exception as e:

print(f"Error reading file: e")

if __name__ == "__main__":

main()

` ` `

This approach is especially beneficial for large datasets, allowing Python to utilize libraries like Pandas for efficient data handling and manipulation.

As we delve deeper into these collaborative processes between VBA and Python, it's important to be aware of common pitfalls. Data type mismatches can lead to errors that disrupt productivity; therefore, ensuring consistency when passing numerical values between VBA and Python is essential. Additionally, be vigilant about whitespace or formatting discrepancies when transferring textual data.

Integrating robust logging in both environments enhances your debugging capabilities. Logging provides insights into each step's performance, enabling you to quickly identify where issues may arise. By embedding logs in both your VBA code and Python scripts, you create a comprehensive view of the entire process flow.

With experience comes expertise. As you apply these techniques to your automation projects, you will discover new opportunities for collaboration between VBA and Python that elevate your workflows beyond mere efficiency into realms of innovation and insight generation.

Mastering these collaborative efforts empowers professionals not only to automate tasks but also to transform their approach to complex challenges through seamless integration of powerful programming languages tailored for different tasks.

Interoperability best practices

Interoperability between Python and VBA significantly enhances our ability to manage data in Excel, leveraging the strengths of both environments. To fully utilize this potential, it is crucial to implement best practices that ensure seamless communication and reduce the risk of errors in your automation processes.

A key principle for effective interoperability is establishing a clear data exchange format. Whether you're passing data directly through command-line arguments or using temporary files, consistency in formatting is vital. Take this example, when sending numeric values from VBA to Python, ensure they are converted into a standard format that Python can easily interpret. A common approach is to use comma-separated values (CSV), which simplifies parsing on both ends.

Let's explore a practical scenario: automating the generation of monthly sales reports. Your VBA script could extract relevant data from various worksheets and save it into a CSV file, which acts as an intermediary between the two languages. Here's how you can achieve this:

In VBA, after compiling your sales data, you can save it into a CSV file with the following code:

```vba
Sub SaveSalesDataToCSV(salesData As Variant)

Dim csvFilePath As String

csvFilePath = ThisWorkbook.Path & "\sales_data.csv


Open csvFilePath For Output As \#1

For i = LBound(salesData) To UBound(salesData)

Print \#1, salesData(i, 1) ' Write each item to the CSV

Next i

Close \#1


Shell "python analyze_sales.py", vbNormalFocus ' Trigger Python script execution

End Sub
```

On the Python side, you can read the CSV file like this:

```python
import pandas as pd

def main():
try:
sales_data = pd.read_csv('sales_data.csv', header=None)
total_sales = sales_data.sum().values[0]
print(f"Total Sales: total_sales")

except Exception as e:
print(f"Error reading file: e")

if __name__ == "__main__":
main()
```

This method ensures that all extracted data is systematically stored and readily accessible for analysis or visualization by your Python script.

Another important consideration is error handling. When dealing with two different programming languages, discrepancies may arise due to type mismatches or invalid inputs. Implementing robust error-catching mechanisms in both environments allows you to address these issues proactively. For example, while reading from a CSV in Python, handle potential errors during file access or data conversion gracefully:

```python
try:
```

```python
sales_data = pd.read_csv('sales_data.csv', header=None)
except FileNotFoundError:
print("CSV file not found.")
except pd.errors.EmptyDataError:
print("No data found in the CSV.")
except Exception as e:
print(f"An error occurred: e")
```

Additionally, consider employing logging techniques in both scripts to monitor operations over time. This not only aids debugging but also provides insights into performance and areas for optimization. In your VBA code, you might use:

```vba
Sub LogMessage(message As String)
Dim logFile As String
logFile = ThisWorkbook.Path & "\automation_log.txt

Open logFile For Append As \#1
Print \#1, Now() & ": " & message
Close \#1
End Sub
```

Similarly, in Python:

```python
import logging
```

```
logging.basicConfig(filename='automation_log.txt',
level=logging.INFO)

def main():

try:

sales_data = pd.read_csv('sales_data.csv', header=None)

total_sales = sales_data.sum().values[0]

logging.info(f"Total Sales calculated successfully: total_sales")


except Exception as e:

logging.error(f"Error encountered: e")
` ` `
```

Maintaining logs across both platforms provides visibility into each step of your process—essential for troubleshooting and ensuring smooth operation.

Lastly, always consider scalability. As your datasets grow larger and more complex, implementing strategies like batch processing or modular script design can help manage increased workloads effectively. Breaking larger tasks into smaller sub-tasks not only simplifies debugging but also enhances clarity.

The collaborative power of VBA and Python goes beyond mere task completion; it transforms how we approach complex challenges within Excel automation. By adhering to these best practices for interoperability, you position yourself not just as an executor of tasks but as an innovator capable of elevating organizational processes through seamless integration and effective problem-solving strategies. Your expertise will resonate throughout your work environment, inspiring others to embrace automation with confidence and creativity.

CHAPTER 6: DATABASE CONNECTIVITY AND EXCEL

Introduction to database integration

Database integration is a crucial step in fully leveraging Excel automation with Python. As organizations increasingly depend on data-driven decision-making, the ability to connect and manipulate data from various databases becomes essential. This integration not only boosts efficiency but also enhances the analytical capabilities of your Excel workflows.

To begin this journey, it's important to familiarize yourself with the types of databases commonly used alongside Excel. Relational databases like MySQL, PostgreSQL, and SQLite are popular due to their structured nature, which facilitates easy querying and data manipulation. In contrast, NoSQL databases such as MongoDB offer flexibility for unstructured data, making them suitable for scenarios where traditional relational models may not suffice.

The first step in connecting Python to a database involves choosing the right library. Libraries like SQLAlchemy provide an abstraction layer that simplifies database interactions by offering a unified interface across different database systems. Alternatively, PyODBC allows for direct connections using ODBC drivers, providing versatility across various environments.

Let's look at a practical example using SQLite, a lightweight database often employed for local applications. Here's how to set up a connection to an SQLite database and perform basic operations:

1. Install the SQLite library (if you haven't already):

```
` ` `

pip install sqlite3
` ` `
```

1. **Create a connection and execute queries:

```python
import sqlite3

def connect_to_database(db_name):

try:

conn = sqlite3.connect(db_name)

cursor = conn.cursor()

print("Connection established.")

return conn, cursor

except sqlite3.Error as e:

print(f"Error connecting to database: e")

def create_table(cursor):

cursor.execute('''

CREATE TABLE IF NOT EXISTS sales (
```

```
id INTEGER PRIMARY KEY,
product TEXT NOT NULL,
amount REAL NOT NULL,
date TEXT NOT NULL
)
''')
print("Table created.")

def insert_data(cursor, product, amount, date):
cursor.execute('''
INSERT INTO sales (product, amount, date)
VALUES (?, ?, ?)
''', (product, amount, date))
print("Data inserted.")

\#\# Main execution
db_name = 'sales_data.db'
conn, cursor = connect_to_database(db_name)
create_table(cursor)
insert_data(cursor, 'Widget', 19.99, '2023-10-01')

conn.commit()
conn.close()
```
```
```

This code snippet shows how to establish a connection to an SQLite database, create a table for sales data, and insert new records. Each function serves a specific purpose, helping keep your code organized and manageable.

Once your data is stored in the database, retrieving it for analysis in Excel is straightforward. Here's how to fetch the sales data from your SQLite database:

```python
def fetch_sales_data(cursor):

cursor.execute('SELECT * FROM sales')

rows = cursor.fetchall()

return rows


\#\# Fetching data

sales_data = fetch_sales_data(cursor)

for row in sales_data:

print(row)
```

This function retrieves all records from the sales table and prints them out. You can now process this data further or export it directly into an Excel file for visualization.

Exporting retrieved data into Excel is seamless with Pandas. Here's how you can do it:

```python
import pandas as pd


def export_to_excel(data, filename):
```

```
df = pd.DataFrame(data, columns=['ID', 'Product', 'Amount', 'Date'])

df.to_excel(filename, index=False)

print(f"Data exported to filename.")


export_to_excel(sales_data, 'sales_report.xlsx')
` ` `
```

This simple process creates an Excel file containing all your sales records—ready for analysis or reporting.

Additionally, implementing security measures around your database connections is essential. Ensure that sensitive data is encrypted both during transit and at rest. Using parameterized queries helps prevent SQL injection attacks—an important best practice when handling user-generated input.

By incorporating these strategies, you will not only enhance your technical skills but also establish yourself as a reliable steward of data within your organization. Leveraging Python's strengths in managing databases alongside Excel's powerful analytics tools will foster an environment where informed decisions are based on accurate insights drawn from rich datasets.

Connecting to SQL databases with Python

To fully leverage Python for Excel automation, mastering the connection to SQL databases is crucial. This capability allows for dynamic data manipulation and retrieval, transforming static spreadsheets into powerful analytical tools. As organizations grow and evolve, integrating data from various sources becomes essential for informed decision-making.

Connecting Python to different databases significantly expands your capabilities. While we've previously explored SQLite, the principles are similarly applicable to other relational databases like MySQL and PostgreSQL. Each database has its unique features, yet they share common access methods through Python.

Let's delve into connecting Python to a MySQL database, a widely used choice due to its robustness and scalability. First, you'll need to install the MySQL Connector library:

```bash
pip install mysql-connector-python
```

After installation, you can establish a connection and perform operations akin to those we executed with SQLite. Here's a basic example of connecting to a MySQL database and creating a table to store customer information:

```python
import mysql.connector


def connect_to_mysql_database(host, user, password, database):

try:

conn = mysql.connector.connect(

host=host,

user=user,

password=password,

database=database

)

cursor = conn.cursor()

print("Connection established.")
```

```python
    return conn, cursor
except mysql.connector.Error as e:
    print(f"Error connecting to database: e")

def create_customer_table(cursor):
    cursor.execute('''
CREATE TABLE IF NOT EXISTS customers (
id INT AUTO_INCREMENT PRIMARY KEY,
name VARCHAR(100) NOT NULL,
email VARCHAR(100) NOT NULL,
join_date DATE NOT NULL
)
''')
    print("Customer table created.")

\#\# Main execution
host = 'localhost'
user = 'your_username'
password = 'your_password'
database = 'your_database_name'

conn, cursor = connect_to_mysql_database(host, user, password, database)
create_customer_table(cursor)
```

` ` `

In this example, remember to replace your_username, your_password, and your_database_name with your actual database credentials. The function above creates a table named customers designed to hold customer details.

After setting up the table, you can insert data into it using the following method:

` ` `python

def insert_customer_data(cursor, name, email, join_date):

cursor.execute('''

INSERT INTO customers (name, email, join_date)

VALUES (%s, %s, %s)

''', (name, email, join_date))

print("Customer data inserted.")

\#\# Inserting sample customer data

insert_customer_data(cursor, 'John Doe', 'john@example.com', '2023-10-01')

conn.commit() \# Commit the transaction
` ` `

Inserting records is straightforward. Using parameterized queries enhances security by reducing the risk of SQL injection attacks.

Retrieving data is just as important. Here's how you can fetch customer information from the customers table:

` ` `python

def fetch_customer_data(cursor):

```
cursor.execute('SELECT * FROM customers')

rows = cursor.fetchall()

return rows


\#\# Fetching data

customer_data = fetch_customer_data(cursor)

for row in customer_data:

print(row)
```
``` ` ` ` ```

This snippet retrieves all entries from the customers table and prints them. To utilize this data effectively within Excel, you can export it using Pandas:

``` ` ` `python```
```python
import pandas as pd


def export_customers_to_excel(data, filename):

df = pd.DataFrame(data, columns=['ID', 'Name', 'Email', 'Join Date'])

df.to_excel(filename, index=False)

print(f"Customer data exported to filename.")


export_customers_to_excel(customer_data,
'customer_report.xlsx')
```
``` ` ` ` ```

This efficient method generates an Excel file containing all customer records, enabling you to take full advantage of
```

Excel's analytical capabilities.

As you explore integration with various SQL databases and utilize Python libraries like MySQL Connector or SQLAlchemy for ORM functionality, consider delving into advanced features such as stored procedures or triggers in your SQL environment. These can automate certain actions directly within the database.

Security should always be a priority in your integration efforts. Implement encryption for sensitive data and use secure connections (like SSL/TLS) when accessing remote databases. Regularly updating your libraries and monitoring access logs will further enhance your security posture.

In the end, mastering these techniques not only enables you to connect Python with SQL databases but also positions you as a valuable asset in any data-driven organization. Your ability to leverage robust database solutions alongside Excel's analytical power will significantly streamline workflows and enhance productivity in your role.

Retrieving data from databases to Excel

Retrieving data from SQL databases to Excel opens the door to creating dynamic reports that reflect the most current information. This capability supports informed decision-making and boosts overall productivity. Once you've established a connection to a SQL database, the next step is to efficiently pull data into your Excel spreadsheets for analysis or reporting. This streamlined process not only simplifies data handling but also enhances collaboration among teams that rely on up-to-date information.

To get started, it's essential to have a clear understanding of the data structure you wish to retrieve. Familiarity with table names, fields, and their relationships will significantly ease the extraction process. Take this example, if you're looking to extract customer details, we can build on the previous example where we created a customers table in MySQL. Our focus now shifts to querying this data and importing it into Excel.

Assuming you've already set up your connection using the earlier provided code, here's how to effectively retrieve and manipulate this data:

```python
def fetch_customer_data(cursor):

cursor.execute('SELECT * FROM customers')

rows = cursor.fetchall()

return rows


\#\# Fetching customer data

customer_data = fetch_customer_data(cursor)
```

This straightforward function executes a SQL query that selects all records from the customers table and returns them as a list of tuples, with each tuple representing a row in the table.

Next, to facilitate interaction with Excel, using Pandas is highly effective due to its robust data manipulation capabilities. After fetching the customer data, converting it into a DataFrame makes for easy manipulation before exporting:

```python
import pandas as pd


def convert_to_dataframe(data):

df = pd.DataFrame(data, columns=['ID', 'Name', 'Email', 'Join Date'])
```

return df

customer_df = convert_to_dataframe(customer_data)

print(customer_df)

` ` `

This code snippet transforms the retrieved customer information into a Pandas DataFrame, simplifying management and visualization. You can perform various operations such as filtering or sorting directly within this DataFrame prior to exporting it to Excel.

Now let's explore how to export this DataFrame into an Excel file. This step ensures your data is not only retrievable but also formatted in a way that's suitable for presentation:

` ` `python

def export_to_excel(df, filename):

df.to_excel(filename, index=False)

print(f"Data exported to filename successfully.")

export_to_excel(customer_df, 'customer_report.xlsx')

` ` `

With this function, you can easily create an Excel report named customer_report.xlsx, containing all customer records organized neatly in tabular form.

If your objective extends beyond simply retrieving data—such as generating regular reports—you can automate this process using scheduling tools like cron jobs or Windows Task Scheduler. Automating report generation not only saves time but also ensures accuracy by consistently working with fresh data pulled directly from your SQL database.

Consider enhancing your data retrieval process by adding filters or parameters to your SQL queries based on specific criteria. For example, if you wish to retrieve only customers who joined after a certain date:

```python
def fetch_recent_customers(cursor, date):

query = 'SELECT * FROM customers WHERE join_date > %s'

cursor.execute(query, (date,))

return cursor.fetchall()


recent_customers = fetch_recent_customers(cursor, '2023-01-01')
```

Utilizing dynamic queries allows you to tailor your reports according to business needs without requiring manual adjustments.

As you refine your automation skills, think about incorporating advanced functionalities such as creating pivot tables directly in Excel post-export or using visualization libraries like Matplotlib within Python to generate charts before exporting them as images into Excel. These enhancements will elevate your reporting capabilities and provide deeper insights at a glance.

Throughout this process, security considerations are paramount. Always validate user inputs when constructing SQL queries to mitigate risks associated with SQL injection attacks. Additionally, ensure that sensitive information is handled appropriately when exporting or displaying data.

By mastering these retrieval techniques and automating routine tasks related to Excel reporting, you position yourself as an invaluable asset within any organization focused on data-driven decision-making. Your ability to extract real-time insights from databases into familiar interfaces like Excel not only accelerates workflows but also empowers colleagues with actionable intelligence.

Writing data back to databases

Writing data back to databases after processing or analyzing it in Excel is crucial for maintaining data integrity and facilitating collaborative workflows. After transforming your data into actionable insights in Excel, it's essential to ensure these updates are reflected in the original database. This not only streamlines operations but also keeps all stakeholders aligned with the latest information.

To begin, verify that your connection to the database is still active. If you've been using an established connection, this should be a straightforward step. Take this example, imagine you've modified customer records in Excel and now need to push those changes back to a SQL database.

Start by preparing your updated data for insertion. Depending on how you've structured your changes, you'll likely have a DataFrame containing new or modified entries that need to be reflected in the database. Here's an example of how to prepare and write this data back using Pandas:

```python
def update_customer_data(cursor, df):

for index, row in df.iterrows():

cursor.execute('UPDATE customers SET Name=%s, Email=%s WHERE ID=%s', (row['Name'], row['Email'], row['ID']))

print("Customer data updated successfully.")
```

In this function, we iterate through each row of the

DataFrame. The execute method sends an update query for each record based on its unique ID, ensuring that only relevant records are modified.

After creating this function, you can call it by passing your database cursor and the DataFrame:

```python
update_customer_data(cursor, customer_df)
```

This action will loop through each customer entry in customer_df, updating their names and emails accordingly in the SQL database.

If you need to add entirely new entries instead of updating existing ones, you can implement an insert statement:

```python
def insert_new_customers(cursor, df):

for index, row in df.iterrows():

cursor.execute('INSERT INTO customers (Name, Email) VALUES (%s, %s)', (row['Name'], row['Email']))

print("New customers added successfully.")
```

This function demonstrates how to insert new records directly into the customers table from your DataFrame.

Before executing any updates or inserts, it's important to manage transactions carefully. You can use transaction control commands like commit and rollback to ensure data consistency:

```python
try:

\#\# Update or insert operations here
```

connection.commit()

except Exception as e:

connection.rollback()

print(f"An error occurred: e")

` ` `

This snippet ensures that if an error occurs during SQL command execution, any changes made during that transaction can be undone.

When working with large datasets or batch updates that might slow down performance, consider leveraging bulk operations provided by libraries like SQLAlchemy or executing multiple rows at once with a single query. For example:

` ` `python

def bulk_insert_customers(cursor, df):

values = [tuple(x) for x in df.to_numpy()]

cursor.executemany('INSERT INTO customers (Name, Email) VALUES (%s, %s)', values)

print("Bulk insert completed successfully.")

` ` `

Using executemany allows you to insert multiple rows at once efficiently, rather than executing separate insert commands individually.

As you continue developing these skills, consider incorporating logging mechanisms within your functions. This will help track changes made back to the database and assist with troubleshooting if issues arise later:

` ` `python

import logging

```
logging.basicConfig(filename='database_updates.log',
level=logging.INFO)


def log_update(customer_id):

logging.info(f"Customer    customer_id    updated    at
datetime.now()")
` ` `
```

With proper logging set up alongside your update functions, you'll gain valuable insights into when and what changes were made—enhancing accountability within your automation processes.

In the end, mastering the process of writing data back to databases not only allows you to manage information more effectively but also reinforces your role as a key contributor within any data-driven organization. Your ability to keep databases current while providing teams with refined analysis tools lays a strong foundation for impactful decision-making across all levels of business operations.

Automating reporting workflows

Automating reporting workflows effectively bridges the gap between data analysis and actionable insights, empowering organizations to make informed decisions swiftly. This integration simplifies the transformation of raw data into visually engaging reports, ultimately enhancing communication and collaboration among stakeholders. By utilizing Python to automate these tasks, you not only save time but also reduce the risk of human error, leading to a more efficient reporting cycle.

The journey toward automating reporting begins with identifying the key metrics and data sources that are relevant to your reports. For example, if your responsibility involves generating monthly sales reports, you should compile all necessary data from sources such as databases, APIs, or CSV files. With this information at hand, you can create a consolidated view that highlights crucial metrics like total sales, revenue growth, and customer acquisition.

Once you've determined the essential data points for your report, the next step is to establish a dynamic reporting structure in Excel. Leveraging Python libraries such as Pandas alongside OpenPyXL or XlsxWriter enables robust manipulation of your data before exporting it into Excel. Here's a straightforward workflow to follow:

1. Data Extraction: Retrieve data from various sources.

2. Data Transformation: Clean and format the data as needed.

3. Report Generation: Populate an Excel template with the processed data.

Let's illustrate this with an example:

```python
import pandas as pd

import openpyxl


\#\# Step 1: Data extraction

sales_data = pd.read_csv('monthly_sales.csv')


\#\# Step 2: Data transformation

sales_summary = sales_data.groupby('Product').agg('Sales': 'sum', 'Revenue': 'sum').reset_index()
```

\#\# Step 3: Report generation

with   pd.ExcelWriter('Monthly_Sales_Report.xlsx', engine='openpyxl') as writer:

sales_summary.to_excel(writer,   sheet_name='Sales Summary', index=False)

` ` `

In this example, we begin by loading sales data from a CSV file into a Pandas DataFrame. We then group the data by product to calculate total sales and revenue before writing it to an Excel workbook. The pd.ExcelWriter function facilitates efficient management of multiple sheets if needed.

Enhancing the report's visual appeal is equally important. Consider adding charts that showcase trends over time or comparisons among different products. By using libraries like Matplotlib or Seaborn alongside Excel, you can transform your reports from simple tables into compelling visual narratives:

` ` `python

import matplotlib.pyplot as plt

\#\# Generate a bar chart

plt.figure(figsize=(10, 6))

plt.bar(sales_summary['Product'], sales_summary['Revenue'])

plt.title('Monthly Revenue by Product')

plt.xlabel('Product')

plt.ylabel('Revenue')

plt.xticks(rotation=45)

plt.tight_layout()

plt.savefig('monthly_revenue_chart.png')

` ` `

Once you've created visual elements such as charts or graphs, you can easily insert them into your Excel report using OpenPyXL:

` ` `python

from openpyxl import load_workbook

from openpyxl.drawing.image import Image

\#\# Load existing workbook

wb = load_workbook('Monthly_Sales_Report.xlsx')

ws = wb['Sales Summary']

\#\# Insert chart image

img = Image('monthly_revenue_chart.png')

ws.add_image(img, 'D5') \# Specify where to place the image

wb.save('Monthly_Sales_Report.xlsx')

` ` `

Adding these visuals not only enhances comprehension but also increases engagement with your report.

Also, scheduling automated reports introduces another level of efficiency. You can utilize libraries like schedule or APScheduler to run your report generation scripts at defined intervals—whether daily, weekly, or monthly. Take this example:

```python
import schedule
import time

def job():
print("Generating report...")
\#\# Place all code related to report generation here

schedule.every().month.at("10:00").do(job)

while True:
schedule.run_pending()
time.sleep(60) \# Wait one minute before checking again
```

This automation ensures that stakeholders receive timely insights without manual intervention each time.

As you refine your reporting processes through the integration of Python and Excel, consider developing templates that standardize formatting and styles across reports. Consistency fosters clarity and professionalism in presentation while minimizing setup time for future reports.

To wrap things up, automating reporting workflows not only streamlines operations but also enhances decision-making capabilities within an organization. By harnessing the powerful libraries of Python in conjunction with Excel's functionalities, you position yourself as an invaluable resource capable of delivering critical insights efficiently—a skill that is increasingly essential in today's fast-paced business landscape.

Handling large datasets efficiently

To begin, it's important to understand Excel's limitations when dealing with large datasets. Although Excel can handle up to 1,048,576 rows and 16,384 columns, performance issues often arise well before these limits are reached. A common scenario involves importing extensive data from a CSV file or database into Excel for analysis. Rather than attempting to load everything at once—which can result in long load times and a frustrating user experience—it's advisable to break the data into manageable chunks.

The Pandas library in Python offers powerful tools for handling large datasets effectively. For example, you can read portions of your dataset using the chunksize parameter in pd.read_csv(), allowing you to process each chunk individually without overwhelming your system's memory:

```python
import pandas as pd


\#\# Processing a large CSV file in chunks

chunk_size = 10000 \# Adjust based on available memory

for chunk in pd.read_csv('large_dataset.csv', chunksize=chunk_size):

\#\# Process each chunk

process_data(chunk) \# Define your processing function here
```

By defining a function like process_data(), you can analyze or manipulate each chunk before proceeding to the next one. This method helps maintain low memory usage and improves processing speed.

When working with datasets larger than your available

memory, consider utilizing Dask, a flexible parallel computing library for analytics. Dask DataFrames function similarly to Pandas but can scale beyond memory limits by parallelizing operations across multiple CPU cores or even distributed systems:

```python
import dask.dataframe as dd


\#\# Reading a large dataset with Dask

dask_df = dd.read_csv('large_dataset.csv')


\#\# Example operation: compute mean of a column

mean_value = dask_df['column_name'].mean().compute()

print(mean_value)
```

This example highlights Dask's lazy evaluation feature; computations are executed only when explicitly requested with .compute(). This functionality significantly enhances efficiency for large-scale data operations.

After processing your data efficiently, you'll likely need to perform transformations before exporting it back into Excel. This is where cleaning and manipulating your dataset becomes vital. Utilizing functions such as dropna(), fillna(), and various filtering techniques will help maintain data integrity:

```python
\#\# Cleaning data: removing rows with missing values

cleaned_data = dask_df.dropna()
```

\#\# Filtering based on conditions

filtered_data = cleaned_data[cleaned_data['sales'] > 1000]
```
` ` `
```

By incorporating these operations into your processing pipeline, you ensure that only relevant and clean data is transferred into Excel.

Once your transformations are complete, exporting the cleaned dataset back into an Excel workbook should also be efficient. Libraries like OpenPyXL or XlsxWriter can assist with this step effectively without compromising performance:

```python
import dask.dataframe as dd
```

\#\# Assuming cleaned_data is ready for export as a Pandas DataFrame

cleaned_data.to_excel('Cleaned_Data.xlsx', index=False)
```
` ` `
```

If you're dealing with extremely large datasets, consider compressing your files during export to minimize storage space requirements while maintaining accessibility.

Lastly, always keep performance optimization techniques in mind when handling large datasets. Profiling tools such as %timeit in Jupyter Notebooks or Python's built-in time module can help identify bottlenecks in your code, allowing for timely adjustments before they become larger issues:

```python
import time
```

```
start_time = time.time()

\#\# Your data processing code here

end_time = time.time()
print(f"Processing time: end_time - start_time seconds")
` ` `
```

Identifying inefficiencies enables you to fine-tune your scripts for better performance.

In summary, leveraging Python's capabilities for handling large datasets opens doors to robust analytical processes without the constraints posed by traditional tools like Excel. By employing methods such as chunking data reads, utilizing libraries like Dask, performing targeted transformations, and focusing on efficient exports, you can effectively manage substantial volumes of information while preserving clarity and precision throughout your workflows.

Security considerations for database access

Ensuring security when accessing databases is crucial in professional environments, especially when dealing with sensitive data. The integrity and privacy of information are paramount, making it essential for anyone involved in data analysis and automation to understand the potential vulnerabilities associated with database connections and transactions.

To begin with, it's important to adhere to secure coding principles and best practices when connecting to databases. One effective approach is to use parameterized queries instead of concatenating strings to form SQL statements. This practice not only enhances security by preventing SQL injection attacks but also results in cleaner, more maintainable code. Take this example, consider the following example using Python's sqlite3 library:

```python
import sqlite3

\#\# Connect to the database
connection = sqlite3.connect('database.db')

\#\# Prepare a parameterized query
user_id = 5
query = "SELECT * FROM users WHERE id = ?
cursor = connection.execute(query, (user_id,))

\#\# Fetch the result
results = cursor.fetchall()
```

In this snippet, user input is handled safely, ensuring that even if malicious data is entered, it won't compromise the integrity of your SQL commands.

Next, it's vital to implement access control measures. Limit database access by granting permissions based on specific roles within your organization. The principle of least privilege dictates that users should have only the access necessary for their job functions, which minimizes the risks associated with unauthorized data access or modifications. Regularly reviewing these permissions is also essential for maintaining a secure environment.

For storing credentials for database connections, prioritize using environment variables or secret management services instead of hardcoding them in your scripts. Tools like python-decouple can help you manage sensitive information securely, keeping your codebase clean. An example configuration might look like this:

```python
from decouple import config

db_user = config('DB_USER')
db_password = config('DB_PASSWORD')
```

By keeping sensitive configurations outside your codebase, you significantly reduce the risk of exposing them in version control systems or public repositories.

It's also crucial to ensure that any data exchanged between your Python application and the database is encrypted both in transit and at rest. Utilizing SSL/TLS for connections creates a secure channel that protects data from eavesdropping and tampering. Most modern database management systems provide built-in support for encrypted connections, so be sure to enable this feature.

Additionally, consider the implications of logging. While logging errors and events is essential for monitoring system health, it can unintentionally expose sensitive information if not managed correctly. Adopting logging best practices —such as anonymizing user data before logging and using configurable log levels—can help prevent unnecessary exposure in production environments.

For organizations subject to compliance regulations like GDPR or HIPAA, understanding the legal landscape surrounding data storage and access is vital. Ensure that personal data processing aligns with relevant regulations and maintain documentation of consent where applicable. This not only protects your organization from legal repercussions but also builds trust with clients and stakeholders.

As you design automated workflows involving databases, it's wise to proactively consider disaster recovery strategies as well. Regularly backing up your databases and testing restoration procedures will ensure that you can quickly recover from potential breaches or data losses with minimal downtime.

Lastly, cultivating a culture of security awareness within your team is essential. Educate colleagues about common security risks related to database access and empower them to adopt secure practices in their daily workflows. Resources such as security training sessions or workshops can enhance understanding and promote vigilance across all levels of the organization.

Navigating security considerations in database access extends beyond mere compliance; it's about instilling confidence in your processes and safeguarding valuable organizational assets from potential threats. By integrating these principles into your workflows, you not only protect data but also enhance the reliability and reputation of your analytical capabilities within Excel and beyond.

CHAPTER 7: WEB SCRAPING AND EXCEL AUTOMATION

Introduction to web scraping

At its essence, web scraping involves programmatically fetching and parsing HTML pages to obtain relevant data. Take this example, imagine you need to compile a list of product prices from an e-commerce site. Rather than manually browsing through each page and copying information into a spreadsheet, you can automate this task using Python. Automating such processes not only saves time but also reduces the risk of human error—an important consideration when managing large datasets.

To begin your web scraping journey, it's essential to understand some foundational concepts. At the heart of web scraping are HTTP requests, which facilitate communication between browsers and servers. When you enter a URL in your browser, an HTTP GET request is sent to retrieve the desired page. Similarly, in Python, libraries like Requests enable you to send these requests programmatically. Here's a simple example:

```python
import requests
```

```
url = 'https://example.com'

response = requests.get(url)

if response.status_code == 200:

html_content = response.text

print("Page fetched successfully!")

else:

print("Failed to retrieve page")

```
```

In this code snippet, we utilize the Requests library to access a webpage and verify the success of our request by checking the status code. A 200 status code indicates that the request was successful; any other code suggests an issue that may need further investigation.

Once you have retrieved the HTML content, the next step is parsing it. This is where BeautifulSoup excels—a powerful library tailored for extracting data from HTML and XML documents with ease. With your HTML content in hand, you can load it into BeautifulSoup for analysis:

```python
from bs4 import BeautifulSoup

soup = BeautifulSoup(html_content, 'html.parser')

titles = soup.find_all('h1') \# Example: find all <h1> tags

for title in titles:
```
```

```
print(title.text)
```
` ` `

This example demonstrates how to extract text from all <h1> tags on a webpage using BeautifulSoup. By navigating the structure of the HTML document through BeautifulSoup's API, you can target specific elements containing valuable data.

However, web scraping presents its own set of challenges. Many websites implement measures such as CAPTCHAs or require user authentication to access their content. Additionally, ethical considerations should not be overlooked —always review a website's terms of service before scraping its content and adhere to robots.txt directives that indicate which sections should not be accessed programmatically.

Another important aspect of web scraping involves dealing with dynamic content generated by JavaScript frameworks like React or Angular. Traditional scraping methods may fall short since such pages often load additional data asynchronously after the initial page load. In these cases, tools like Selenium become invaluable. Selenium automates browsers and allows for interaction with JavaScript-heavy sites as if you were navigating them manually:

` ` `python

```
from selenium import webdriver


driver = webdriver.Chrome()

driver.get(url)


\#\# Wait until elements are loaded

titles = driver.find_elements_by_tag_name('h1')
```

```
for title in titles:

print(title.text)


driver.quit()
```
` ` `

This example illustrates how Selenium can be employed to open a webpage and scrape data that isn't immediately visible in the static HTML.

As we delve deeper into web scraping throughout this book, you'll discover its practical applications within Excel automation—enabling you to compile datasets automatically for reporting or analysis directly from live online sources. The true power lies not just in retrieving data but also in transforming it into actionable insights that drive decision-making.

Your newfound ability to automate data extraction will significantly enhance your workflows and position you as an innovative professional adept at leveraging technology for greater efficiency. Embracing these techniques opens up avenues for personal development while elevating your contributions within your organization, making you a catalyst for innovation and strategic growth.

Setting up the scraping environment

Setting up your scraping environment is a crucial step in your web scraping journey. This phase transforms theoretical knowledge into practical application, enabling you to leverage the full capabilities of Python and its libraries. A well-configured environment streamlines your workflow and reduces the likelihood of issues as you begin extracting data from various websites.

To get started, ensure that you have Python installed on your machine. If you haven't installed it yet, visit the official Python website to download the latest version. The installation process is straightforward—simply follow the prompts and be sure to check the option that adds Python to your system PATH. This will allow you to run Python scripts from any command line interface, enhancing your development experience.

Once Python is installed, the next step is setting up a virtual environment. This practice is essential for managing dependencies specific to your projects while avoiding conflicts with other projects or system-level packages. To create a virtual environment, navigate to your desired project directory in the terminal or command prompt and run:

```bash
python -m venv my_scraping_env
```

After creating the environment, activate it using one of the following commands based on your operating system:

- For Windows:

```bash
my_scraping_env
```

- For macOS/Linux:

```bash
source my_scraping_env/bin/activate
```

With your virtual environment activated, it's time to install some essential libraries for web scraping. The two primary libraries you'll need are Requests for making HTTP requests and BeautifulSoup for parsing HTML content. You can install these libraries using pip, Python's package installer:

``` bash

pip install requests beautifulsoup4
```

If you intend to scrape dynamic content that relies on JavaScript, you'll also need Selenium. Install it with:

``` bash

pip install selenium
```

Additionally, Selenium requires a web driver compatible with the browser you plan to automate. Take this example, if you're using Chrome, you'll need ChromeDriver. Download it from its official site and ensure it's accessible via your PATH or specify its location when initializing Selenium in your scripts.

Now that you have set up your environment with all necessary libraries and tools, consider organizing your project files effectively. Creating a directory structure that separates different components of your scraping project—such as scripts, data outputs, logs, and configurations—will help maintain clarity as your project evolves. A simple structure might look like this:

```

my_scraping_project/
|
├── scripts/
|   └── scraper.py
|
├── data/
|   └── output.csv
```

```
|
└── logs/
└── scraping_log.txt
` ` `
```

This organization fosters clarity and makes it easier to manage as projects scale.

Next, configure logging for better tracking of your scraping activities. By utilizing Python's built-in logging library, you can monitor both successes and failures during data extraction. Here's a basic setup for logging within your script:

```python
import logging

logging.basicConfig(filename='logs/scraping_log.txt', level=logging.INFO,

format='%(asctime)s - %(levelname)s - %(message)s')


logging.info('Starting web scraping...')
```

With logging in place, every time you run your script, it will generate a log file detailing the execution—an invaluable tool for troubleshooting when things don't go as planned.

As you prepare for actual scraping tasks, take time to familiarize yourself with the structure of any website you plan to scrape by reviewing it using browser developer tools (accessible by right-clicking on elements and selecting "Inspect"). Understanding how data is organized within HTML tags will significantly simplify writing effective extraction logic later.

As you move forward, always keep ethical considerations at the forefront of your actions. Respect robots.txt files and adhere to website terms of service; these guidelines are often established for good reason. Following them not only protects others but also enhances the credibility of web scrapers as a whole.

By establishing a solid foundation through this setup process, you're positioning yourself for successful web scraping endeavors ahead. Your organized approach, combined with a keen understanding of both technical skills and ethical considerations, equips you well in this field—preparing you not just for success but also paving the way toward innovative applications of scraped data within Excel automation workflows. The ability to gather real-time information seamlessly will empower you to make informed decisions that drive impactful results in any domain you're working within.

Retrieving data from websites

To retrieve data from websites, it's essential to apply the knowledge you've gained during your environment setup. Let's put that theory into practice by exploring the process of extracting information. This is where your web scraping ambitions truly begin, transforming static web pages into dynamic datasets that are ready for analysis.

Start by selecting a target website that contains the data you wish to collect. Take this example, you might choose a site that lists job postings or product prices. If you opt for a job listing site, your goal would be to extract job titles, company names, and links from the listings. Open your browser and inspect the webpage structure using the developer tools—just right-click on the page and select "Inspect." Familiarize yourself with the HTML tags that hold the information you want; this understanding will inform your scraping strategy.

Now, let's delve into how you can retrieve this data using Python's Requests and BeautifulSoup libraries. Begin by making an HTTP request to fetch the content of the webpage:

```python
import requests
from bs4 import BeautifulSoup

\#\# URL of the webpage you want to scrape
url = 'https://example.com/job-listings'

\#\# Send an HTTP request and get the response
response = requests.get(url)

\#\# Check if the request was successful
if response.status_code == 200:
\#\# Parse the page content
soup = BeautifulSoup(response.text, 'html.parser')
else:
print(f"Failed to retrieve data: response.status_code")
```

Once you've retrieved and parsed the HTML content, it's time to locate and extract specific elements. Using BeautifulSoup, you can find all job listing entries on the page. Here's an example of how to extract job titles along with their corresponding company names:

```python
\#\# Find all job listings on the page
job_listings = soup.find_all('div', class_='job-listing')
```

```python
for job in job_listings:
title = job.find('h2', class_='job-title').text.strip() \# Job title
company = job.find('span', class_='company-name').text.strip() \# Company name

print(f"Job Title: title, Company: company")
```
```

This snippet searches for div elements with a specific class name that identifies each job listing. The find method retrieves nested tags—such as h2 for titles or span for company names—allowing for straightforward extraction of relevant text.

However, some pages load data dynamically via JavaScript after the initial page load. In such cases, utilizing Selenium is essential. Selenium automates a web browser to interact effectively with these dynamic elements. Here's how you can achieve similar results using Selenium:

```python
from selenium import webdriver


\#\# Set up Selenium WebDriver (ensure ChromeDriver is installed)
driver = webdriver.Chrome()


\#\# Navigate to the target URL
driver.get(url)


\#\# Allow some time for JavaScript content to load
```
```

```
driver.implicitly_wait(10) \# seconds
```

```
\#\# Locate job listings after full page load
```

```
job_elements    =    driver.find_elements_by_class_name('job-
listing')
```

```
for job in job_elements:
```

```
title = job.find_element_by_class_name('job-title').text.strip()
```

```
company    =    job.find_element_by_class_name('company-
name').text.strip()
```

```
print(f"Job Title: title, Company: company")
```

```
\#\# Close the browser window when done
```

```
driver.quit()
```
``` ` ` ` ```

This approach allows your script to interact with a fully rendered page before scraping its contents.

After retrieving the data, the next step is to store it in a structured format for later use in Excel or further analysis. A simple and versatile option is to save it as a CSV file:
``` ` ` `python ```

```
import csv
```

```
\#\# Save data into a CSV file
```

```
with    open('data/job_listings.csv',    mode='w',    newline=",
encoding='utf-8') as file:
```

```
writer = csv.writer(file)

\#\# Write header row
writer.writerow(['Job Title', 'Company'])

\#\# Write rows containing each job's information
for job in job_listings:
title = job.find('h2', class_='job-title').text.strip()
company = job.find('span', class_='company-name').text.strip()
writer.writerow([title, company])
` ` `
```

Executing this code after extracting jobs using either Requests or Selenium will create a CSV file that can be easily imported into Excel.

It's crucial to keep ethical considerations in mind while scraping; always respect robots.txt files and website terms of service guidelines. Regularly assess whether your scraping activities remain within legal bounds and considerate of server load—not every website appreciates automated requests.

Mastering the skill of retrieving meaningful data from websites opens up vast opportunities for enhancing Excel automation workflows. As you become proficient in these techniques, think about how this capability can enrich your analytical tasks or improve decision-making processes at work —transforming static web pages into dynamic insights is no small feat!

Cleaning and preparing web data for Excel

For web scraping, the process doesn't conclude with merely

retrieving data; the next vital step is cleaning and preparing this data for effective use in Excel. Raw data often presents various challenges—irrelevant information, inconsistent formats, and extraneous characters—that can hinder analysis. The objective here is to transform this unstructured raw data into a clean, structured format that is ready for immediate use or further processing.

Let's first delve into what cleaning entails. This typically involves removing unwanted whitespace, correcting inconsistencies in data formats (such as dates), and addressing missing values. Take this example, if you've scraped job listings from a website, you might encounter job titles with extra spaces or varying capitalization styles. To tackle these inconsistencies in Python, consider the following example:

```python
\#\# Sample list of job titles scraped from a website

job_titles = [" Software Engineer ", "Data Analyst", "senior Developer", "QA Tester"]


\#\# Clean job titles by stripping whitespace and normalizing case

cleaned_titles = [title.strip().title() for title in job_titles]


print(cleaned_titles)
```

In this snippet, we use list comprehension to create a new list that eliminates unnecessary spaces and standardizes capitalization across job titles. Such transformations are essential for ensuring that your data integrates smoothly into reports.

Next, let's address missing values. If your scraped dataset

includes entries where the company name is missing, you might choose to fill these gaps with a placeholder like "Not Specified" or remove those entries altogether, depending on your analytical needs. Here's how you can handle this situation:

```python
job_data = [

"title": "Software Engineer", "company": "Tech Corp",

"title": "Data Analyst", "company": None,

"title": "Senior Developer", "company": "Dev Solutions",

"title": "QA Tester", "company": ""

]


\#\# Clean company names: replace None or empty strings with 'Not Specified'

for job in job_data:

if not job["company"]:

job["company"] = 'Not Specified'


print(job_data)
```

In this code block, we iterate over each job entry and replace missing company names accordingly. This practice not only enhances consistency but also improves visualization when the data is imported into Excel.

Once you have cleaned the basic structure of your dataset, it's time to prepare it for Excel output. If your goal is to facilitate further analysis within Excel's interface, organizing your data as a DataFrame using Pandas can be especially beneficial. Pandas offers powerful functionalities that simplify dataset manipulation before exporting:

```python
import pandas as pd

\#\# Create a DataFrame from cleaned job data

df = pd.DataFrame(job_data)


\#\# Preview the DataFrame

print(df)


\#\# Export to Excel format

df.to_excel('job_listings_cleaned.xlsx', index=False)
```

This approach allows you to take full advantage of Pandas to format your data neatly within an Excel file. The to_excel() method streamlines the process of generating well-organized sheets that are ready for analysis or reporting.

Additionally, consider situations where specific columns require type conversions—for instance, transforming date strings into datetime objects to facilitate time series analyses later on. If numerical values were scraped as strings (like salary ranges), converting them into integers or floats will enable accurate calculations and visualizations within Excel.

The intricacies of cleaning and preparing web-scraped data are crucial if you aim for precision in your analyses. It demands diligence and attention to detail but serves as a solid foundation for any analytical project you undertake.

Each step in this process enhances your ability not only to analyze but also to extract actionable insights from seemingly chaotic datasets. The cleaner and more structured your input is, the more reliable and insightful your outputs will be— an essential aspect when making business decisions based on collected data.

As you become more proficient at cleaning and preparing web-scraped datasets for Excel integration, reflect on how these skills benefit not just individual projects but also broader organizational efficiencies and decision-making processes. With every dataset refined and each report generated seamlessly through automation, you're significantly contributing to your team's analytics efforts— empowering smarter choices backed by clean insights derived from raw web data.

Automating regular data extraction

Automating regular data extraction can significantly streamline workflow processes. After you've cleaned and prepared your web-scraped data, the next step is to implement automation that consistently pulls the latest information from websites. This not only saves you time but also ensures that your analyses are based on the most up-to-date data available.

To establish a routine for regular data extraction, Python provides several powerful libraries, with BeautifulSoup and Requests being among the most popular for scraping tasks. When you combine these tools with scheduling libraries like Schedule or APScheduler, you can run your extraction scripts at set intervals—whether hourly, daily, or weekly. This automation frees you to concentrate on analysis rather than manual updates.

Imagine you're extracting stock prices from a financial news website. You would start by creating a function that scrapes the required information:

```python
import requests
from bs4 import BeautifulSoup

def fetch_stock_prices(stock_symbol):
url = f"https://example.com/stocks/stock_symbol
response = requests.get(url)

\#\# Check if request was successful
if response.status_code == 200:
soup = BeautifulSoup(response.text, 'html.parser')
price = soup.find("span", class_="price").text
return price
else:
print(f"Error fetching data for stock_symbol: response.status_code")
return None

\#\# Example usage
stock_price = fetch_stock_prices("AAPL")
print(f"Current Apple Stock Price: stock_price")
```

In this script, the fetch_stock_prices function takes a stock symbol as an argument and retrieves its current price from a specified webpage. It also includes error handling to address any potential issues during the request process.

Next, let's look at how to automate this function using the Schedule library. You can easily set up a job that runs this function at defined intervals:

```python
import schedule

import time


def job():

stock_symbol = "AAPL

price = fetch_stock_prices(stock_symbol)

if price:

print(f"The latest price for stock_symbol is price")


\#\# Schedule job every hour

schedule.every(1).hours.do(job)


while True:

schedule.run_pending()

time.sleep(1)

```

In this example, the job function calls fetch_stock_prices to get the current stock price for Apple every hour. The continuous loop checks if any scheduled jobs are due to execute.

Once you have retrieved this data, it's essential to consider what to do with it. You might want to log it into an Excel file or database to keep track of historical prices over time. Using

Pandas simplifies this process:

```python
import pandas as pd

\#\# Initialize an empty DataFrame (or load an existing one)
dataframe_columns = ['Timestamp', 'Stock Symbol', 'Price']
df = pd.DataFrame(columns=dataframe_columns)

def log_to_excel(stock_symbol, price):
global df  \# Referencing global DataFrame

\#\# Append new entry
new_entry =
'Timestamp': pd.Timestamp.now(),
'Stock Symbol': stock_symbol,
'Price': price,


df = df.append(new_entry, ignore_index=True)

\#\# Export to Excel (appending new data)
df.to_excel('stock_prices_log.xlsx', index=False)

\#\# Update log within job function after fetching prices
def job():
```

```
stock_symbol = "AAPL

price = fetch_stock_prices(stock_symbol)

if price:

log_to_excel(stock_symbol, price)
`  `  `
```

With each automated extraction, the latest prices are logged into an Excel file named stock_prices_log.xlsx, resulting in a continuously updating dataset that is ideal for generating reports and visualizations.

Another benefit of automation is consistency in data quality and formatting. By clearly defining your functions and proactively handling errors, you can minimize human mistakes that often occur during manual tasks.

However, it's important to be mindful of ethical considerations when scraping websites. Always review a site's robots.txt file and terms of service before automating any extraction processes to ensure compliance with their guidelines.

As you integrate these strategies into your routine, consider how they not only enhance personal productivity but also improve organizational responsiveness. Automation empowers teams to quickly adapt based on fresh insights derived from real-time data—a crucial advantage in today's fast-paced business environment.

By establishing reliable automation routines for regular data extraction, you'll be better equipped to make informed decisions and uncover deeper insights from ongoing trends reflected in your datasets. This approach truly unlocks the potential of your analytical endeavors.

Handling dynamic websites and authentication

Web scraping dynamic websites that require authentication presents unique challenges compared to static pages. Unlike static sites, dynamic ones often load content through JavaScript, necessitating a different strategy for effective data extraction. When user authentication is involved—whether through login forms or API tokens—the process becomes even more intricate, requiring additional steps to access the desired information.

To navigate this complexity, let's explore how to programmatically handle login processes. Take this example, if you want to scrape data from a website that requires you to log in first, you can utilize the Requests library to create a session. This session allows you to maintain cookies across multiple requests, ensuring that you remain logged in while fetching content.

Here's an example that demonstrates how to log into a hypothetical site and retrieve data after authentication:

```python
import requests

from bs4 import BeautifulSoup


\#\# Start a session

session = requests.Session()


\#\# Define login URL and credentials

login_url = "https://example.com/login

payload =

'username': 'your_username',

'password': 'your_password'
```

```
\#\# Log in to the site
response = session.post(login_url, data=payload)

\#\# Check if login was successful
if response.ok:
print("Login successful!")
else:
print("Login failed!")

\#\# Now that we're logged in, we can access protected pages
data_url = "https://example.com/protected-data
data_response = session.get(data_url)

if data_response.ok:
soup = BeautifulSoup(data_response.text, 'html.parser')
\#\# Extract desired information
desired_data = soup.find("div", class_="data-class").text
print(f"Extracted Data: desired_data")
else:
print("Failed to retrieve protected data.")
` ` `
```

In this script, we establish a session with requests.Session(), which simplifies cookie management. After logging in with the provided credentials via a POST request, we verify the success of the login before proceeding to fetch content from a restricted page.

However, many dynamic sites implement additional security measures such as CAPTCHA verification or token-based authentication systems. In such cases, using libraries like Selenium can be advantageous, as they allow for automated browser interactions and facilitate navigation through complex logins or JavaScript-rendered content.

For example:

```python
from selenium import webdriver

\#\# Initialize WebDriver (ensure ChromeDriver is installed)
driver = webdriver.Chrome()

\#\# Navigate to login page
driver.get('https://example.com/login')

\#\# Input username and password
username_input = driver.find_element_by_name('username')
password_input = driver.find_element_by_name('password')

username_input.send_keys('your_username')
password_input.send_keys('your_password')

\#\# Submit the form
```

```
login_button          =          driver.find_element_by_xpath('//
button[@type="submit"]')

login_button.click()


\#\# After logging in, navigate to the desired page and scrape
data

driver.get('https://example.com/protected-data')

desired_data_element                                    =
driver.find_element_by_class_name('data-class')

print(f"Extracted Data: desired_data_element.text")


\#\# Clean up: close the browser window after extracting data

driver.quit()
```

` ` `

With Selenium, you can interact with web elements just as if you were using a browser manually. This functionality is especially useful for addressing scenarios involving dynamic content loading or intricate user interactions.

As you engage in web scraping, it's essential to consider ethical implications when working with sites that have authentication requirements. Always comply with their terms of service and remain aware of any rate limits they impose on your requests.

Effectively handling dynamic websites significantly enhances your ability to extract valuable insights from various sources. As you implement these strategies for managing authentication and dynamically loaded content, think about their broader applications—enabling richer analyses through real-time data access across multiple domains.

By embracing these techniques, you not only empower yourself as an analyst but also position your organization at the forefront of leveraging diverse datasets for informed decision-making.

Integrating web-scraped data into Excel workbooks

Integrating web-scraped data into Excel workbooks can transform raw data into actionable insights, allowing you to leverage Python's capabilities to bridge the gap between web data and Excel, where analysis and visualization can occur. Once you've successfully scraped data from a website, the next step is ensuring it flows seamlessly into your Excel workbooks, ready for further analysis or reporting.

To start this integration, you'll want to utilize libraries such as Pandas and OpenPyXL, which are essential tools for data manipulation and Excel file management. Begin by installing these libraries in your Python environment:

```bash
pip install pandas openpyxl
```

With the libraries set up, you can convert your scraped data into a Pandas DataFrame. This structure is intuitive and powerful, allowing for easy manipulation before exporting to Excel. Take this example, suppose you've extracted a list of product names and prices from an e-commerce site. You can format this data like so:

```python
import pandas as pd

\#\# Sample data extracted from web scraping
data =
```

'Product Name': ['Widget A', 'Widget B', 'Widget C'],

'Price': [19.99, 29.99, 39.99]

\#\# Create a DataFrame

df = pd.DataFrame(data)

` ` `

Once your DataFrame is established, exporting it to an Excel workbook is straightforward. You can use OpenPyXL or take advantage of Pandas' built-in capabilities:

` ` `python

\#\# Exporting DataFrame to Excel

output_file = 'products.xlsx'

df.to_excel(output_file, index=False)

` ` `

This command will generate an Excel file named products.xlsx, containing your scraped data organized in a clear tabular format.

However, integrating web-scraped data into existing workbooks often requires more than simply appending new sheets. You may need to merge this new information with existing datasets or format it according to specific requirements. Let's examine how to open an existing workbook, add new data, and save those changes.

To modify an existing workbook using OpenPyXL, you first need to load the workbook:

` ` `python

from openpyxl import load_workbook

```
\#\# Load an existing workbook
workbook = load_workbook('existing_workbook.xlsx')
sheet = workbook.active

\#\# Assuming you want to start writing from row 2 onwards
for index, row in df.iterrows():
    sheet.cell(row=index + 2, column=1).value = row['Product Name']
    sheet.cell(row=index + 2, column=2).value = row['Price']

\#\# Save the modified workbook
workbook.save('updated_workbook.xlsx')
```

In this snippet, existing_workbook.xlsx is opened, and new product names and prices are written starting from row 2 (assuming row 1 contains headers). The updated content is then saved as updated_workbook.xlsx, preserving all previous data while effectively integrating your newly scraped information.

Formatting plays a crucial role in presenting integrated data clearly within Excel. OpenPyXL offers various formatting options—such as adjusting column widths or applying styles —to enhance readability:

```python
from openpyxl.styles import Font

\#\# Set header font style
```

```
for cell in sheet["1:1"]:

cell.font = Font(bold=True)


\#\# Adjust column widths

sheet.column_dimensions['A'].width = 30   \# Width for Product Name column

sheet.column_dimensions['B'].width = 15   \# Width for Price column


\#\# Save changes again after formatting

workbook.save('formatted_workbook.xlsx')
` ` `
```

Incorporating these formatting features ensures that anyone viewing the integrated workbook can quickly grasp key information without unnecessary confusion.

As you explore deeper integration of web-scraped data with Python and Excel workflows, consider how automation can further streamline these processes. You could develop scripts that periodically scrape updated content from websites and automatically integrate it into your reports or dashboards—saving time while keeping information current.

This synergy between web scraping and Excel not only enhances your analytical capabilities but also equips you with robust strategies for decision-making based on real-time insights. The ability to manipulate vast datasets seamlessly positions you as a valuable asset within any organization striving for data-driven excellence.

Legal and ethical considerations in web scraping

Web scraping presents powerful opportunities for extracting

data from online sources, but it's essential to approach this practice with a keen awareness of the legal and ethical landscape. The internet serves as a vast repository of information, yet not all of it is available for unrestricted use. Understanding the boundaries of what is permissible when scraping data is crucial for maintaining your integrity and avoiding potential legal issues.

Central to these considerations are the terms of service (ToS) of the websites you plan to scrape. Many sites clearly outline their policies regarding automated access and data usage. Ignoring these terms can lead to serious consequences, including cease-and-desist orders or lawsuits. Therefore, before initiating any scraping activities, it is prudent to thoroughly review these agreements. Take this example, platforms like LinkedIn and Amazon have strict policies against unauthorized scraping, and violating them can put you in a difficult position.

Another important aspect to keep in mind is copyright law. The data you wish to scrape may be protected under intellectual property rights, which means you cannot freely take it without permission. This is particularly relevant for original content such as articles, images, and multimedia. Just because information is publicly accessible does not imply that it is free to use without restrictions. Always ensure proper attribution when necessary, and if you're uncertain about using specific content, it's best to seek clarification.

Data privacy regulations also play a significant role in ethical web scraping practices. Laws like the General Data Protection Regulation (GDPR) in Europe establish strict guidelines for handling personal data. If your scraping activities involve collecting personal information—such as email addresses or contact details—you must comply with these regulations. This typically requires obtaining explicit consent from individuals before collecting their information or ensuring that any scraped data is anonymized to protect user privacy.

In addition to legal considerations, it's important to think about the impact of your scraping activities on website performance and user experience. Excessive scraping requests can burden a server, leading to slowdowns or crashes that affect legitimate users. To mitigate this risk, adopt polite scraping techniques such as rate limiting—sending requests at intervals rather than all at once—to minimize your impact on the site you're accessing. Respectful scraping fosters a healthier online ecosystem where data sharing can occur without disrupting service availability.

When considering ethical scraping practices, transparency is key. If you are collecting data for research or analytics purposes, consider informing website owners about your activities, especially if your work could be beneficial to them or align with their interests. Building positive relationships can open doors for collaboration opportunities where both parties can derive value from shared data.

As technology evolves, so does the discourse surrounding ethical scraping practices. Engaging in industry discussions —whether through forums, conferences, or webinars—can help you stay informed about best practices and emerging standards in this area.

In summary, while web scraping offers a wealth of possibilities for data extraction and analysis, it's vital to approach this tool responsibly. Familiarizing yourself with the legal guidelines and ethical practices that govern your interactions with web content will not only protect you but also contribute to a more respectful digital environment where valuable information can flow freely without compromising rights or accessibility.

In the end, the intersection of law and ethics in web scraping highlights the importance of responsible behavior in all your automation endeavors. With a solid understanding of these principles guiding your practices, you'll be well-equipped to leverage web-sourced insights without venturing into murky waters.

CHAPTER 8: DATA VISUALIZATION WITH PYTHON AND EXCEL

Importance of data visualization

Data visualization has evolved into a vital skill in today's data-driven world, serving as a cornerstone of effective communication. The adage "A picture is worth a thousand words" rings particularly true when it comes to presenting complex information. Visualizations distill intricate data into easily digestible formats, enabling audiences to quickly grasp trends and insights. This clarity not only enhances understanding but also supports informed decision-making across various sectors.

To illustrate this point, consider the impact of presenting raw data in a table versus displaying it through a graph or chart. A well-crafted visualization can reveal patterns and correlations that might remain hidden in a sea of numbers. For example, if you have quarterly sales figures from multiple regions, plotting this data on a line graph can vividly showcase growth trends over time, making it easier for stakeholders to identify thriving areas and those needing attention. Engaging visualizations invite your audience into the narrative that your data tells, fostering deeper connections and facilitating discussion.

The role of visualization extends beyond clarity; it also plays a crucial part in persuasion. In corporate settings where decisions hinge on data presentations, the ability to communicate findings compellingly can significantly influence project approvals and resource allocations. Striking visuals can evoke emotions and prompt reactions—critical elements in persuading your audience. Take this example, a powerful bar chart illustrating an unexpected rise in customer satisfaction can inspire management to invest further in customer service improvements.

Yet, the art of data presentation should not stop at creating appealing charts. Effective storytelling with data marries narrative techniques with visual elements to craft an engaging viewer experience. By structuring your presentation around key insights and supporting them with relevant visuals, you guide your audience through your analysis step-by-step. This approach transforms passive observers into active participants who can engage with and contribute to discussions about your findings.

To create impactful visualizations, a solid grasp of design principles is essential. Elements such as color schemes, font choices, and layout all contribute to the effectiveness of your presentation. For example, using contrasting colors can help differentiate between datasets on a graph without overwhelming the viewer. Consistency across visual elements reinforces clarity and strengthens your message.

In addition, interactivity has emerged as a transformative feature in modern data visualization tools. Allowing users to engage with the data—filtering results or drilling down into specifics—creates an immersive experience that static images cannot provide. Tools like Tableau and Power BI facilitate this interactivity, enabling users to explore insights at their own pace, which enhances information retention.

Automating visualizations further enhances their utility in business contexts. By leveraging Python libraries such as Matplotlib or Seaborn, you can streamline the creation of dynamic graphs directly from Excel data sources. Imagine the efficiency of generating real-time dashboards that automatically update as new information enters your spreadsheets—this capability not only saves time but also ensures that decision-makers always have access to the latest insights.

For professionals seeking to excel in data handling and reporting, mastering visualization techniques is essential. The combination of analytical skills and creative storytelling transforms how insights are communicated within organizations. Those who can present findings visually distinguish themselves as leaders who inspire action based on informed decisions.

In summary, embracing the significance of data visualization means acknowledging its dual role: clarifying complex datasets while shaping organizational narratives through compelling storytelling. By dedicating time to hone these skills, you'll enhance both your analytical capabilities and your communication effectiveness—an invaluable combination that can elevate any professional's career trajectory.

Using Matplotlib and Seaborn with Excel

Integrating Matplotlib and Seaborn into your Excel automation workflow significantly enhances your data visualization capabilities. These powerful Python libraries enable you to create visually appealing and informative plots, transforming raw data into engaging graphics that promote deeper understanding and insights. Let's explore how you can harness these tools to produce professional-grade visualizations directly from your Excel datasets.

Matplotlib is the foundational library for creating static, animated, and interactive visualizations in Python. It offers a wide array of features, allowing you to design everything from simple line graphs to intricate 3D plots. To begin using Matplotlib, first ensure it's installed in your Python environment by running the following command in your terminal or command prompt:

```bash
pip install matplotlib
```

Once you have Matplotlib installed, creating a basic plot is straightforward. Take this example, if you have sales data stored in an Excel file named "sales_data.xlsx," you might start by reading the data using Pandas, then visualize it with Matplotlib:

```python
import pandas as pd
import matplotlib.pyplot as plt

\#\# Load the data from an Excel file
data = pd.read_excel('sales_data.xlsx')

\#\# Assuming 'Year' and 'Sales' are columns in your dataset
plt.plot(data['Year'], data['Sales'])
plt.title('Yearly Sales Trends')
plt.xlabel('Year')
plt.ylabel('Sales')
plt.grid(True)
plt.show()
```

This code snippet reads the sales data and generates a simple line chart illustrating yearly trends. The plt.show() function displays the plot, giving you immediate feedback on your visualization efforts.

Seaborn builds upon Matplotlib, offering a higher-level interface for creating attractive statistical graphics with less code. It integrates seamlessly with Pandas DataFrames and includes several built-in themes that enhance the aesthetics of your plots effortlessly. To install Seaborn, simply run:

```bash
pip install seaborn
```

Once installed, you can create more sophisticated visualizations using similar sales data. For example, here's how to generate a bar plot that showcases sales by product category:

```python
import seaborn as sns

\#\# Load your data again if necessary; using the same dataset
data = pd.read_excel('sales_data.xlsx')

\#\# Create a bar plot using Seaborn
sns.barplot(x='Product Category', y='Sales', data=data)
plt.title('Sales by Product Category')
plt.xticks(rotation=45)
plt.show()
```

This approach automatically applies aesthetic improvements

like color palettes and labeling styles, enhancing readability and engagement.

To further streamline your Excel workflows, consider automating reports that generate charts alongside your datasets. By scripting this process in Python, you can eliminate the manual steps typically involved in updating reports after new data entries. Imagine sending out quarterly performance summaries featuring dynamically generated graphs based on the latest figures every time.

You can also save Matplotlib figures directly into Excel workbooks using libraries like OpenPyXL or XlsxWriter. Take this example:

```python
from openpyxl import Workbook

\#\# Create a workbook and add a worksheet
wb = Workbook()
ws = wb.active

\#\# Save the plot to a file
plot_file = 'yearly_sales_trends.png'
plt.savefig(plot_file)

\#\# Insert the image into Excel
from openpyxl.drawing.image import Image
img = Image(plot_file)
ws.add_image(img, 'A1')
```

\#\# Save the workbook

wb.save('sales_report_with_plots.xlsx')

` ` `

In this example, you not only create visualizations programmatically but also embed them directly into an Excel report—an effective enhancement for presenting your analysis.

As professionals increasingly rely on clear visual narratives to communicate their findings, mastering tools like Matplotlib and Seaborn becomes essential. These libraries empower you to not just present data but also to persuade stakeholders through thoughtful visual storytelling rooted in robust analysis.

With these skills at your disposal, you position yourself as more than just a number cruncher; you become a valued communicator capable of transforming complex datasets into actionable insights—an invaluable asset in today's data-driven decision-making landscape.

Creating Excel-compatible visualizations

Creating visually compelling and informative graphics is essential for effectively conveying insights from your data. By utilizing Matplotlib and Seaborn, you can develop Excel-compatible visualizations that not only enhance your reports but also capture your audience's attention. These powerful libraries enable you to transform complex datasets into easily understandable graphics, making it simpler for stakeholders to grasp the underlying narratives.

To begin your journey into data visualization, first ensure that both libraries are properly installed in your Python environment. If you haven't yet set them up, simply run the following commands:

```bash
pip install matplotlib seaborn
```

Once everything is configured, you can start creating basic visualizations. For example, let's consider a dataset containing monthly sales figures stored in an Excel file named "monthly_sales.xlsx." A great way to illustrate these figures is through a simple line plot. Here's how to do it:

```python
import pandas as pd
import matplotlib.pyplot as plt

\#\# Load the data from the Excel file
data = pd.read_excel('monthly_sales.xlsx')

\#\# Generate a line plot for the sales data
plt.plot(data['Month'], data['Sales'], marker='o')
plt.title('Monthly Sales Overview')
plt.xlabel('Month')
plt.ylabel('Sales (\()')
plt.grid(True)
plt.xticks(rotation=45)
plt.tight_layout() \# Ensures everything fits well in the figure
plt.show()
```

This example produces a straightforward line chart that

highlights sales trends over the months. The addition of markers enhances clarity, allowing viewers to quickly identify specific data points.

For a more visually appealing option, Seaborn offers built-in themes and color palettes that can elevate your graphics. When dealing with categorical data, such as product sales by region, Seaborn makes it easy to create attractive bar plots with minimal effort. Here's how you can accomplish this:

```python
import seaborn as sns


\#\# Load your data again if necessary; using the same dataset

data = pd.read_excel('monthly_sales.xlsx')


\#\# Create a bar plot using Seaborn

sns.set_theme(style="whitegrid")  \# Set the theme for better aesthetics

sns.barplot(x='Region', y='Sales', data=data, palette='viridis')

plt.title('Sales Distribution by Region')

plt.xticks(rotation=30)

plt.tight_layout()

plt.show()
```

The selection of a color palette allows for improved visual contrast and accessibility, ensuring that your audience can easily interpret the results.

To further streamline your reporting process, consider automating these visualization tasks so they update with new data entries automatically. This method not only saves time but also ensures consistency across reports.

If you wish to embed your visualizations directly into Excel reports, libraries such as OpenPyXL or XlsxWriter are invaluable. Below is an example of how to save a plot and insert it into an Excel workbook using OpenPyXL:

```python
from openpyxl import Workbook

from openpyxl.drawing.image import Image


\#\# Create a new workbook and select the active worksheet

wb = Workbook()

ws = wb.active


\#\# Save the plot as an image file

plot_filename = 'monthly_sales_overview.png'

plt.savefig(plot_filename) \# Save the figure


\#\# Insert the saved image into Excel

img = Image(plot_filename)

ws.add_image(img, 'A1') \# Specify where to place the image


\#\# Save the workbook with embedded chart

wb.save('monthly_sales_report.xlsx')
```

This code snippet efficiently integrates generated plots into an Excel report, simplifying the process of sharing insights with colleagues or clients. The final product appears polished and professional, reinforcing your commitment to quality analysis.

In today's business landscape, visual storytelling has become increasingly vital for decision-making based on clear data interpretations. By mastering Matplotlib and Seaborn, you transition from merely processing numbers to becoming a professional who effectively communicates findings through engaging visuals.

With these skills at your disposal, you're not just presenting data—you're crafting narratives that resonate and drive action among stakeholders. This capability positions you as an invaluable contributor in any data-driven team or organization. Embrace these techniques, and watch your ability to influence decisions through compelling visual narratives flourish.

Best practices for visual data representation

Visual data representation plays a crucial role in effective communication, particularly when conveying complex information. The aim is not only to create visually appealing graphics but also to enhance clarity and impact. To achieve this, several best practices can guide you in crafting visualizations that resonate with your audience while maintaining the accuracy and integrity of the data.

Choosing the right type of chart or graph is fundamental. Different data types are best represented by specific visual formats. Take this example, line graphs effectively showcase time series data, allowing viewers to identify trends over time. In contrast, categorical data is more appropriately illustrated with bar charts or pie charts, which facilitate easy comparisons among different groups. Understanding the nature of your data will inform your choice, ensuring that the selected visualization conveys its intended message clearly.

Simplicity is another key element in design. Visual overload

—characterized by excessive colors, cluttered layouts, or too much text—can confuse rather than clarify. Aim for a clean and focused design that highlights key insights without unnecessary distractions. A limited color palette often creates a cohesive look while directing attention to the most critical areas. For example, if you want to emphasize a specific category within a bar chart, using a distinct color for that bar while keeping others neutral can effectively draw the viewer's eye.

Incorporating labels and annotations enhances understanding as well. Each axis should be clearly labeled with appropriate units of measurement. Additionally, tooltips can provide further context in interactive visualizations, enriching the user experience. Take this example, when presenting sales data across different regions, labeling not only the regions but also including sales figures directly on or above the bars offers immediate context and minimizes confusion.

And, it's essential to tell a story with your data. A well-crafted narrative makes statistics more engaging and memorable. This involves not just presenting numbers but also contextualizing them within a broader framework or trend. For example, when showcasing quarterly profits over several years, weaving in relevant historical events or market shifts can provide insights that mere numbers might overlook. This storytelling approach helps stakeholders grasp the significance of the data rather than viewing it as isolated figures.

Consistency across all visual elements reinforces professionalism and aids comprehension. Maintaining uniform font styles, sizes, and colors throughout your visualizations creates an easy-to-follow narrative for the viewer. If you're using Excel alongside Python-generated visualizations, ensure they share similar aesthetics to maintain coherence—this not only reinforces brand identity but also makes reports more digestible.

Accessibility should also be a priority in your visual representations. Ensure your visuals are usable by people with disabilities by adhering to color contrast guidelines and providing alternative text descriptions for images or complex graphs. Tools like color blindness simulators can help assess whether your visuals are inclusive enough for all audiences.

Finally, feedback is invaluable in refining your visuals. Share drafts with colleagues or stakeholders who can offer constructive criticism before finalizing your designs. Engaging others broadens perspectives and can illuminate potential misinterpretations that may arise from viewing your work too closely.

In summary, effective visual data representation hinges on thoughtful selection of visualization types, a commitment to simplicity and clarity, integration of contextual storytelling elements, consistency across designs, prioritization of accessibility, and openness to feedback for refinement. Each of these practices not only enhances how data is displayed but significantly impacts how it is understood and acted upon by its audience. By implementing these principles, you can create compelling visuals that elevate analytical insights derived from Python-driven Excel automation to new heights.

Automating visualization updates

Automating visualization updates in Excel using Python offers a powerful way to integrate fresh data and create dynamic visual stories. As you embark on this journey, it's essential to prioritize keeping your visualizations current and aligned with the latest data trends. The true advantage of automation lies in its ability to save time while ensuring that stakeholders have immediate access to the most relevant insights.

To start automating your visualization updates, consider utilizing libraries like Matplotlib, Seaborn, and Pandas. These tools not only help you create stunning visualizations but also enable you to update them effortlessly as new data becomes available. By establishing a process that refreshes your visuals automatically, you can eliminate the repetitive task of manual updates.

Let's explore this with a practical example. Imagine you have a dataset containing monthly sales figures across various product categories, stored in an Excel file named sales_data.xlsx. You can create a function that reads this data and generates a line chart illustrating sales trends over time.

Here's a sample script to set up your automation:

```python
import pandas as pd

import matplotlib.pyplot as plt


def update_sales_visualization():

\#\# Load data from Excel

df = pd.read_excel('sales_data.xlsx', sheet_name='Monthly Sales')


\#\# Ensure dates are in datetime format

df['Date'] = pd.to_datetime(df['Date'])


\#\# Create a line plot for sales trends

plt.figure(figsize=(10, 6))

for category in df['Category'].unique():

subset = df[df['Category'] == category]

plt.plot(subset['Date'], subset['Sales'], label=category)
```

```
plt.title('Monthly Sales Trends')

plt.xlabel('Date')

plt.ylabel('Sales Amount')

plt.legend()

\#\# Save the updated figure

plt.savefig('monthly_sales_trends.png')

plt.close()

\#\# Call the function to update the visualization

update_sales_visualization()

` ` `
```

This code snippet illustrates how to automate the updating of your sales visualization. By simply running the update_sales_visualization function, your chart will reflect any changes made to the sales_data.xlsx file without requiring you to recreate it manually each time.

For ongoing projects with frequent data updates, consider scheduling this script to run at specific intervals using task schedulers like Windows Task Scheduler or cron jobs on Unix-based systems. This approach ensures that your reports and presentations are always based on the most recent information, which is crucial for informed decision-making.

Integrating these automated visualizations into your Excel reports significantly enhances their value. By employing tools such as OpenPyXL or XlsxWriter, you can embed your updated charts directly into Excel spreadsheets, providing users with instant access to fresh insights. Here's a brief example of how you can add an image of the updated chart into an Excel workbook:

```python
from openpyxl import Workbook

from openpyxl.drawing.image import Image


def embed_chart_in_excel():

wb = Workbook()

ws = wb.active

ws.title = "Sales Report


\#\# Insert chart image

img = Image('monthly_sales_trends.png')

ws.add_image(img, 'A1') \# Positioning it at cell A1


wb.save("updated_sales_report.xlsx")


\#\# Embed the updated chart in an Excel file

embed_chart_in_excel()
```

This functionality seamlessly ties everything together—data is processed and visualized in Python, then integrated into an Excel report. Automating visualization updates not only streamlines workflows but also enhances collaboration within teams by ensuring everyone has access to timely information.

As you continue refining your skills in automating these processes, take the opportunity to explore new visualization techniques and frameworks. Each enhancement will significantly impact how effectively you communicate insights from your analyses. In the end, combining automated updates with thoughtful design principles allows you to craft impactful narratives that resonate with your audience and promote data-driven decision-making throughout your organization.

Exporting Python visualizations to Excel

Exporting Python visualizations to Excel is an essential step in transforming raw data into actionable reports. This functionality enhances the visibility of your findings and facilitates seamless integration into existing workflows, making it easier for stakeholders to access and interpret critical information. In this exploration, we will focus on utilizing libraries that enable the direct export of visualizations into Excel spreadsheets.

To start, consider combining Matplotlib or Seaborn for creating your visualizations with OpenPyXL or XlsxWriter for embedding them into Excel files. This combination allows you to produce visually appealing graphics while ensuring they fit within a broader data analysis context. Take this example, imagine presenting sales performance metrics or operational statistics in a manner that not only informs but also captivates your audience.

Let's look at a practical scenario: suppose you've created a bar chart illustrating quarterly revenue across various departments. To export this visualization to an Excel file, follow these steps:

1. Create the Visualization: Generate the desired plot using Matplotlib.

2. Save the Plot as an Image: Save the generated plot as a PNG file.

3. Embed the Image in Excel: Use OpenPyXL to insert

this image into a designated location within your Excel sheet.

Here's how you can implement this:

```python
import pandas as pd

import matplotlib.pyplot as plt

from openpyxl import Workbook

from openpyxl.drawing.image import Image


\#\# Sample data

data = 'Department': ['Sales', 'Marketing', 'HR', 'Finance'],

'Revenue': [25000, 15000, 10000, 20000]

df = pd.DataFrame(data)


\#\# Create a bar chart

plt.figure(figsize=(8, 5))

plt.bar(df['Department'], df['Revenue'], color='blue')

plt.title('Quarterly Revenue by Department')

plt.xlabel('Department')

plt.ylabel('Revenue')

plt.xticks(rotation=45)

plt.tight_layout()


\#\# Save the figure

plt.savefig('quarterly_revenue.png')
```

```
plt.close()

\#\# Create a new Excel workbook and add the image
def embed_chart_in_excel():
wb = Workbook()
ws = wb.active
ws.title = "Quarterly Report

\#\# Insert chart image
img = Image('quarterly_revenue.png')
ws.add_image(img, 'A1') \# Positioning it at cell A1

wb.save("quarterly_report.xlsx")

\#\# Call the function to embed the chart in Excel
embed_chart_in_excel()
` ` `
```

In this example, you first generate a bar chart that represents quarterly revenue by department. After saving the visualization as an image file, the script creates a new Excel workbook and embeds the chart within it. The add_image method places your visual representation directly into cell A1 of the newly created worksheet.

This approach not only enhances clarity and visual appeal in your reports but also simplifies data presentations during meetings or collaborative sessions. By establishing a consistent update mechanism for your charts and reports, you create an environment where decision-makers are well-informed and can act swiftly based on accurate information.

To further optimize your workflow, consider automating these processes with task schedulers or cron jobs. Automating the entire pipeline—from data acquisition to visualization generation and export—ensures that every report is up-to-date while minimizing manual errors associated with repetitive tasks.

As you enhance your skills in Python and Excel integration, reflect on how exporting visualizations adds value beyond aesthetics. It fosters clearer communication of insights and supports informed decision-making across teams. With each new visualization and report you create, you're not just sharing data; you're crafting compelling narratives that drive action within your organization.

Mastering this process will position you at the forefront of data-driven innovation, empowering you to lead meaningful discussions and influence outcomes based on insights derived from robust analytical practices.

Enhancing Excel charts with external libraries

Integrating external libraries to enhance Excel charts can significantly boost your data visualization capabilities. As you explore more sophisticated charting options, libraries such as Plotly and Bokeh provide dynamic, interactive visualizations that can elevate your Excel reports. Unlike the static charts produced by traditional methods, these tools allow users to engage with data directly, offering features like zooming, hovering, and clicking for deeper insights.

Take this example, consider using Plotly to create an interactive line chart that tracks sales trends over time. Presenting data in an engaging format not only aids in effectively communicating findings but also crafts a compelling narrative around the numbers. Here's a step-by-step guide to get you started:

1. Install Plotly: First, ensure that you have the Plotly library installed. You can easily do this using pip:

```bash
pip install plotly
```

1. Create the Interactive Visualization: Use Plotly's expressive API to build a line chart.
2. Export as HTML: Instead of embedding static images in Excel, save your interactive charts as HTML files and link them within your spreadsheets.

Here's a concise example illustrating these steps:

```python
import pandas as pd
import plotly.express as px

\#\# Sample data
data =
'Month': ['Jan', 'Feb', 'Mar', 'Apr', 'May'],
'Sales': [15000, 20000, 18000, 25000, 30000]

df = pd.DataFrame(data)

\#\# Create an interactive line chart
fig = px.line(df, x='Month', y='Sales', title='Monthly Sales Trend')
fig.write_html('monthly_sales_trend.html')
```

` ` `

By running this script, you'll generate an interactive line chart stored as an HTML file. While direct embedding into Excel may not retain interactivity when converted to static images, you can hyperlink the HTML file within your workbook for easy access. To do this:

- Open Excel and select a cell for the link.
- Right-click and choose "Hyperlink."
- Browse for the monthly_sales_trend.html file and create the link.

This approach allows stakeholders instant access to detailed visualizations without cluttering your Excel report with images or sacrificing interactivity.

As you enhance your Python skills alongside your Excel expertise, remember that these tools complement one another in achieving comprehensive data storytelling. Integrating advanced visualization techniques from external libraries with Excel's traditional capabilities not only improves aesthetic appeal but also deepens analytical insight.

When presenting complex datasets or financial information, consider which visualizations will resonate most with your audience. While Matplotlib is excellent for basic plots, Plotly excels in scenarios where interactivity engages decision-makers more effectively. Thoughtfully selecting visualization types will lead to better comprehension and facilitate productive discussions among colleagues or clients.

Incorporating these advanced techniques into your workflow gives you a strategic edge in any professional setting—enabling clearer communication of insights while fostering proactive engagement with key metrics and trends.

As you embark on this journey, remember that mastering these visualization strategies goes beyond technical skills;

it's about transforming decision-making within your organization through impactful storytelling driven by data.

Storytelling with data: Case studies

Data storytelling transforms raw numbers into engaging narratives that resonate with audiences, and case studies serve as perfect illustrations of this concept. They showcase how organizations leverage data to inform decisions, innovate processes, and achieve impressive outcomes. By exploring real-world applications of Python and Excel automation, you can uncover effective practices and strategies that elevate data analysis from simple reporting to impactful storytelling.

Take this example, consider a retail company grappling with inventory management issues. With inconsistent stock levels and frequent out-of-stock situations, they turned to data analysis for a solution. By utilizing Python scripts to automate the extraction and analysis of sales data from Excel, they were able to identify purchasing patterns and peak sales periods. Incorporating predictive analytics enabled them to forecast demand more accurately, ultimately optimizing their inventory levels.

To visualize these insights, the company leveraged Excel's charting features alongside Python libraries like Matplotlib and Seaborn. They developed dashboards that not only displayed historical sales trends but also featured predictive models highlighting future inventory needs. Stakeholders could interact with these visualizations, adjusting parameters such as seasonality or promotional events to see how these factors influenced stock requirements. This interactivity was crucial in fostering discussions among departments and aligning marketing strategies with inventory management.

Another compelling case study involved a healthcare organization aiming to enhance patient outcomes through data-driven decision-making. They employed Python scripts to analyze patient data stored in Excel spreadsheets, focusing on factors like treatment efficacy and recovery times. By consolidating this information into user-friendly dashboards, the organization could visualize patient demographics alongside treatment results.

The real breakthrough occurred when they integrated external libraries like Plotly to create interactive visualizations, allowing doctors to explore correlations between treatments and outcomes dynamically. This engagement encouraged medical staff to discuss findings during team meetings, leading to collaborative decision-making on best practices for patient care. The result was a notable improvement in recovery rates and increased patient satisfaction.

In the finance sector, one firm streamlined its quarterly reporting processes—tasks that once consumed weeks—by implementing automation techniques. By writing Python scripts that pulled data from multiple Excel files covering everything from revenue projections to expenditure tracking, they generated comprehensive reports in a fraction of the time. Here too, visualization tools provided by libraries such as Bokeh transformed complex financial data into clear, interactive charts that illustrated trends over time.

This automated approach not only saved countless hours of labor but also reduced errors typically associated with manual data entry. Presentations became more dynamic as stakeholders accessed live charts during meetings instead of static slides. This shift fostered a culture of data-driven decision-making where team members felt empowered to ask questions about the financial health of projects in real-time.

These case studies highlight how automation can revitalize traditional business practices. They demonstrate that by harnessing Python's capabilities alongside Excel's strengths, organizations can unlock insights that inform strategies and inspire action.

Engaging with these narratives reveals common themes:

collaboration across teams, embracing technology for efficiency, and emphasizing visual communication of complex data. As you reflect on these examples, consider how similar approaches could be adapted in your own work environment.

Think about your current processes—what tasks are repetitive? Where could visualization enhance the communication of important messages? The answers to these questions will guide you as you begin crafting your own narrative around the data at your disposal.

In summary, storytelling through data is an art form enriched by automation techniques. By learning from these successful case studies, you can apply similar methodologies within your organization. In the end, it's about transforming insights into stories that drive meaningful change—stories built on collaboration and powered by advanced tools like Python and Excel working together seamlessly.

CHAPTER 9: ADVANCED EXCEL REPORTING WITH PYTHON

Designing comprehensive reports

Designing comprehensive reports in Excel using Python goes beyond simply presenting data; it's about crafting a narrative that informs, persuades, and guides decision-making. A well-designed report effectively communicates insights, making clarity and impact paramount. To achieve this, you can harness Python's automation capabilities alongside Excel's formatting features, resulting in reports that are both professional in appearance and practical in function.

Start by understanding your audience. Knowing who will read the report influences both its content and presentation style. For example, a technical team may prefer detailed data and complex analyses, while executives often seek high-level insights and visual summaries. By tailoring your reports to meet these diverse needs, you ensure that your message resonates with its intended recipients.

As you begin the report design process, define your key objectives. What questions should the report answer? What decisions will it inform? Once these objectives are clear, structure your report accordingly. Organize it into sections such as an executive summary, methodology, findings, and recommendations. This logical flow enhances comprehension and enriches the narrative quality of your reporting.

Utilizing Python can significantly streamline data collection and analysis before reaching Excel. Writing scripts to pull data from various sources—such as databases or external APIs—automates the data-gathering process. Take this example, consider automating the retrieval of sales figures from a company database to create a monthly performance report. Libraries like Pandas make data manipulation straightforward.

Here's a simple example of how to pull sales data into Python:

```python
import pandas as pd

\#\# Load sales data from an Excel file

sales_data = pd.read_excel('sales_data.xlsx')


\#\# Perform some basic analysis

total_sales = sales_data['Sales'].sum()

average_sales = sales_data['Sales'].mean()


print(f'Total Sales: total_sales')

print(f'Average Sales: average_sales')
```

After processing this data, exporting it back into Excel for visualization is seamless. You can format the output using libraries like XlsxWriter to create visually appealing reports directly from Python. For example:

```python
import xlsxwriter

\#\# Create a new Excel file and add a worksheet
workbook = xlsxwriter.Workbook('Sales_Report.xlsx')
worksheet = workbook.add_worksheet()

\#\# Write some data headers
worksheet.write('A1', 'Total Sales')
worksheet.write('B1', 'Average Sales')

\#\# Write calculated values
worksheet.write('A2', total_sales)
worksheet.write('B2', average_sales)

\#\# Close the workbook
workbook.close()
```

Incorporating visualizations is key to enhancing comprehension and retention within reports. Charts can illustrate trends over time or comparisons among different categories. By integrating libraries such as Matplotlib or Seaborn with your Python scripts, you can create dynamic visualizations that enrich your reports. Take this example:

```python
import matplotlib.pyplot as plt
```

```
\#\# Plotting the sales data

plt.figure(figsize=(10, 6))

plt.plot(sales_data['Date'], sales_data['Sales'], marker='o')

plt.title('Sales Over Time')

plt.xlabel('Date')

plt.ylabel('Sales')

plt.grid()

plt.xticks(rotation=45)

plt.tight_layout()

plt.savefig('sales_over_time.png') \# Save plot as an image
` ` `
```

Embedding these visuals directly into your Excel report creates a more engaging experience for viewers. Use features in XlsxWriter to insert images or charts seamlessly into your worksheets.

As you refine your reporting process, consider advanced formatting techniques that enhance clarity without overwhelming the reader. Consistency in fonts, colors, and styles helps guide viewers through your narrative effectively. Additionally, employing conditional formatting within Excel can dynamically highlight key figures or trends based on specific criteria—drawing attention where it matters most.

Incorporating interactivity into your reports can further elevate their impact. Utilizing tools like Excel's slicers or PivotTables enables users to filter data themselves, empowering them to explore insights tailored to their specific interests.

Reflecting on the overall design of your reports is essential for continuous improvement. After generating several reports, gather feedback from stakeholders about what works well and what could be refined. This iterative approach not only enhances your reporting skills but also fosters collaboration among teams as they share insights derived from these documents.

In the end, the goal is to transform raw data into actionable insights through well-designed reports that tell a compelling story. By embracing automation with Python while leveraging Excel's strengths in presentation and interaction, you create reports that do more than inform—they inspire action and drive strategic decisions within your organization.

Automating regular report generation

Automating regular report generation harnesses the principles of effective reporting and enhances them through Python's powerful capabilities. By transforming the tedious task of report creation into a streamlined and efficient workflow, automation not only saves time but also minimizes errors. The goal is to produce reports that facilitate timely decision-making and boost overall productivity.

Central to this automation is the ability to schedule reports to run at specified intervals—be it daily, weekly, or monthly—without any manual effort. This guarantees that stakeholders consistently have access to up-to-date information without needing to remember to request or generate reports themselves. You can easily set up automated scripts using task schedulers like Cron for Unix systems or Task Scheduler for Windows, allowing your scripts to execute smoothly in the background.

Consider the process of automatically generating a monthly sales report. You can write a Python script that fetches sales data from a database, processes it, formats it, and exports it to Excel—all without any manual intervention after the initial setup.

Here's a basic outline of what such a script might look like:

```python
import pandas as pd
import datetime
from sqlalchemy import create_engine

\#\# Create a database connection
engine = create_engine('sqlite:///sales.db')

\#\# Define the date range for the report
end_date = datetime.datetime.now()
start_date = end_date - pd.DateOffset(months=1)

\#\# Query to retrieve sales data for the past month
query = f""
SELECT * FROM sales_data WHERE sale_date BETWEEN 'start_date' AND 'end_date'
"

\#\# Load data into a DataFrame
sales_data = pd.read_sql(query, engine)

\#\# Perform analysis and aggregation as needed
monthly_summary = sales_data.groupby('product_id').agg(
```

```python
'sales_amount': 'sum',
'quantity_sold': 'sum'
).reset_index()
```

\#\# Export summary to Excel

```python
monthly_summary.to_excel('Monthly_Sales_Report.xlsx', index=False)
```
```

In this example, we connect to a SQLite database containing sales data, query records from the past month, aggregate information by product ID, and export the summarized data directly into an Excel file. Each time this script runs, it generates an updated report reflecting the latest data.

To enhance this automation further, consider incorporating error handling mechanisms. Take this example, if your database becomes temporarily unavailable, you would want your script to fail gracefully rather than crash completely. Here's how you might improve your script:

```python
try:
sales_data = pd.read_sql(query, engine)
except Exception as e:
print(f"Error occurred: e")
\#\# Optionally send an alert email or log the error for further investigation.
```
```

This addition not only protects your automation process against unexpected failures but also provides valuable insights into potential operational issues during data retrieval.

And, utilizing templates can significantly streamline your report design process. Instead of formatting each report from scratch, you can create an Excel template with predefined styles and layouts. Your Python script can then populate this template with new data every time it runs. Libraries like OpenPyXL make it easy to load existing Excel files and modify them as needed.

Here's how you might leverage OpenPyXL with a template:

```python
from openpyxl import load_workbook

\#\# Load existing workbook as template
template_path = 'Sales_Report_Template.xlsx'
wb = load_workbook(template_path)
ws = wb.active

\#\# Fill in template with new data
ws['A2'] = total_sales  \# Example: inserting total sales into cell A2

\#\# Save the modified workbook as a new file
wb.save('Automated_Sales_Report.xlsx')
```

Using templates ensures consistency across reports while also reducing time spent on formatting tasks.

As your automated reporting system evolves, consider integrating advanced features such as interactive dashboards or real-time data updates using web technologies like Flask or Dash. These tools allow users to interact dynamically with their reports, enhancing their ability to derive insights directly from live data streams.

Gathering feedback remains crucial even in automated processes. Encourage report recipients to share their thoughts on both content and usability. Their insights can guide refinements that enhance clarity and functionality in future iterations.

Incorporating automation into your reporting workflow fundamentally transforms how information is shared within an organization. It empowers teams with timely insights while freeing up valuable human resources for more strategic tasks. In the end, consistent automation fosters an environment where informed decisions can thrive based on readily available information—all thanks to well-crafted Python scripts designed for seamless Excel integration.

Utilizing templates for consistency

Automation flourishes on consistency, and one of the most effective ways to achieve this is through the use of templates. By generating reports with a standardized layout and style, you not only save time but also enhance the ease with which stakeholders can navigate the presented information. Integrating templates into your automated reporting workflow can be transformative, providing uniformity across documents and allowing you to concentrate on content rather than formatting.

Let's explore how to create and utilize templates effectively. Take this example, consider an Excel template designed for your monthly performance report. This template includes designated sections for key performance indicators (KPIs), charts, and summary tables. Rather than manually adjusting formatting each month, your Python script can populate this pre-designed template with fresh data every time it runs, ensuring that the final report maintains a professional appearance.

To create such a template, begin by designing an Excel file that clearly lays out all necessary sections. Save this file as "Performance_Report_Template.xlsx." Now, whenever you run your automation script, it can dynamically fill this template with updated data while preserving its core structure.

Here's how you might implement this using Python's OpenPyXL library:

```python
from openpyxl import load_workbook

\#\# Load the Excel template
template_path = 'Performance_Report_Template.xlsx'
workbook = load_workbook(template_path)
worksheet = workbook.active

\#\# Example data to fill into the report
data_to_fill =
'Total Sales': 15000,
'Total Expenses': 8000,
'Net Profit': 7000,

\#\# Fill in the template
worksheet['B2'] = data_to_fill['Total Sales']    \# Assuming B2 is
```

Total Sales cell

```
worksheet['B3'] = data_to_fill['Total Expenses']   \# B3 for Total Expenses

worksheet['B4'] = data_to_fill['Net Profit']     \# B4 for Net Profit


\#\# Save the populated report as a new file

workbook.save('Monthly_Performance_Report.xlsx')
```
``` `

In this script, we load an existing workbook based on our predefined template and fill specific cells with new data representing total sales, expenses, and profit figures. The outcome is a fresh report that adheres to established guidelines.

For even greater sophistication, consider incorporating dynamic elements within your templates. Excel offers features such as pivot tables and charts that can automatically update when the underlying data changes. By linking these elements directly to your populated data ranges through your Python script, you not only enhance consistency but also add interactivity to your reports.

As you develop these templates, remember to include clear documentation within your scripts regarding the origin of each piece of data. This practice will save time during future adjustments or troubleshooting. A well-commented codebase serves as a guide for yourself and a valuable resource for anyone else who may work on it later.

And, templates foster collaboration among team members. When everyone uses the same format, comparing results across different periods or departments becomes much simpler. A standardized approach enhances communication around performance metrics and enables quicker responses to
```

trends observed within those metrics.

As you assess your automated reports, seek feedback from users about clarity and usability. If stakeholders find certain sections unclear or cumbersome, you can swiftly adjust your template for future iterations. Building a culture of continuous improvement into your processes allows you to gather insights regularly and refine both content and presentation to meet evolving needs.

With well-structured templates in place, automation evolves from merely generating reports into creating valuable insights that are presented in an organized manner. This clarity enhances decision-making capabilities throughout the organization by providing stakeholders with reliable and easily understandable information at their fingertips.

In the end, embracing templates in your reporting process not only promotes efficiency but also cultivates a culture of professionalism and coherence throughout any business environment. As Python automates these tasks behind the scenes, you reclaim precious time—time that can be reinvested in strategic thinking and analysis rather than repetitive formatting tasks.

Advanced formatting techniques

Creating visually appealing and informative Excel reports involves more than merely populating cells with data; it requires advanced formatting techniques that enhance readability and professionalism. These techniques enable you to manipulate the visual elements of Excel spreadsheets, ensuring that the information presented is not only accurate but also engaging.

One effective tool in your formatting toolkit is cell styles. By using predefined or custom styles for headers, data rows, and key figures, you can significantly improve the visual hierarchy of your reports. For example, making headers bold, increasing their font size, and applying a distinct background color creates a clear separation between different sections. This approach guides the reader's eye and emphasizes critical information.

You can apply these styles programmatically using Python's OpenPyXL library. Here's a snippet demonstrating how to style your headers:

```python
from openpyxl.styles import Font, PatternFill


\#\# Load the Excel workbook

workbook = load_workbook('Monthly_Performance_Report.xlsx')

worksheet = workbook.active


\#\# Define styles

header_font = Font(bold=True, size=12)

header_fill = PatternFill(start_color="FFC0CB", end_color="FFC0CB", fill_type="solid")


\#\# Apply styles to header row

for cell in worksheet["1:1"]:  \# Assuming row 1 contains headers

cell.font = header_font

cell.fill = header_fill


\#\# Save the workbook with updated styles

workbook.save('Styled_Monthly_Performance_Report.xlsx')
```

` ` `

In this example, we style the first row of our report by making the text bold and applying a pink background fill. Such small changes can have a significant impact on how stakeholders perceive the report at a glance.

Another advanced technique is conditional formatting, which dynamically applies formats based on specific criteria. Take this example, you might want to highlight cells with values below a certain threshold or use color scales to effectively visualize trends in performance metrics.

Implementing conditional formatting with OpenPyXL is straightforward:

` ` `python

from openpyxl.formatting.rule import CellIsRule

\#\# Load the workbook again

workbook   =
load_workbook('Styled_Monthly_Performance_Report.xlsx')

worksheet = workbook.active

\#\# Apply conditional formatting to highlight low sales figures

sales_column = 'B' \# Assuming sales figures are in column B

rule = CellIsRule(operator='lessThan', formula=['10000'], stopIfTrue=True,

fill=PatternFill(start_color='FF9999', end_color='FF9999', fill_type='solid'))

worksheet.conditional_formatting.add(f'sales_column2:sales

_column100', rule) \# Adjust range as necessary

\#\# Save changes

workbook.save('Conditional_Formatted_Report.xlsx')
` ` `

This snippet demonstrates how to highlight sales figures below)10,000 in red. Such visual cues quickly alert decision-makers, facilitating prompt actions where necessary.

Incorporating charts into your reports further enhances both aesthetics and clarity. Visualizing data trends through line graphs or pie charts helps convey complex information succinctly. Here's how you can insert a simple chart using OpenPyXL:

` ` `python

from openpyxl.chart import BarChart, Reference

\#\# Load the workbook again

workbook   =
load_workbook('Conditional_Formatted_Report.xlsx')

worksheet = workbook.active

\#\# Create a bar chart for sales data

bar_chart = BarChart()

data_reference = Reference(worksheet,

min_col=2,

min_row=1,

max_col=2,

max_row=100) \# Adjust as needed for actual data range

bar_chart.add_data(data_reference, titles_from_data=True)

bar_chart.title = "Monthly Sales Performance

worksheet.add_chart(bar_chart, "E5") \# Adjust position as necessary

\#\# Save updated workbook with chart

workbook.save('Report_with_Chart.xlsx')

` ` `

This example illustrates how to create a bar chart that visualizes monthly sales performance directly within your Excel file. By embedding such visuals into your reports, you help stakeholders quickly grasp trends without sifting through rows of raw data.

Lastly, when finalizing report layouts, it's essential to consider alignment and spacing. Properly aligned text and consistent spacing create an organized appearance that contributes to easy reading and comprehension. Leveraging these advanced formatting techniques not only elevates the presentation of your automated reports but also fosters engagement from those who rely on this information for decision-making.

As you implement these practices into your automation workflow using Python for Excel tasks, remember that every detail counts. From bolding headers to applying dynamic visual cues through conditional formatting and integrating insightful charts—these elements transform ordinary reports into powerful tools that drive business strategy forward.

In summary, employing advanced formatting techniques enhances both functionality and professionalism in automated Excel reporting processes. This focus on presentation equips stakeholders with clear insights while allowing you to reclaim valuable time previously spent on manual adjustments—all while reinforcing your reputation as an innovative leader within your organization.

Adding interactivity to Excel reports

Integrating interactivity into Excel reports can significantly enhance the user experience, allowing stakeholders to engage with data in meaningful ways. By transforming static reports into dynamic resources, interactivity facilitates deeper insights and immediate analysis—an essential capability in today's fast-paced business environment where users need to quickly extract actionable information.

One of the simplest yet effective methods for adding interactivity is through drop-down lists. By using data validation to create drop-down menus, you can enable users to select specific parameters for analysis. For example, consider a sales report where users can filter results by region or product category. Here's how to create a drop-down list using OpenPyXL:

```python
from openpyxl import Workbook

from openpyxl.worksheet.datavalidation import DataValidation


\#\# Create a new workbook and access the active worksheet

workbook = Workbook()

worksheet = workbook.active


\#\# Define the options for your drop-down list
```

```python
options = ['North', 'South', 'East', 'West']

\#\# Create a data validation object for the drop-down list
data_validation        =        DataValidation(type="list",
formula1="'North,South,East,West'", showDropDown=True)

\#\# Apply the data validation to a specific cell (e.g., A1)
worksheet.add_data_validation(data_validation)

data_validation.add(worksheet["A1"])

\#\# Save the workbook
workbook.save('Sales_Report_with_Dropdown.xlsx')
```

With this implementation, users can select their preferred region from a drop-down menu in cell A1 of the Excel report, allowing for a tailored view of sales data that enhances both personalization and efficiency.

Another effective way to boost interactivity is by incorporating slicers, which provide an easy method for filtering PivotTables without navigating complex menus. Slicers display visual buttons representing different categories, allowing users to filter data directly on their dashboard or report.

For those using Pandas alongside OpenPyXL, creating an interactive dashboard becomes even more engaging by integrating visualizations from libraries like Matplotlib or Plotly. Take this example, you might use Plotly to create an interactive chart within an Excel context:

```python
```

```
import plotly.express as px

import pandas as pd

\#\# Sample sales data

data =

'Region': ['North', 'South', 'East', 'West'],

'Sales': [12000, 15000, 17000, 13000]


df = pd.DataFrame(data)


\#\# Create an interactive bar chart

fig = px.bar(df, x='Region', y='Sales', title='Sales by Region')


\#\# Save this figure as an HTML file that can be linked from Excel

fig.write_html('Sales_Bar_Chart.html')
` ` `
```

By saving your visualization as an HTML file, you can link it within your Excel report for seamless access. Users can click on this link to view detailed charts, enabling them to hover over bars for precise figures or dynamically select regions.

In addition to these features, incorporating form controls like sliders or checkboxes can further enhance interactivity. Sliders allow users to set parameters such as date ranges or thresholds dynamically, which is especially useful when analyzing time series data. While implementing sliders directly within Excel requires manual setup through the Developer tab and ActiveX controls, automating adjustments via Python scripts can significantly streamline the process.

Hyperlinks also serve as a valuable tool for navigation within larger reports. They can direct readers to specific sections of interest or external resources for deeper exploration of topics related to your datasets. Here's how to create hyperlinks using OpenPyXL:

```python
from openpyxl import Workbook

\#\# Create a new workbook and add hyperlinks
workbook = Workbook()
worksheet = workbook.active


\#\# Set hyperlink in cell A1 pointing to an external resource
(e.g., report summary)
hyperlink_url = "https://www.example.com/report_summary
worksheet['A1'].value = "View Report Summary
worksheet['A1'].hyperlink = hyperlink_url


\#\# Save workbook
workbook.save('Report_with_Hyperlink.xlsx')
```

This code creates a clickable link in cell A1 that directs users straight to further reading on report summaries, expanding their understanding without cluttering the main document.

Finally, embedding comments within cells fosters collaboration by providing prompts or explanations about specific metrics directly tied into your automated reports.

By incorporating these interactive elements into your reporting processes using Python and Excel frameworks like OpenPyXL and Pandas, you not only enrich user engagement but also empower decision-makers. This transformation from passive data consumption to active exploration allows stakeholders to make informed decisions swiftly. Remember, enhancing user empowerment leads directly to increased productivity while ensuring that vital insights are always just a click away.

Exporting reports in various formats

Exporting reports in various formats is a vital aspect of the automation process, enabling stakeholders to access and manipulate data in ways that meet their specific requirements. Whether sharing a polished PDF for a board meeting, generating an HTML document for online access, or saving data as CSV files for in-depth analysis, efficient export capabilities can significantly streamline workflows and enhance collaboration.

Excel naturally supports saving files in multiple formats, and Python can automate these exports seamlessly. A straightforward way to export an Excel report is by utilizing libraries like openpyxl and pandas, both of which offer features to create Excel files that can be easily converted into other formats.

Let's start with exporting an Excel file directly to CSV format. This approach is especially beneficial for large datasets that need to be shared quickly without the added complexity of formatting:

```python
import pandas as pd


\#\# Sample data frame
```

```python
data =
'Product': ['A', 'B', 'C'],
'Sales': [100, 200, 300]

df = pd.DataFrame(data)

\#\# Exporting the DataFrame to a CSV file
df.to_csv('Sales_Report.csv', index=False)
```
` ` `

Using the to_csv() method ensures that your report is not only easy to share but also universally accessible across different platforms. The index=False parameter prevents Pandas from including row indices in the CSV file.

For exporting Excel files in other formats, such as PDF, you can use the xlsxwriter library in conjunction with pandas. Here's how to set up your Excel workbook for PDF conversion:

` ` `python

```python
import pandas as pd

\#\# Creating a DataFrame
data =
'Region': ['North', 'South', 'East', 'West'],
'Sales': [12000, 15000, 17000, 13000]

df = pd.DataFrame(data)
```

```
\#\# Write the DataFrame to an Excel file

excel_file = 'Sales_Report.xlsx'

df.to_excel(excel_file, index=False)


\#\# Use XlsxWriter for PDF conversion (requires Excel installed)

import xlsxwriter


workbook = xlsxwriter.Workbook('Sales_Report.pdf')

worksheet = workbook.add_worksheet()


\#\# Write data from DataFrame into worksheet

for row_num, value in enumerate(df.values):

worksheet.write_row(row_num, 0, value)


workbook.close()
```
` ` `

This example demonstrates writing to an Excel file first and outlines how you might prepare it for PDF conversion with a professional layout. However, it's important to note that while XlsxWriter does not support direct PDF conversion, it enables you to format your data effectively for manual export via Excel.

For those looking for greater automation across different formats—including HTML—Python provides robust options. Take this example:

```python
\#\# Exporting directly from Pandas to HTML
html_output = df.to_html('Sales_Report.html')
```

This code generates an HTML table viewable in any web browser, making it particularly useful for sharing reports with stakeholders who may not have Excel installed.

Another critical aspect of exporting reports is customizing outputs based on audience needs. For example, some stakeholders may only require summarized data while others need detailed analyses. Implementing conditional exports based on user preferences can be essential. Utilizing functions or classes within Python can help streamline this process.

You might create a function tailored for this purpose:

```python
def export_report(dataframe, format_type):

if format_type == 'csv':

dataframe.to_csv('Sales_Report.csv', index=False)

elif format_type == 'html':

dataframe.to_html('Sales_Report.html')

elif format_type == 'pdf':

\#\# Logic to convert to pdf as shown earlier would go here.

pass


export_report(df, 'csv')  \# Adjust as necessary for different formats.
```

This modular approach provides flexibility, allowing you to modify the function based on evolving requirements without overhauling your entire report generation pipeline.

Finally, always consider the security implications when exporting sensitive information. Employ encryption methods when necessary and ensure compliance with relevant regulations regarding data protection during any exports.

As you explore these various methods of exporting reports using Python's libraries—whether through traditional formats like CSV or more complex paths such as PDFs—you'll discover opportunities that not only enhance usability but also empower your stakeholders with immediate access to vital insights tailored to their needs.

Integrating Python reports into business workflows

Integrating Python reports into existing business workflows is a crucial step in enhancing productivity and improving decision-making capabilities. When automated reports are seamlessly incorporated, they can deliver real-time insights, significantly reducing the time between data collection and actionable analysis. Imagine the benefits of receiving a daily sales report that is automatically generated from your database, formatted in Excel, and enriched with visualizations that highlight trends and anomalies—all ready for your review before you even arrive at your desk.

Consider the case of Sarah, a project manager at a mid-sized firm, who faced the challenging task of compiling weekly progress reports. Previously, this involved laboriously sifting through various data sources and manually formatting charts in Excel—an effort that consumed valuable time and limited her ability to conduct deeper analysis. Recognizing the potential for improvement, Sarah decided to leverage Python's capabilities to automate her reporting process. Utilizing libraries such as Pandas for data manipulation and Matplotlib for visualization, she developed a script over a few weeks that extracted necessary data from their SQL database, compiled it into a DataFrame, created visualizations, and output everything into an Excel file ready for distribution.

Sarah structured her workflow thoughtfully. She began by identifying the data inputs required for her reports, which included metrics from project management tools, resource allocation spreadsheets, and client feedback forms. Using Pandas, she efficiently merged these datasets into one cohesive DataFrame with the pd.merge() function. An important part of her process was employing the groupby function to aggregate data effectively based on project milestones.

```python
` ` `python
import pandas as pd

\#\# Sample DataFrames
df1 = pd.DataFrame(
'Project': ['A', 'B', 'C', 'A', 'B'],
'Completion_Status': [20, 50, 75, 45, 60]
)

df2 = pd.DataFrame(
'Project': ['A', 'B', 'C'],
'Client_Feedback': ['Positive', 'Neutral', 'Negative']
)

\#\# Merging DataFrames
merged_df                                                    =
pd.merge(df1.groupby('Project').sum().reset_index(),      df2,
```

on='Project')

```
` ` `
```

This integrated approach allowed Sarah to clearly visualize completion percentages alongside client feedback—insights that had previously been obscured by manual processes.

Automating report generation not only saves time but also significantly reduces human error. After implementing her automated reporting process for a month, Sarah discovered discrepancies that had gone unnoticed before. Take this example, one data source recorded project statuses inaccurately due to a faulty input method; this issue became apparent when comparing automated outputs against manual entries over time.

To further enhance usability within her team's workflow, Sarah introduced conditional formatting to automatically highlight critical metrics in her reports. She established conditions in her Excel output so that completion percentages below 30% would be marked in red—an effective visual cue for quick identification of problem areas. This was made possible using libraries like XlsxWriter:

```python
` ` `python
import xlsxwriter

workbook = xlsxwriter.Workbook('Project_Report.xlsx')

worksheet = workbook.add_worksheet()

\#\# Example data writing

worksheet.write('A1', 'Project')

worksheet.write('B1', 'Completion Status')
```

```
\#\# Write data dynamically

for index, row in merged_df.iterrows():

worksheet.write(index + 1, 0, row['Project'])

worksheet.write(index + 1, 1, row['Completion_Status'])


\#\# Conditional Formatting

worksheet.conditional_format('B2:B10', 'type': 'cell',

'criteria': '<',

'value': 30,

'format': workbook.add_format('bg_color': '\#FF0000'))


workbook.close()
```
` ` `

As these reports became part of Sarah's routine workflow and were shared weekly across her team's communication channels—such as Slack or email—engagement improved significantly. Team members felt more informed and empowered to make decisions based on the latest insights.

To fully embed such reports into business processes, it's essential to create feedback loops where decisions based on automated reports are continuously reviewed and refined. Regular discussions among stakeholders about these reports during team meetings or strategy sessions enable adjustments to be made in Python scripts—whether that involves changing tracked metrics or modifying how insights are presented.

Incorporating automated reporting within existing workflows not only enhances efficiency but also fosters a culture of data-driven decision-making. In today's fast-paced business environment, it is vital for organizations to cultivate an atmosphere where ongoing improvements can occur without overwhelming employees with additional tasks; automation allows them to focus on what truly matters: interpreting data rather than merely collecting it.

Sarah's experience exemplifies just one of many possibilities available to organizations willing to embrace Python-based automation fully. By effectively leveraging these tools within their workflows, companies can promote innovation and agility—essential qualities for staying competitive in an ever-evolving marketplace.

CHAPTER 10: BUILDING DASHBOARDS IN EXCEL WITH PYTHON

Understanding dashboard components

Understanding the components of a dashboard is essential for creating effective and informative visualizations. A well-designed dashboard acts as a dynamic interface, enabling users to interact with data in real time and extract insights at a glance. Let's begin by examining the key elements that make up a robust dashboard: data visualizations, key performance indicators (KPIs), interactivity, and layout design.

At the heart of any dashboard is data visualization. This crucial element transforms complex datasets into intuitive graphical representations—such as charts, graphs, and maps—that convey information quickly and clearly. For example, a sales dashboard might feature bar charts illustrating monthly revenue trends alongside pie charts representing market share by product category. Each type of visualization has its strengths: bar charts are excellent for comparing quantities, while line graphs are ideal for displaying trends over time.

To further illustrate this point, consider a scenario in which a company tracks its sales performance across different regions. By utilizing Python libraries like Matplotlib or Seaborn, you can create compelling visualizations directly from your data. Here's how to generate a simple bar chart using Matplotlib:

```python
import matplotlib.pyplot as plt

\#\# Sample data
regions = ['North', 'South', 'East', 'West']
sales = [150000, 200000, 170000, 120000]

plt.bar(regions, sales, color='skyblue')
plt.title('Sales Performance by Region')
plt.xlabel('Region')
plt.ylabel('Sales (\()')
plt.show()
```

This straightforward code snippet generates a clear representation of sales performance across regions. Such visualizations not only make data more digestible but also help stakeholders quickly identify trends and areas that need attention.

Next, let's discuss key performance indicators (KPIs). These quantifiable measures assess an organization's success in achieving its objectives. In the context of a dashboard, KPIs serve as benchmarks for performance evaluation. Take this example, if your goal is to enhance customer satisfaction scores, displaying the latest survey results alongside previous scores can create context and urgency around improvement efforts.

Imagine how Sarah from our earlier example could enrich

her project reports by integrating KPIs into her dashboard layout. By including metrics such as on-time delivery rates or budget adherence percentages, she could provide stakeholders with immediate insights into project health. This approach empowers her team to make informed decisions more swiftly.

Another critical aspect of modern dashboards is interactivity. Users should be able to manipulate elements—such as filtering by date ranges or drilling down into specific categories—to gain deeper insights tailored to their needs. Python's Dash library offers robust tools for building interactive dashboards where users can explore data dynamically.

Here's a quick example demonstrating how to create an interactive dashboard using Dash:

```python
import dash

from dash import dcc

from dash import html


app = dash.Dash(__name__)


app.layout = html.Div([

dcc.Graph(

id='example-graph',

figure=

'data': [

'x': regions, 'y': sales, 'type': 'bar', 'name': 'Sales',

],

'layout':
```

```
'title': 'Interactive Sales Performance'


),
dcc.Dropdown(
id='region-dropdown',
options=['label': region, 'value': region for region in regions],
value='North'
)
])


if __name__ == '__main__':
app.run_server(debug=True)
```
` ` `

This script sets up a basic web-based dashboard featuring an interactive bar chart and a dropdown menu that allows users to dynamically select different regions.

The layout design of your dashboard is also vital for enhancing user experience. A clean and organized structure enables viewers to navigate information effortlessly without feeling overwhelmed. Consider using grid layouts to separate distinct sections; for instance, place KPIs at the top for immediate visibility while allocating larger areas for detailed visualizations below.

Remember that simplicity often leads to effectiveness in design; avoid cluttering your dashboard with excessive information or overly complex visualizations that may confuse rather than inform users. Maintaining consistency in colors and fonts helps enhance readability while keeping focus on the data.

In summary, dashboards are most effective when they combine clear data visualizations with meaningful KPIs and interactivity within a thoughtfully structured layout. By understanding how each component contributes to the overall function of your dashboard, you will be well-equipped to create engaging tools that facilitate better decision-making processes within your organization.

Design principles for effective dashboards

One fundamental principle is the prioritization of critical information. When creating your dashboard, identify the key metrics most relevant to users. For example, in a financial dashboard for a team, focus on displaying figures like revenue, expenses, and profit margins prominently. This strategic placement allows for swift assessments of financial health. Employing visual hierarchies—such as larger fonts for important metrics or well-positioned graphs—can effectively direct attention where it's needed most.

Consider a marketing team tracking campaign performance. If their primary objective is to monitor conversion rates alongside customer acquisition costs, these metrics should be visually distinct through contrasting colors or larger graphical elements. A thoughtfully structured layout ensures that users can easily focus on these critical KPIs without sifting through extensive data.

Context is equally vital in dashboard design. Metrics can be misleading without the appropriate background or historical data for comparison. Take this example, displaying last month's sales figures alongside current ones allows stakeholders to assess trends effectively. Here's how you might implement this in your Python dashboard using Matplotlib:

```python
```

```
import matplotlib.pyplot as plt

\#\# Sample data
months = ['January', 'February', 'March', 'April']
last_month_sales = [30000, 35000, 28000, 40000]
current_month_sales = [32000, 37000, 30000, 42000]

plt.plot(months, last_month_sales, label='Last Month',
marker='o')
plt.plot(months, current_month_sales, label='Current Month',
marker='o')
plt.title('Sales Comparison: Last Month vs Current Month')
plt.xlabel('Month')
plt.ylabel('Sales (\))')
plt.legend()
plt.show()
```

This code generates a line graph that clearly illustrates changes over time—demonstrating how visualizations can convey context alongside raw numbers.

Interactivity further enhances dashboards by allowing users to customize their views according to specific needs. Features like filters and drill-down capabilities enable users to explore data at varying levels without feeling overwhelmed by excessive details initially. Utilizing libraries such as Plotly or Dash not only facilitates the creation of these interactive elements but also enriches user engagement with the data.

For example, if stakeholders want to analyze sales

performance by product category across different regions, an interactive dropdown could allow them to select specific categories while simultaneously updating corresponding graphs based on their selection.

Here's an illustration of how you can build interactivity with Dash:

```python
import dash

from dash import dcc

from dash import html

from dash.dependencies import Input, Output


app = dash.Dash(__name__)


app.layout = html.Div([

dcc.Dropdown(

id='category-dropdown',

options=[

'label': 'Electronics', 'value': 'Electronics',

'label': 'Clothing', 'value': 'Clothing',

'label': 'Home Goods', 'value': 'Home Goods'

],

value='Electronics'

),

dcc.Graph(id='sales-graph')

])
```

```
@app.callback(
Output('sales-graph', 'figure'),
Input('category-dropdown', 'value')
)
def update_graph(selected_category):
\#\# This would normally pull real data based on selection.
\#\# For demonstration purposes:
sales_data =
'Electronics': [2000, 2500],
'Clothing': [1500, 1700],
'Home Goods': [800, 900]


return
'data': ['x': ['Q1', 'Q2'],
'y': sales_data[selected_category],
'type': 'bar'],
'layout': 'title': f'Sales Data for selected_category'


if __name__ == '__main__':
app.run_server(debug=True)
```
` ` `

This script demonstrates how interactivity can transform a static representation into a dynamic tool that adapts based on user input.

Finally, strive for aesthetic simplicity in your designs. Overly complicated dashboards with cluttered visuals can impede comprehension rather than enhance it. Effectively using whitespace serves as a buffer between different sections and allows viewers' eyes to rest amidst complex information flows.

To wrap things up, effective dashboard design merges prioritized critical information with contextually rich visuals and engaging interactivity—all while maintaining aesthetic clarity and simplicity. By adhering to these principles as you develop dashboards using Python and Excel integrations, you empower stakeholders across your organization with tools that inform and inspire action based on clear insights derived from comprehensive data analysis.

Real-time data updates and Python

Real-time data updates in dashboards mark a significant advancement in how we visualize and engage with information. This capability allows for immediate feedback from your data, which not only enhances decision-making but also encourages a proactive response to business challenges. By integrating real-time data into your Python-driven Excel dashboards, you enhance the user experience and deliver timely insights that can inform strategic actions.

To enable real-time data updates, the first step is to establish a reliable source of live data. Whether drawing from an API, a database, or streaming data, maintaining a stable and efficient connection is crucial. For example, if you're monitoring financial markets, connecting to a stock price API can provide you with the latest pricing information for display on your dashboard. Python's requests library simplifies this process, allowing you to easily fetch and parse JSON responses.

Here's a straightforward example of how to retrieve stock price data from an API:

```python
import requests

def get_stock_price(symbol):
url = f'https://api.example.com/stocks/symbol'
response = requests.get(url)
if response.status_code == 200:
return response.json()['price']
else:
raise Exception("Error fetching stock price")

\#\# Example usage
print(get_stock_price('AAPL'))
```

This function retrieves the current price of a specified stock symbol. By integrating this functionality into your dashboard, users receive the most current data each time they refresh or interact with it.

Next, we can explore how to visualize this data dynamically in Excel using Python. The openpyxl library enables programmatic updates to cell values. By scheduling regular updates or triggering them based on specific events, you ensure users always see the latest information. Take this example, if you want to refresh an Excel sheet with the latest stock prices every minute:

```python
```

```
import openpyxl
import time

\#\# Load workbook and select sheet
workbook = openpyxl.load_workbook('stocks.xlsx')
sheet = workbook.active

while True:
stock_price = get_stock_price('AAPL')
sheet['B2'] = stock_price \# Update cell B2 with new price
workbook.save('stocks.xlsx')
time.sleep(60) \# Wait for 60 seconds before the next update
```

This code snippet demonstrates how to continuously fetch updated stock prices and save them in an Excel file. Automating these updates enhances efficiency while reducing the risk of human error associated with manual entries.

For creating visually compelling real-time dashboards, libraries like Dash can streamline the process even further. Dash enables you to build web applications for your dashboards that automatically refresh when new data becomes available, eliminating the need for user-initiated refreshes. This interactivity is achieved through callbacks that respond to changes and update components accordingly.

Consider this enhanced example where we integrate live data into a Dash application:

```python
import dash
```

```
from dash import dcc, html

from dash.dependencies import Input, Output

import pandas as pd


app = dash.Dash(__name__)


app.layout = html.Div([

dcc.Graph(id='live-stock-graph'),

dcc.Interval(id='interval-component', interval=60000)    \#
Updates every minute

])


@app.callback(

Output('live-stock-graph', 'figure'),

Input('interval-component', 'n_intervals')

)

def update_graph(n):

\#\# Fetch new stock price for demonstration purposes

stock_price = get_stock_price('AAPL')


\#\# Prepare data for plotting

df = pd.DataFrame('Time': [pd.Timestamp.now()], 'Price':
[stock_price])


return
```

```
'data': ['x': df['Time'], 'y': df['Price'], 'type': 'line'],
'layout': 'title': 'Live Stock Price'


if __name__ == '__main__':
app.run_server(debug=True)
```

This Dash application uses an Interval component that triggers updates every minute without requiring any manual intervention from users. Given that real-time information is vital in many sectors—finance being just one—this setup offers tremendous value by keeping stakeholders informed instantly.

However, it's essential to manage data flow thoughtfully to avoid overwhelming users with constant changes. Implementing features like alerts or notifications for significant fluctuations can help maintain clarity while ensuring users remain engaged with critical developments.

To wrap things up, by embracing real-time data updates within your dashboards built on Python and Excel integrations, you are not only enhancing user experience but also equipping decision-makers with timely insights. This capability allows organizations to respond swiftly and accurately to emerging trends and challenges, ultimately strengthening their competitive edge in an increasingly dynamic landscape.

Integrating interactive elements

Integrating interactive elements into your Python-driven Excel dashboards transforms static reports into dynamic experiences that engage users and enhance decision-making. By incorporating these elements, you create a more immersive environment where users can explore data at their own pace, leading to deeper insights. Interactivity can manifest in various ways, such as drop-down menus for data filtering or buttons that trigger specific actions, all contributing to a more user-friendly interface.

To begin incorporating interactivity, consider using ipywidgets, a powerful library designed for creating user interface elements in Jupyter Notebooks. This tool is especially beneficial for developing prototypes or conducting exploratory analyses. Take this example, you could allow users to select specific stocks for analysis by implementing a simple drop-down menu:

```python
import ipywidgets as widgets

from IPython.display import display


\#\# Create a drop-down widget for stock selection

stock_selector = widgets.Dropdown(

options=['AAPL', 'GOOGL', 'MSFT'],

description='Select Stock:',

)


display(stock_selector)
```

Once the widget is set up, you can link it to functions that update visualizations based on user selections. This real-time responsiveness encourages deeper interaction with the data. For example, when a stock is selected from the drop-down menu, you can fetch its latest price and display it in an Excel sheet:

```python
def on_stock_change(change):

stock_price = get_stock_price(change['new'])

sheet['B2'] = stock_price \# Update cell B2 with new price

workbook.save('stocks.xlsx')


\#\# Link the widget's value change to the function

stock_selector.observe(on_stock_change, names='value')
```

By adding this interactivity to your Excel environment, you empower users to control what they want to see, thereby increasing engagement and satisfaction.

Another significant enhancement involves using sliders and buttons for data manipulation. Imagine allowing users to filter data based on price ranges or time periods. With ipywidgets, you can create a slider that adjusts these parameters dynamically—particularly useful in financial modeling where varying inputs yield different outputs.

For example, here's how you might implement a slider for adjusting price thresholds:

```python
price_slider = widgets.FloatSlider(

value=100,

min=0,

max=500,

step=1,

description='Price Threshold:',
```

)

display(price_slider)

def update_price_threshold(change):

filtered_data   =
filter_data_by_price_threshold(price_slider.value) \# Custom
function for filtering data

display_filtered_data(filtered_data) \# Function to visualize
filtered data

price_slider.observe(update_price_threshold, names='value')
` ` `

This implementation allows users to easily adjust values while observing immediate updates in their visualizations or Excel sheets. Such real-time feedback is crucial for making informed decisions quickly.

Additionally, buttons can serve as actionable items that trigger specific scripts or processes directly from the dashboard interface. If you are automating reports or executing heavy calculations that should run only upon user request, incorporating buttons enhances user control while effectively managing system resources.

Take this example:

` ` `python

run_button = widgets.Button(description="Run Analysis")

def run_analysis(b):

```
perform_complex_analysis()    \# Custom function that
performs analysis

print("Analysis complete!")


run_button.on_click(run_analysis)

display(run_button)
` ` `
```

This button gives users control over when intensive tasks are executed, rather than running them automatically at every refresh.

And, incorporating interactive visualizations using libraries such as Plotly allows for richer data exploration directly within dashboards. You can create plots where hovering over points reveals detailed information or where clicking on sections filters associated datasets automatically.

As you enhance interactivity in your dashboards, keep user experience at the forefront. Thoughtful design choices—such as intuitive layouts and clear labeling—ensure that users can easily navigate your dashboard's features without feeling overwhelmed.

The ultimate goal of integrating these interactive elements is not merely about adding features; it's about enhancing the storytelling aspect of your data. Users transition from being mere observers to active participants in their analysis, which leads to deeper insights and better retention of information.

In the end, merging interactivity with real-time data capabilities enriches both the experience and effectiveness of your Python-Excel dashboards. As organizations increasingly rely on quick decision-making powered by immediate access to relevant information, mastering these integrations will distinguish you as an innovator in your field.

Case studies of successful dashboards

Successful dashboards in Python-driven Excel automation are built on a foundation of integrating interactive elements through thoughtful design and practical application. Real-world case studies demonstrate how these principles are applied to create impactful tools that not only address business needs but also empower users.

Take, for example, a dashboard created for a financial services firm that aimed to enhance its client reporting process. The firm faced challenges with static reports that demanded manual updates and lacked real-time insights. By leveraging Python in conjunction with Excel, they developed an interactive dashboard that enabled financial analysts to visualize data dynamically. With integrated filters, users could easily segment client portfolios by asset class, risk level, and performance metrics—all within an intuitive interface.

A standout feature of this dashboard was a time-series analysis tool that illustrated investment performance across various periods. Users could adjust date ranges using sliders, instantly visualizing shifts in portfolio value and performance indicators. This real-time data manipulation not only saved hours of manual effort but also equipped clients with customized insights during meetings, significantly boosting client satisfaction.

In another compelling instance, a healthcare organization sought a comprehensive solution to track patient outcomes across different departments. They implemented a dashboard that aggregated data from multiple sources—patient records, treatment plans, and follow-up results—into a single Excel workbook powered by Python scripts. Featuring interactive charts and heat maps, this dashboard allowed healthcare providers to quickly assess treatment efficacy across demographics and conditions.

The dashboard included dropdown menus for filtering

data by department or treatment type, facilitating quick trend identification. Take this example, selecting a specific treatment protocol would refresh all relevant graphs and tables, highlighting patient recovery rates or complications linked to that protocol. Such insights led to improved care protocols based on empirical evidence rather than anecdotal observations.

In the realm of retail analytics, another organization developed a sales dashboard that integrated live sales data with historical trends. By utilizing buttons within the Excel interface to trigger complex Python scripts for predictive modeling, store managers gained immediate access to forecasted sales figures based on current performance metrics. This capability enabled informed inventory decisions ahead of seasonal fluctuations.

For example, when managers pressed the "Run Forecast" button on their dashboard, they received instant feedback about projected sales trends for the upcoming quarter. Graphs dynamically updated to reflect anticipated changes in consumer behavior based on previous years' data—empowering managers to make proactive adjustments in staffing and stock levels before peak shopping periods.

These case studies underscore the transformative power of interactivity and its profound impact on decision-making processes across various sectors. A common thread emerges: effective dashboards serve as bridges between raw data and actionable insights through user engagement.

A vital takeaway from these examples is the significance of user-centric design when developing dashboards. Each organization customized its approach based on specific user needs and industry requirements—whether simplifying complex datasets for financial analysts or providing detailed patient care insights for healthcare professionals.

This focus on user experience enhances adoption rates within organizations, ensuring that employees feel confident using these advanced tools rather than overwhelmed by their complexity. As you embark on your journey to develop similar dashboards, keep these principles in mind: understand your audience's needs, prioritize usability, and ensure that every interactive element serves a clear purpose in enhancing comprehension and engagement.

By studying these successful implementations, you can draw inspiration for your projects while recognizing that each context will require unique adaptations based on industry demands and user preferences. In the end, the combination of functionality and intuitive design elevates dashboards from mere reporting tools to essential components of strategic decision-making frameworks in modern organizations.

Challenges and solutions in dashboard creation

Creating effective dashboards presents a variety of challenges that can hinder user experience and reduce the impact of visualizations. These obstacles often arise from issues related to data integration, performance limitations, and barriers to user engagement. By recognizing these hurdles, we can implement strategic solutions that enhance both functionality and usability.

A primary challenge is ensuring that data from diverse sources integrates smoothly into the dashboard. For example, a business might utilize different systems for sales tracking, inventory management, and customer relationship management (CRM). Consolidating this data can be complex. Establishing a reliable data pipeline is crucial in such scenarios. Python's Pandas library can streamline this process by enabling developers to efficiently clean, transform, and merge datasets before they are displayed on the dashboard.

Take, for instance, a retail company struggling to unify its sales data from various regional offices. By utilizing Python scripts to automate data extraction from multiple CSV files or

APIs, they created a centralized database that the dashboard could easily access. This not only simplified the data management process but also ensured that decision-makers had real-time insights readily available.

Another frequent issue arises when dashboards become slow or unresponsive due to large datasets or complex calculations. Users expect immediate feedback when interacting with dashboard elements; delays can lead to frustration. To mitigate this, employing performance optimization techniques is essential. For example, reducing the volume of data loaded initially by applying filters or aggregating information before display can significantly improve responsiveness.

In one case, a logistics company experienced lag with its shipment tracking dashboard during live data updates. By optimizing queries to retrieve only necessary information —such as current shipments within a specific timeframe— they improved load times, allowing users to visualize critical metrics quickly without unnecessary delays.

User engagement adds another layer of complexity to dashboard creation. If users find dashboards overwhelming or difficult to navigate, they are less likely to use them effectively. Therefore, adopting user-centric design principles is vital. This includes conducting user research to identify specific needs and preferences and designing interactive elements that enhance usability.

For example, instead of overwhelming users with all available data at once, consider incorporating dropdown menus or toggle switches that allow customization of their views. A marketing team might find this functionality beneficial when analyzing campaign performance; they could easily select various metrics like click-through rates or conversion rates from a user-friendly menu rather than sifting through numerous charts and tables.

And, providing tooltips or brief explanations for complex

visualizations can help demystify data points for users unfamiliar with certain metrics or terminology. This approach fosters confidence in using the dashboard and enhances overall user satisfaction.

Addressing these challenges with practical solutions not only improves the user experience but also encourages adoption across organizations. When users feel empowered to interact meaningfully with their dashboards—whether through real-time data manipulation or streamlined access to critical insights—they are more likely to embrace these tools as integral parts of their decision-making processes.

In the end, building successful dashboards requires a balance between technical expertise and an understanding of user needs. By leveraging Python's capabilities for data management while prioritizing intuitive design principles, you can create dashboards that inform, engage, and inspire action within your organization. Such strategic frameworks transform raw data into actionable insights that empower teams across various sectors to make informed decisions based on comprehensive analysis rather than guesswork.

Evaluating dashboard performance and feedback

Evaluating the performance of a dashboard and gathering user feedback are essential steps in ensuring that the tool remains effective and relevant. Once a dashboard is deployed, the focus shifts from creation to ongoing assessment. This iterative process involves analyzing how well the dashboard meets user expectations and identifying areas for improvement.

One key component of evaluating dashboard performance is monitoring user engagement metrics. Analytics tools can track which features users interact with most frequently, how long they spend on specific sections, and where they may lose interest. For example, if analytics show that users consistently avoid a particular chart or metric, it may indicate confusion or a lack of interest. Revisiting the design and usability of such elements can lead to significant enhancements.

Consider a sales dashboard featuring multiple charts that detail performance across various regions. If data indicates that users are only engaging with two out of ten visualizations, it raises an important question: Are those visuals genuinely providing value? By identifying underutilized elements, developers can streamline content and focus on what truly resonates with users. This approach not only improves clarity but also aligns the dashboard more closely with user needs.

In addition to analytics, gathering direct feedback from users offers another layer of insight into dashboard effectiveness. Conducting surveys or informal interviews can provide valuable information about user experiences, preferences, and pain points. Questions might explore usability—such as how intuitive navigation is—or content relevance—whether the data presented supports their decision-making processes.

Take this example, after launching a new financial dashboard, a finance team might express difficulties in quickly accessing certain reports. Collecting this feedback enables developers to prioritize adjustments that enhance efficiency—perhaps by reconfiguring menu layouts or providing quick access links to frequently used reports.

Creating an environment where users feel comfortable sharing their thoughts fosters continuous improvement. Establishing channels for ongoing feedback—such as forums or regular check-in meetings—encourages users to voice concerns and suggestions proactively. This open dialogue not only builds trust but also empowers users by making them feel like stakeholders in the development process.

Performance metrics should also encompass load times and responsiveness under varying conditions. A dashboard that performs well during off-peak hours but struggles under heavy traffic may require optimization. Implementing techniques such as caching frequently accessed data or utilizing lazy loading can significantly enhance performance without compromising functionality.

For example, if an organization's project management dashboard begins to lag as more users access it simultaneously, analyzing server performance data and optimizing backend queries can help ensure that all users receive timely updates, regardless of system load.

Incorporating user feedback into ongoing development is crucial for maintaining relevance. Regularly updating dashboards based on analytical insights and user input ensures they evolve alongside business needs and technological advancements. This adaptive approach transforms static tools into dynamic resources capable of addressing real-world challenges.

In the end, effectively evaluating dashboard performance requires a blend of quantitative metrics and qualitative insights. Combining usage analytics with direct user feedback provides a comprehensive understanding of how well a dashboard functions in practice. By prioritizing these evaluations, organizations can create dashboards that not only fulfill their intended purpose but also deeply engage users —leading to informed decision-making grounded in reliable data analysis.

As you continue refining your dashboards through this evaluation process, remember that the goal extends beyond mere visual appeal; it's about developing powerful tools that foster clarity and support actionable insights across your organization's landscape.

CHAPTER 11: SCALABILITY AND PERFORMANCE OPTIMIZATION

Identifying performance bottlenecks

Identifying performance bottlenecks in Excel automation tasks is essential for maximizing efficiency and minimizing downtime. Whether you're running complex scripts to handle large datasets or developing automated reports, recognizing where slowdowns occur can save valuable time and resources. The diagnostic journey begins with monitoring key operations and pinpointing the sources of delays.

To effectively identify these bottlenecks, start by thoroughly examining your scripts. Profiling tools, such as Python's built-in cProfile module, can provide detailed statistics on where time is being spent during execution. For example, profiling a script that processes sales data may reveal that a significant portion of the runtime is consumed by a particular function or a data retrieval operation. Here's how to implement cProfile:

```python
import cProfile

import pandas as pd
```

```
def process_data():

\#\# Simulated data processing task

df = pd.read_csv('sales_data.csv')

\#\# Perform some complex operations

df['Profit'] = df['Revenue'] - df['Cost']

return df


cProfile.run('process_data()')
```
` ` `

Once you've identified specific functions or methods as potential bottlenecks, it's crucial to analyze them more closely. This may involve reviewing the logic within those functions or checking external dependencies like database connections or file I/O operations. Take this example, if reading data from an Excel file is taking longer than expected, consider whether the file format contributes to the delay. Opting for efficient formats such as binary (like Parquet) instead of CSV or XLSX may lead to performance improvements.

Also, if your automation involves multiple steps that sequentially depend on one another—such as reading data, processing it, and writing it back to Excel—it's beneficial to measure the time taken for each step individually. This approach helps in understanding which part of the chain requires attention. Here's a simple timing example:

` ` `python

import time

start_time = time.time()

```
\#\# Step 1: Read data
data = pd.read_excel('data.xlsx')
print(f"Read time: time.time() - start_time:.2f seconds")

start_time = time.time()
\#\# Step 2: Process data
processed_data = data.groupby('Category').sum()
print(f"Processing time: time.time() - start_time:.2f seconds")

start_time = time.time()
\#\# Step 3: Write back to Excel
processed_data.to_excel('processed_data.xlsx')
print(f"Write time: time.time() - start_time:.2f seconds")
```

This breakdown not only highlights where delays occur but also illustrates how different sections interact with one another.

In addition to analyzing execution times, it's important to consider resource utilization metrics such as memory usage and CPU load. Tools like memory_profiler can track how much memory different parts of your code consume, helping identify memory leaks or inefficiencies during data handling processes. Here's a quick example of using memory_profiler:

```python
from memory_profiler import profile

@profile
```

```
def process_large_data():

\#\# Processing logic here

pass


process_large_data()
```
` ` `

Monitoring these metrics ensures that your scripts run smoothly without overloading system resources.

Another key element in identifying performance bottlenecks is understanding user behavior and system load during execution. If a script runs efficiently in isolation but encounters issues when executed alongside others, this discrepancy may indicate contention for resources. Reviewing system logs during peak usage times can clarify any traffic-related slowdowns.

And, regularly benchmarking various approaches within your automation tasks can uncover better-performing alternatives. For example, if one method of aggregating data is slower than another technique (such as using vectorized operations instead of loops), revising your approach could result in significant performance gains.

In the end, recognizing and resolving performance bottlenecks requires systematic monitoring and analysis of both code and environmental factors. By employing profiling tools and measuring individual task durations while being mindful of system interactions, you can enhance your Python scripts for Excel automation significantly.

As you navigate these assessments and optimizations, remember that even small improvements can accumulate over time. Each enhancement not only refines the immediate task but also contributes to a more resilient automation framework capable of adapting to evolving business needs.

Efficient data processing techniques

Efficient data processing techniques are crucial for enhancing the performance of your Python scripts when automating Excel tasks. As datasets expand and automation grows in complexity, the demand for streamlined processes becomes increasingly important. The key to success lies in harnessing Python's capabilities while optimizing data handling throughout your workflows.

One foundational approach is to utilize vectorized operations whenever possible. Libraries like Pandas are designed with this principle, enabling you to perform calculations on entire columns or rows without resorting to slower iterative methods. For example, instead of looping through a dataset to calculate profit margins, you can achieve this in a single line:

```python
import pandas as pd

\#\# Sample DataFrame
data =
'Revenue': [200, 300, 150],
'Cost': [100, 150, 80]

df = pd.DataFrame(data)

\#\# Vectorized operation to calculate profit margin
df['Profit Margin'] = (df['Revenue'] - df['Cost']) / df['Revenue']
```

This approach not only simplifies your code but also

significantly boosts performance by minimizing the overhead associated with loops.

In addition to vectorization, choosing efficient data formats for storage and retrieval can further enhance performance. While Excel files (XLSX) are user-friendly, they may not be optimal for large datasets due to slower read and write speeds compared to binary formats. Utilizing formats like Parquet or Feather can considerably reduce processing times:

```python
\#\# Saving a DataFrame as a Parquet file

df.to_parquet('sales_data.parquet')


\#\# Reading back the Parquet file

df = pd.read_parquet('sales_data.parquet')
```

These formats are optimized for speed and can be particularly beneficial when working with extensive datasets.

Memory management is another critical aspect that ensures smooth automation. When handling large files or executing complex operations, actively monitoring and controlling memory usage becomes essential. One effective method is chunking—processing data in smaller subsets instead of loading everything into memory at once:

```python
chunksize = 10000 \# Number of rows per chunk

for chunk in pd.read_csv('large_dataset.csv', chunksize=chunksize):

\#\# Process each chunk here

process_chunk(chunk)
```

` ` `

By breaking the workload into manageable pieces, you can minimize the risk of memory overload and maintain a responsive automation process.

Incorporating parallel processing can also yield substantial efficiency gains. Python's concurrent.futures module allows for simultaneous execution of multiple tasks, which is particularly useful for independent operations that do not depend on each other's results:

` ` `python

from concurrent.futures import ThreadPoolExecutor

def process_file(file_path):

df = pd.read_excel(file_path)

\#\# Perform processing...

return df

file_paths = ['file1.xlsx', 'file2.xlsx', 'file3.xlsx']

with ThreadPoolExecutor() as executor:

results = list(executor.map(process_file, file_paths))

` ` `

In this scenario, three Excel files are processed concurrently, greatly reducing overall execution time compared to sequential processing.

Lastly, leveraging lazy evaluation techniques can further improve efficiency. Libraries such as Dask allow you to work with large datasets that may not fit into memory by employing out-of-core computation and deferred execution. Dask's DataFrames are similar to those in Pandas but are designed for scalability, enabling seamless processing without overloading resources.

By implementing these efficient data processing techniques —vectorization, optimal file formats, chunking strategies, parallel execution, and lazy evaluation—you can transform how your scripts interact with Excel data. This approach not only enhances performance but also leads to more maintainable code that adapts well as project requirements evolve.

As you integrate these techniques into your automation practices, reflect on how they align with your specific workflows and challenges. Each optimization presents an opportunity not only for immediate gains but also for building robust solutions capable of meeting future demands in data processing and reporting.

Memory management in large Excel files

Effectively managing memory while working with large Excel files is essential for maintaining optimal performance and preventing crashes or slowdowns. As Excel files increase in size, they often incorporate numerous formulas, formatting, and potentially thousands of rows of data. This complexity necessitates a solid understanding of how Python interacts with these files and how to handle memory usage efficiently.

The first step in tackling memory management is to recognize the limitations of your computing environment. Python can consume significant amounts of memory, particularly when utilizing libraries like Pandas or OpenPyXL. When dealing with large datasets, it's easy to run out of system memory, resulting in sluggish performance or unexpected failures. Take this example, while loading a 500MB Excel file into a Pandas DataFrame may seem straightforward, it can quickly deplete your available RAM if your machine has limited resources.

To mitigate this risk, consider using the dtype parameter when reading Excel files with Pandas. By explicitly specifying the data types for each column, you can significantly reduce memory consumption. Here's a practical example:

```python
import pandas as pd


\#\# Specify data types for each column
data_types =
'id': 'int32',
'name': 'str',
'value': 'float32'



\#\# Load the Excel file with specified dtypes
df = pd.read_excel('large_file.xlsx', dtype=data_types)
```

This snippet ensures that numerical columns utilize the least amount of memory necessary. If you are working with very large datasets, consider incorporating the chunksize parameter. This allows you to process the data in smaller batches rather than loading everything into memory at once:

```python
chunk_size = 10000  \# Number of rows per chunk

for chunk in pd.read_excel('large_file.xlsx', chunksize=chunk_size):

process(chunk) \# Replace with your data processing function
```

` ` `

By iteratively processing chunks, you limit the maximum amount of data loaded at any one time, which helps keep your memory footprint manageable.

Another effective technique is to utilize the gc module from Python's standard library for garbage collection. Explicitly invoking garbage collection can help free up memory that is no longer needed:

` ` ` python

import gc

\#\# After processing your DataFrame

del df \# Delete the DataFrame object

gc.collect() \# Run garbage collection

` ` `

This method ensures that Python reclaims any unreferenced memory space.

When writing back to Excel after processing, it's important to consider how you structure your output files. Excessive formatting or styling can unnecessarily inflate file sizes. Focus on essential formatting elements unless specific styles are required for reporting purposes.

Additionally, always monitor your environment's available resources while running scripts that involve large files. Monitoring tools can help you identify when you're approaching system limits, allowing you to adjust accordingly. Take this example, using system monitors or tools like memory_profiler can provide insights into the memory consumption of different parts of your script.

Lastly, if compatibility allows, consider employing alternative file formats for very large datasets. CSV files are generally more lightweight than Excel formats and can be loaded into Pandas without incurring the overhead associated with complex Excel structures:

```python
\#\# Reading a CSV instead

df = pd.read_csv('large_file.csv')
```

Adopting more efficient data storage and handling practices will not only streamline your workflows but also enhance overall productivity by minimizing wait times and crashes related to high-memory operations.

Navigating large Excel files requires a blend of strategy and technical skill. By leveraging efficient coding practices and remaining vigilant about resource management throughout your data manipulation processes, you can ensure that your projects remain scalable and manageable even under demanding conditions.

Parallel processing with Python

Parallel processing can significantly boost the speed and efficiency of your Python scripts, particularly when working with large datasets in Excel automation. By leveraging the capabilities of multiple processors, you can perform data operations concurrently rather than sequentially, effectively reducing overall execution time. This approach is especially advantageous in tasks like data cleaning or analysis, where independent operations can be executed across various segments of data.

To implement parallel processing in Python, the multiprocessing library offers a powerful framework. This library allows you to spawn multiple processes that run simultaneously, maximizing CPU utilization. For example, consider a large Excel file that requires extensive data manipulation before generating reports. By dividing the workload among several processes, you can transform tasks that might typically take minutes into mere seconds.

Here's a straightforward yet effective example demonstrating how to read and process data using parallel processing:

```python
import pandas as pd

from multiprocessing import Pool


\#\# Function to process each chunk

def process_chunk(chunk):

\#\# Example operation: Calculate the square of a specific column

chunk['squared_value'] = chunk['value'] ** 2

return chunk


\#\# Read data in chunks

def read_in_chunks(file_name, chunksize):

for chunk in pd.read_excel(file_name, chunksize=chunksize):

yield chunk


def main():

file_path = 'large_file.xlsx'

chunk_size = 10000  \# Process in chunks of 10,000 rows
```

```
with Pool() as pool:

results = pool.map(process_chunk, read_in_chunks(file_path,
chunk_size))

\#\# Combine results into a single DataFrame

final_df = pd.concat(results)

\#\# Save the processed DataFrame back to Excel

final_df.to_excel('processed_data.xlsx', index=False)

if __name__ == '__main__':

main()
```
` ` `

In this example, the process_chunk function performs a simple calculation by squaring the values in a designated column. The read_in_chunks function facilitates reading the Excel file in manageable pieces. Using Pool, we map our process_chunk function across all these chunks simultaneously.

When engaging in parallel processing, it's essential to manage shared resources effectively. If multiple processes need to write back to shared files or databases at the same time, implementing locking mechanisms is crucial to prevent data corruption or race conditions. Python's multiprocessing provides synchronization tools like Lock, which can help manage access to these shared resources.

Another key consideration is identifying which tasks are suitable for parallel execution. Not all operations benefit from concurrent execution. I/O-bound tasks—such as reading from or writing to files—may not experience significant gains due to inherent waiting times for disk access. In contrast, CPU-bound operations like mathematical computations or complex transformations can see substantial improvements.

While parallel processing can greatly enhance performance, it's important to be mindful of the overhead costs related to process management and memory usage. Avoid launching an excessive number of concurrent processes; instead, aim for a balance that aligns with your system's capabilities.

Lastly, profiling your code is vital for optimizing performance. Tools such as line_profiler or built-in libraries like time can help you measure execution times before and after implementing parallel processing techniques. This guarantees that your efforts lead to meaningful improvements rather than unintended consequences.

By harnessing parallel processing, you not only enhance your Python scripting capabilities but also streamline extensive data operations more efficiently than ever before. With careful implementation and ongoing monitoring, you can transform how you automate complex Excel tasks while maximizing productivity and minimizing wait times.

Streamlining automation scripts

Streamlining automation scripts can significantly enhance efficiency and reduce execution times, particularly for complex Excel tasks. A well-optimized script not only boosts performance but also simplifies your code, making it easier to maintain and extend in the future. The aim is to eliminate redundancy, manage dependencies effectively, and structure your code clearly while adhering to best practices in Python programming.

To begin, focus on modular design principles. Breaking large tasks into smaller, reusable functions makes your scripts more manageable. Each function should have a single responsibility, which simplifies debugging when issues arise. For example, if you need to clean data, perform analysis, and generate reports simultaneously, separating these tasks into distinct functions allows you to pinpoint problems quickly without sifting through extensive code.

Consider this illustrative example:

```python
import pandas as pd

def clean_data(df):
    df.dropna(inplace=True) \# Remove missing values
    return df

def analyze_data(df):
    results = df.describe() \# Get summary statistics
    return results

def save_report(results):
    results.to_excel('analysis_report.xlsx', index=False)

def main():
    df = pd.read_excel('data.xlsx') \# Read the Excel file

    cleaned_df = clean_data(df)
    analysis_results = analyze_data(cleaned_df)
    save_report(analysis_results)
```

```
if __name__ == '__main__':

main()
```

In this example, each function handles a specific task: cleaning data, analyzing it, and saving results. This clear separation enhances readability and simplifies debugging. When unexpected results occur, you can easily target the relevant function rather than navigating a large block of code.

Next, leverage Python's built-in libraries to facilitate efficient data handling. The pandas library is particularly useful for working with Excel files due to its powerful DataFrame structure. It allows for vectorized operations that enable calculations on entire columns at once instead of iterating through rows.

Take this example, instead of using a loop to create a new column based on existing ones:

```python
df['new_column'] = 0

for i in range(len(df)):

df['new_column'][i] = df['column1'][i] * 2 \# Inefficient loop
```

You can achieve the same result with:

```python
df['new_column'] = df['column1'] * 2 \# Vectorized operation
```

This change not only accelerates execution but also clarifies your intentions for others reading your code.

Error handling is another crucial aspect of robust scripting.

342

Implementing try-except blocks ensures your automation runs smoothly even when unexpected issues arise. By catching exceptions and logging errors appropriately, you prevent minor problems from derailing your entire process. Here's an example:

```python
def read_data(file_path):

try:

return pd.read_excel(file_path)

except FileNotFoundError:

print(f"Error: The file file_path does not exist.")

return None
```

With this approach, if the file isn't found, your script provides feedback instead of crashing.

While streamlining scripts emphasizes efficiency, it is equally important to maintain clear documentation within your code. Commenting on complex sections or including docstrings for functions enhances understanding for anyone reviewing or using the script later—including yourself in the future. Good documentation clarifies intent and functionality, reducing the learning curve when revisiting old projects.

As you refine your scripts and processes over time, thorough testing in various scenarios is essential to ensure robustness. Incorporating unit tests where applicable helps validate the functionality of individual components in isolation, giving you confidence that changes made during enhancements do not inadvertently disrupt existing features.

By adopting these strategies—modular design principles, efficient use of libraries like pandas, effective error handling, thorough documentation, and rigorous testing —you'll significantly streamline your automation scripts. This refinement empowers you to automate Excel tasks with greater agility and reliability while laying a solid foundation for future projects. As you continue exploring Python automation for Excel, remember that clarity and maintainability are just as vital as performance; both contribute to creating lasting solutions.

Batch processing for time efficiency

When considering batch processing for improved time efficiency, it's crucial to recognize that the primary objective extends beyond mere task automation. The goal is to maximize performance and minimize execution time. Batch processing enables the handling of large datasets or numerous files simultaneously, thereby streamlining workflows and significantly reducing the need for manual intervention.

Take this example, imagine you are responsible for analyzing sales data across multiple Excel files, each containing hundreds of rows. Instead of processing these files one by one—reading each, executing necessary operations, and then writing back the results—you can utilize batch processing techniques to manage them collectively. This method not only saves time but also enhances productivity by minimizing the overhead associated with repeatedly initializing scripts.

To illustrate this approach, consider using Python's os module alongside pandas for batch file handling. The following code snippet demonstrates how to read multiple Excel files from a directory, process them simultaneously, and combine the results into a single DataFrame:

```python
import pandas as pd

import os
```

```
def load_and_process_files(directory):

combined_data = pd.DataFrame()    \# Create an empty
DataFrame

for filename in os.listdir(directory):

if filename.endswith('.xlsx'):

file_path = os.path.join(directory, filename)

df = pd.read_excel(file_path) \# Read each Excel file

processed_df = process_data(df) \# Process the data as needed

combined_data = pd.concat([combined_data, processed_df],
ignore_index=True)

return combined_data

def process_data(df):

\#\# Example processing: cleaning and filtering

df.dropna(inplace=True)

return df[df['Sales'] > 1000] \# Keep only significant sales

directory_path = 'path/to/excel/files'

final_data = load_and_process_files(directory_path)
` ` `
```

In this example, the load_and_process_files function
efficiently reads every Excel file in the specified directory. By
utilizing pd.concat, it combines all processed data into a single

DataFrame without generating intermediate files or requiring repetitive read-write cycles.

Batch processing is particularly advantageous when it comes to operations such as aggregating or transforming data across multiple datasets. Instead of analyzing each dataset individually and manually merging results—an often labor-intensive process—you can aggregate them all at once. For example:

```python
def aggregate_sales_data(combined_df):

return                combined_df.groupby('Product').agg('Sales':
'sum').reset_index()


aggregated_results = aggregate_sales_data(final_data)

print(aggregated_results)
```

This function groups the combined DataFrame by product and sums up sales figures in one step. This streamlined approach not only enhances performance but also improves clarity by reducing complexity in your analysis pipeline.

However, while implementing batch processes, it's essential to be mindful of memory usage, especially with large datasets. Monitoring the amount of data loaded into memory is crucial. Utilizing the chunksize parameter in pandas can be particularly beneficial when working with exceptionally large files:

```python
for chunk in pd.read_excel(file_path, chunksize=10000):

processed_chunk = process_data(chunk)

combined_data            =            pd.concat([combined_data,
```

processed_chunk], ignore_index=True)
```

This code processes the file in smaller segments rather than loading it entirely into memory at once.

Another important aspect of batch processing is automating tasks that require regular execution—such as updating reports or dashboards. Setting up a scheduled task using Python scripts allows you to automate these updates without manual oversight. Libraries like schedule can assist in defining tasks that run at specified intervals.

For example:

```python
import schedule

import time


def job():

print("Updating reports...")

\#\# Call your function here that performs updates


schedule.every().day.at("10:00").do(job)


while True:

schedule.run_pending()

time.sleep(1)
```

This simple scheduler executes the job daily at 10:00 AM without necessitating constant supervision.
```

Additionally, effective error management is vital when dealing with batch processing of multiple files or extensive datasets. Issues may arise that could disrupt your entire workflow if not handled appropriately. Implementing logging within your batch processes allows you to track progress and errors efficiently:

```python
import logging

logging.basicConfig(filename='batch_processing.log',
level=logging.INFO)

def load_and_process_files(directory):
combined_data = pd.DataFrame()

for filename in os.listdir(directory):
try:
if filename.endswith('.xlsx'):
file_path = os.path.join(directory, filename)
df = pd.read_excel(file_path)
processed_df = process_data(df)
combined_data = pd.concat([combined_data, processed_df],
ignore_index=True)
logging.info(f"Processed filename successfully.")
except Exception as e:
logging.error(f"Failed to process filename: e")
```

```
final_data = load_and_process_files(directory_path)
` ` `
```

With this implementation, even if one file fails during processing, the script logs the error and continues its operations smoothly.

By employing these strategies—simultaneously managing multiple files, leveraging memory-efficient techniques, scheduling automated tasks, and ensuring robust error handling—you can significantly enhance your efficiency when automating Excel processes with Python. Batch processing equips you to handle substantial workloads effortlessly while freeing up valuable time for more strategic initiatives within your organization.

Case studies in optimization

As we explore case studies centered around optimization, the importance of real-world applications becomes evident. Each example presents distinct challenges and showcases innovative solutions designed to boost efficiency and productivity through Python and Excel automation. These cases offer valuable insights that can inspire you to incorporate similar strategies into your own workflows.

Take, for instance, a marketing department grappling with overwhelming weekly reporting demands. Each week, team members manually compiled data from various sources, including sales figures, web analytics, and customer feedback. This labor-intensive process consumed countless hours and was prone to errors. By adopting a Python-based automation solution, the team revolutionized their reporting workflow. Utilizing libraries such as Pandas and OpenPyXL, they automated both data collection and analysis.

The turning point came when they developed a script that not

HAYDEN VAN DER POST

only aggregated data but also generated visual reports directly in Excel. The following code snippet captures the essence of their automation:

```python
import pandas as pd
import openpyxl

\#\# Load sales data
sales_data = pd.read_excel('sales_data.xlsx')
web_data = pd.read_excel('web_data.xlsx')

\#\# Combine datasets
combined_data = pd.merge(sales_data, web_data, on='Date')

\#\# Generate report
report = combined_data.groupby(['Product']).agg('Sales': 'sum', 'Visits': 'mean').reset_index()

\#\# Write to Excel
with pd.ExcelWriter('Weekly_Report.xlsx') as writer:
report.to_excel(writer, sheet_name='Summary', index=False)
```

This approach not only expedited report generation but also enhanced accuracy by reducing human error. So, the marketing team transformed two full days of work into just a few hours, enabling them to focus more on strategic initiatives rather than routine tasks.

Next, we turn our attention to a financial services firm that faced challenges with risk assessment across multiple investment portfolios. Analysts spent an inordinate amount of time running individual calculations based on varying criteria and manually consolidating results into Excel sheets. By leveraging batch processing and Python's SQLAlchemy library for database connectivity, they significantly streamlined their analysis process.

This integration allowed them to pull data directly from SQL databases into Python for processing and then write the results back to Excel files for stakeholder reviews:

```python
from sqlalchemy import create_engine

\#\# Create database connection

engine = create_engine('mysql+pymysql://user:password@host/db_name')

\#\# Query risk metrics from database

query = "SELECT Portfolio_ID, Risk_Score FROM Portfolio_Data

risk_data = pd.read_sql(query, engine)

\#\# Perform risk aggregation

aggregated_risk = risk_data.groupby('Portfolio_ID').agg('Risk_Score': 'mean').reset_index()

\#\# Save back to Excel

aggregated_risk.to_excel('Risk_Assessment_Report.xlsx',
```

index=False)

` ` `

With this automation in place, the firm reduced the time spent on data manipulation from days to just hours, allowing analysts to concentrate on interpreting results rather than gathering them.

Another compelling example involves a healthcare provider managing patient records across various locations. With regulations requiring timely reporting on patient outcomes and operational efficiency metrics, their existing system was cumbersome and vulnerable to inconsistencies due to manual entry errors.

Here, an innovative solution combined web scraping with traditional data processing. The team created scripts that extracted real-time patient satisfaction scores from an external survey tool while simultaneously compiling internal operational data using Python:

` ` `python

import requests

def fetch_satisfaction_scores():

response   =   requests.get('https://api.surveytool.com/satisfaction')

return response.json()   \# Assuming JSON format for simplicity

\#\# Fetch external survey data

satisfaction_scores = fetch_satisfaction_scores()

\#\# Assume patient_data is already loaded as a DataFrame

```
merged_data = pd.merge(patient_data, satisfaction_scores,
on='Patient_ID')


merged_data.to_excel('Patient_Outcome_Report.xlsx',
index=False)
```
` ` `

This combination of real-time data extraction and efficient processing resulted in near-instantaneous access to up-to-date insights, which informed both clinical practices and administrative decisions.

Each case study not only highlights technical implementations but also illustrates the transformative effects these optimizations have had on organizational operations. Whether it involved freeing up hours previously devoted to mundane tasks or enhancing decision-making with timely insights, these transformations demonstrate the power of effective Python automation alongside Excel.

As you consider these examples, think about how similar principles might apply in your own context. What challenges do you encounter in your workflow? How might batch processing or task automation alleviate those pain points? The journey toward optimization is continuous; each challenge presents an opportunity for innovation and improvement through effective automation strategies.

Tools and techniques for performance analysis

In the realm of performance analysis, the tools and techniques you choose can greatly influence your ability to evaluate and enhance your automation processes. Adopting a strategic approach—rather than merely collecting data or running scripts—ensures that you consistently refine your methods for optimal outcomes.

To begin, consider profiling your Python scripts. Utilizing

built-in modules like cProfile can help you identify bottlenecks in your code. Take this example, if you have a script that processes large datasets but runs slower than expected, cProfile can pinpoint which functions consume the most time, enabling you to direct your optimization efforts effectively. Here's a simple implementation:

```python
import cProfile


def data_processing():

\#\# Imagine this function contains intensive data processing tasks

pass


\#\# Profile the data processing function

cProfile.run('data_processing()')
```

After executing this code, you'll receive detailed output indicating the time spent on each function call. This insight allows you to target specific areas for optimization, whether it involves experimenting with more efficient algorithms or revising data structures to improve speed.

Understanding memory consumption is another crucial aspect of performance analysis. Tools like memory_profiler allow you to visualize memory usage over time during script execution. For example:

```python
from memory_profiler import profile
```

```python
@profile
def large_data_processing():
\#\# Simulate memory-intensive operations
data = [x ** 2 for x in range(1000000)]
return sum(data)

large_data_processing()
` ` `
```

Running this code provides insight into how much memory each line consumes, helping you identify sections that may lead to inefficiencies or excessive resource use.

In addition to profiling tools, leveraging visualization libraries such as Matplotlib or Seaborn can create graphical representations of your performance metrics. Plotting execution times over multiple runs can reveal trends or improvements stemming from your optimization efforts. Here's how to create a basic execution time plot:

```python
` ` `python
import matplotlib.pyplot as plt

execution_times = [1.2, 1.0, 0.8, 0.5]  \# Example execution times over iterations
iterations = list(range(1, len(execution_times) + 1))

plt.plot(iterations, execution_times)
plt.title('Execution Time Over Iterations')
```

```python
plt.xlabel('Iteration')

plt.ylabel('Time (seconds)')

plt.show()
```

This visual feedback not only documents progress but also serves as motivation to continue refining your scripts.

Establishing benchmarks for your processes is essential for measuring future performance against a reference point. By documenting current performance levels before implementing changes, you can evaluate the effectiveness of new strategies and determine whether adjustments yield meaningful improvements.

For example, when automating Excel report generation, if certain reports take longer due to complexity or dataset size, creating benchmarks allows you to focus on enhancing those specific areas first.

Continuous monitoring is vital for maintaining an efficient workflow. Automating logging systems within your scripts ensures consistent capture of performance data. Libraries like Loguru simplify logging important events and metrics without cluttering your code with print statements:

```python
from loguru import logger


logger.add("performance.log", rotation="1 MB")  \# Rotate log file after it reaches 1 MB


@logger.catch

def run_automation_task():
```

```
\#\# Task logic here

logger.info("Task started")

pass


run_automation_task()
` ` `
```

By embedding logging into your automation tasks, you create a rich repository of historical performance data that can inform future optimizations and troubleshooting efforts.

Performance analysis transcends mere identification of effective practices; it fosters a mindset geared towards continuous improvement and innovation. As these techniques illustrate, an analytical approach allows for proactive adjustments rather than reactive fixes—an essential distinction in an environment where efficiency is paramount.

Integrate these tools and strategies into your workflows by reflecting on potential inefficiencies and experimenting with the discussed profiling and monitoring techniques. Each step towards understanding and optimizing performance not only enhances individual projects but also significantly boosts overall productivity within your organization.

The potential for improvement is vast; seize the opportunity today to refine how you approach automation tasks through effective performance analysis techniques!

CHAPTER 12: ERROR HANDLING AND DEBUGGING TECHNIQUES

Common error types in Excel automation

Understanding common errors in Excel automation is crucial for anyone looking to optimize their processes. Just like any programming environment, Python's integration with Excel comes with its own set of challenges. Being aware of these pitfalls can save you countless hours of frustration and improve your workflow.

One prevalent issue arises with file handling. For example, if your script attempts to read from a file that either doesn't exist or is currently in use by another application, it can trigger exceptions that halt execution. To manage this gracefully, consider using try-except blocks. This allows you to handle errors without crashing your program. Here's a practical example:

```python
import pandas as pd


try:
df = pd.read_excel('data.xlsx')
```

except FileNotFoundError:

print("The specified file was not found.")

except PermissionError:

print("The file is currently open in another application.")

``` `

By capturing specific exceptions, you provide meaningful feedback to users, enhancing their experience while also simplifying debugging.

Another common error involves data type mismatches. When automating tasks in Excel, it's easy to overlook the types of data you're working with, particularly in large datasets where columns may contain mixed types. Take this example, if you attempt to perform mathematical operations on a string value within a DataFrame, Python will raise a TypeError. To avoid this issue, always validate and clean your data before processing:

``` `python

```python
df['Sales'] = pd.to_numeric(df['Sales'], errors='coerce')   \# Converts non-numeric values to NaN
```

``` `

This line ensures that problematic entries are transformed into NaN (not a number), allowing calculations to proceed smoothly.

Excel formulas also present a fertile ground for errors when executed through Python scripts. Using libraries like OpenPyXL or XlsxWriter, incorrect formula syntax can lead to script failures or erroneous outputs. It's essential to double-check the formula strings being passed into cells:

``` `python

from openpyxl import Workbook

```
wb = Workbook()
ws = wb.active
ws['A1'] = 10
ws['A2'] = 20
ws['A3'] = '=SUM(A1:A2)' \# Ensure formula syntax is correct
wb.save('formulas.xlsx')
```

Misconfigurations in formulas can not only result in runtime errors but may also produce misleading data outputs that affect stakeholders relying on automated reports.

In addition to these issues, it's important to account for unexpected changes in data structures when automating repetitive tasks. Shifts in column names or formats due to upstream changes can disrupt your scripts. To mitigate this risk, implement checks at the beginning of your scripts to confirm that the expected formats and structures are present:

```python
expected_columns = ['Date', 'Sales', 'Region']
if not all(col in df.columns for col in expected_columns):
raise ValueError("The dataset is missing one or more expected columns.")
```

This proactive approach prevents downstream errors and maintains the integrity of your automation process.

Lastly, performance issues often manifest as silent errors that gradually degrade efficiency until they become critical failures. While scripts may run smoothly initially, they might slow down as datasets grow larger. Implementing logging mechanisms can help capture performance metrics during execution, providing insights into potential bottlenecks:

```python
import logging

logging.basicConfig(level=logging.INFO)

def process_data():
logging.info("Data processing started.")
\#\# Processing logic here...
logging.info("Data processing completed.")


process_data()
```

By maintaining logs of execution times and resource usage, you can better identify slowdowns and optimize your scripts accordingly.

In summary, recognizing common error types in Excel automation enables you to react effectively while also proactively enhancing your workflow. Whether facing file handling issues, data type mismatches, formula syntax errors, structural changes in datasets, or performance degradation— each challenge offers an opportunity for growth and learning.

Equipping yourself with knowledge about these pitfalls ensures smoother automation experiences and positions you for innovative problem-solving as you integrate Python more deeply into your Excel processes. Embrace these strategies; they are essential components of mastering Excel automation through Python.

Debugging Python scripts

Debugging Python scripts is an essential skill that significantly enhances the reliability and efficiency of your Excel automation processes. As you integrate Python into your workflows, mastering troubleshooting techniques will save you time and help you avoid frustration. The ability to quickly identify and resolve issues not only boosts your confidence but also improves the overall quality of your projects.

One effective strategy for debugging is utilizing Python's built-in tools, such as the pdb module. This module enables you to set breakpoints and inspect variables at different points in your script, which can be particularly valuable when dealing with complex logic or data manipulations. For example:

```python
import pdb

def calculate_average(data):
pdb.set_trace() \# Set a breakpoint here
total = sum(data)
average = total / len(data)
return average

print(calculate_average([10, 20, 30]))
```

When this script runs, execution pauses at the pdb.set_trace() line, allowing you to examine variables interactively in the console. This makes it easier to pinpoint issues as they arise.

In addition to using debugging tools, strategically placed print statements can provide immediate insights into variable values and control flow throughout your code. Although less sophisticated than a debugger, print statements can be incredibly helpful. Take this example:

```python
def process_data(df):

print("Data before processing:", df.head())

\#\# Processing logic...

print("Data after processing:", df.head())
```

This snippet allows you to visualize how your DataFrame changes before and after processing steps, helping you catch discrepancies early on.

However, relying too heavily on print statements can lead to cluttered output. To streamline this process, consider implementing logging instead. Logging allows you to record messages at different levels of severity (INFO, WARNING, ERROR), providing a comprehensive view of script execution without overwhelming your output:

```python
import logging


logging.basicConfig(level=logging.DEBUG)


def load_data(file_path):

logging.debug(f"Attempting to load data from file_path")

try:

df = pd.read_excel(file_path)

logging.info("Data loaded successfully.")
```

return df

except Exception as e:

logging.error(f"Failed to load data: e")

load_data('data.xlsx')
``` `

By adjusting log levels based on message importance, you can tailor your debugging output effectively.

When working with external libraries like Pandas or OpenPyXL, it's crucial to familiarize yourself with their documentation and common error messages. Many issues stem from misunderstandings about the expected data formats or structures within these libraries. For example, attempting to access a non-existent column in a DataFrame may raise a KeyError. Handling such exceptions with specific error messages can lead to smoother debugging:

``` `python

try:

region_data = df['Region']

except KeyError:

logging.warning("The 'Region' column does not exist in the DataFrame.")
``` `

Additionally, testing your functions independently through unit tests can significantly minimize bugs in larger scripts. By writing tests for individual components—such as data loading or transformation—you ensure that each piece functions correctly before integrating them into broader processes.

Consider using frameworks like unittest or pytest for
```

structured testing:

```python
import unittest

class TestAverageCalculation(unittest.TestCase):

    def test_average(self):
        self.assertEqual(calculate_average([10, 20]), 15)

if __name__ == '__main__':
    unittest.main()
```

This proactive approach to error checking not only boosts your confidence in your scripts but also helps catch potential bugs before they reach production environments.

By understanding and implementing these debugging techniques, you lay a strong foundation for your Excel automation tasks with Python. While errors are inevitable, embracing systematic strategies—from utilizing built-in tools and logging mechanisms to conducting unit tests—will enhance both the reliability of your code and your proficiency as an automation expert.

As you explore Python's capabilities within Excel automation further, remember that every challenge offers an opportunity for growth. Cultivating these debugging skills will empower you to address complex problems more effectively while fostering a mindset geared towards continuous learning and adaptation in an ever-evolving technological landscape.

Error handling best practices

Error handling is an essential aspect of developing resilient Python scripts for Excel automation. When automating tasks, unexpected issues can arise: files may be missing, data might be incorrectly formatted, or network interruptions could disrupt processes. Mastering the art of error management not only strengthens your scripts but also fosters trust in your automated solutions.

A key principle of effective error handling is anticipating potential errors and preparing to address them. Utilizing try-except blocks allows you to catch and manage exceptions gracefully without causing your program to crash. For example, when loading data from an Excel file, you can handle file-related errors in a user-friendly manner:

```python
import pandas as pd


def load_data(file_path):

try:

df = pd.read_excel(file_path)

return df

except FileNotFoundError:

print(f"Error: The file file_path was not found.")

return None

except pd.errors.EmptyDataError:

print("Error: The file is empty.")

return None

except Exception as e:

print(f"An unexpected error occurred: e")
```

return None

```python
data = load_data('data.xlsx')
```

In this example, specific exceptions like FileNotFoundError are caught and handled with clear messages, while a general exception handler addresses any unforeseen issues. This approach keeps users informed about problems while allowing your script to continue running where possible.

Another best practice is validating data before processing it, which can prevent cascading errors caused by invalid inputs. Take this example, if you expect numeric values in a column for calculations, it's prudent to check the data types beforehand:

```python
def calculate_average(df, column_name):

if     column_name     in     df.columns     and pd.api.types.is_numeric_dtype(df[column_name]):

return df[column_name].mean()

else:

print(f"Error: 'column_name' does not exist or is not numeric.")

return None


average = calculate_average(data, 'Sales')
```

In this scenario, validation ensures that attempts to calculate an average are only made on valid numeric data and existing columns. This proactive measure saves time by avoiding unnecessary errors during execution.

Logging serves as another powerful tool for effective error handling. It allows you to track issues without disrupting the flow of execution. Instead of merely printing error messages, you can utilize Python's logging module:

```python
import logging

logging.basicConfig(level=logging.ERROR)

def save_data(df, output_file):
try:
df.to_excel(output_file)
logging.info(f"Data successfully saved to output_file.")
except Exception as e:
logging.error(f"Failed to save data: e")

save_data(data, 'output.xlsx')
```

In this example, successful operations are recorded as INFO messages, while failures generate ERROR logs that can be reviewed later. By leveraging different logging levels (DEBUG, INFO, WARNING, ERROR), you can filter messages based on their severity and importance.

Implementing retries for transient errors—such as temporary connectivity issues—is also advisable in automation scripts. If a task fails due to a network glitch or an unavailable resource, retrying after a brief delay can often resolve the issue:

```python
import time

def fetch_data_with_retry(url, retries=3):
for attempt in range(retries):
try:
response = requests.get(url)
response.raise_for_status()  \# Raises an HTTPError for bad responses
return response.json()
except requests.exceptions.RequestException as e:
print(f"Attempt attempt + 1 failed: e")
time.sleep(2)  \# Wait before retrying
print("All attempts failed.")
return None

data = fetch_data_with_retry('https://api.example.com/data')
```

This strategy provides flexibility while ensuring that temporary setbacks do not derail your automation efforts.

In summary, adopting effective error handling practices significantly enhances the quality and reliability of your Python scripts for Excel automation. By anticipating potential failures with try-except blocks, validating inputs upfront, utilizing logging to monitor progress and issues alike, and implementing retry mechanisms for transient failures, you will create robust systems capable of managing challenges seamlessly.

As you continue to hone these skills on your journey with Python and Excel automation, remember that robust error handling is not just about preventing problems; it's about building solutions that empower users and instill confidence in your automated workflows. Each script refined through thoughtful error management reflects professionalism and dedication—a hallmark of truly impactful automation work.

Logging and monitoring automation tasks

Effective logging and monitoring are crucial for developing reliable Python scripts for Excel automation. These practices not only document processes but also help identify bottlenecks, diagnose issues, and improve overall performance. As you refine your workflows, remember that logging provides a retrospective view of task execution, offering insights into both successes and failures.

When you implement logging in your scripts, it's important to establish clear and meaningful log messages. Each message should convey relevant information succinctly. Take this example, while processing data, you might want to track how many records were successfully processed versus how many encountered errors. Here's an example using Python's logging module:

```python
import logging


logging.basicConfig(level=logging.INFO)


def process_data(df):
success_count = 0
error_count = 0
```

```python
for index, row in df.iterrows():

try:

\#\# Assume some processing happens here

success_count += 1

except Exception as e:

error_count += 1

logging.error(f"Error processing row index: e")


logging.info(f"Processed success_count records successfully with error_count errors.")


\#\# Assuming 'data' is a DataFrame loaded earlier

process_data(data)
```
```

In this snippet, any error that occurs during data processing is logged with a clear indication of which row caused the issue. This facilitates quick isolation of problems within datasets, allowing for efficient troubleshooting.

Monitoring your script's performance during execution is equally important. By implementing metrics, you can observe trends over time—such as rising error rates or extended processing durations—which may signal underlying issues needing attention. A straightforward timer can help you measure execution duration:

```python
import time
```
```

```
def timed_process_data(df):

start_time = time.time()

process_data(df)

elapsed_time = time.time() - start_time

logging.info(f"Data processing completed in elapsed_time:.2f
seconds.")


timed_process_data(data)
` ` `
```

This function wraps the data processing logic with timing code to record how long it takes. Understanding these performance metrics is essential for assessing whether your automation meets efficiency standards or requires adjustments.

You may also want to consider integrating tools that provide real-time monitoring capabilities. For example, Application Performance Management (APM) solutions can offer valuable insights by tracking resource usage and detecting anomalies. This proactive approach can save time by alerting you to potential issues before they escalate into significant failures.

Additionally, establishing a feedback loop within your automation systems can enhance user experience and operational efficiency. Gathering user feedback on specific processes allows you to refine scripts accordingly, fostering continuous improvement.

Incorporating notifications into your scripts can also facilitate prompt responses to emerging issues. By setting up alerts for critical failures through email or messaging apps like Slack, you ensure that responsible parties are informed immediately when something goes wrong:

```python
def notify_failure(message):

\#\# Placeholder for sending notifications (e.g., via email or API)

print(f"ALERT: message")


def save_data_with_notification(df, output_file):

try:

df.to_excel(output_file)

logging.info(f"Data saved successfully to output_file.")

except Exception as e:

notify_failure(f"Failed to save data: e")

logging.error(f"Failed to save data: e")


save_data_with_notification(data, 'output.xlsx')
```

In this example, if the data-saving operation fails, users receive an immediate notification while logs are updated with detailed information about the failure.

Lastly, remember that the effectiveness of your logging and monitoring efforts depends on regular reviews of log files and performance metrics. Consistently analyzing logs helps identify patterns over time and reveals opportunities for optimization.

As you develop your Python automation skills for Excel, adopting robust logging practices and active monitoring will enhance not only the reliability of your solutions but also their acceptance within your organization. By empowering stakeholders with visibility into automated processes, you cultivate trust in technology—ultimately leading to broader adoption of automation initiatives across teams.

Integrating these strategies into your workflow transforms basic automation into a structured framework capable of adapting to evolving needs while maintaining high standards of performance and accountability.

Proactive monitoring and alerts

In today's increasingly automated landscape, proactively monitoring Excel automation tasks is essential. Since these processes often run without direct human oversight, the risk of errors or unexpected outcomes rises significantly. By implementing a proactive monitoring system, you not only protect data integrity but also boost overall operational efficiency.

Imagine an automated script generating weekly sales reports. If something goes wrong—such as a lost data connection or a formula failure—those inaccuracies can lead to critical business decisions based on flawed information. Integrating monitoring capabilities into your Python scripts allows you to establish checkpoints that verify key actions and alert you to any deviations from the expected flow.

One effective way to implement monitoring is through logging. Python's built-in logging library enables you to capture events and errors in detail. For example, while automating the report generation process, your script could log important milestones like "Report generation started," "Data retrieval complete," and "Report saved successfully." In the event of an error, the log will document the incident along with relevant details, facilitating quick diagnosis.

Here's how you can incorporate logging into your automation script:

```python
import logging

\#\# Configure the logger
logging.basicConfig(filename='automation_log.log',
level=logging.INFO)

def generate_report():
try:
logging.info('Report generation started.')
\#\# Simulating data retrieval
retrieve_data()

\#\# Simulating report generation logic
create_excel_report()

logging.info('Report generated successfully.')
except Exception as e:
logging.error(f'Error during report generation: e')

def retrieve_data():
\#\# Simulated function for data retrieval
pass

def create_excel_report():
```

```
\#\# Simulated function for creating an Excel report

pass


generate_report()
```
```

This setup creates a straightforward log file that tracks the state of your automation process at various points. When issues arise, you have an immediate reference point for swift troubleshooting.

In addition to logging, setting up alerts is crucial for proactive monitoring. Email notifications within your scripts provide a direct line of communication regarding issues that require immediate attention. Take this example, if your script detects a failure to connect to the database or identifies missing data essential for report generation, sending an email alert can help you respond before any significant fallout occurs.

Integrating this feature into your existing workflow might look like this:

```python
import smtplib

from email.mime.text import MIMEText


def send_alert(message):

msg = MIMEText(message)

msg['Subject'] = 'Automation Alert'

msg['From'] = 'your_email@example.com'

msg['To'] = 'recipient@example.com'
```
```

```
with smtplib.SMTP('smtp.example.com') as server:

server.login('your_email@example.com', 'your_password')

server.send_message(msg)


\#\# In your generate_report function

if not db_connection_successful:

send_alert('Database connection failed during report
generation.')
` ` `
```

By incorporating alert mechanisms alongside structured logging, you establish a robust safety net around your automated tasks. This dual approach ensures that even when you're not actively monitoring processes, you're informed about their status and can take prompt action if needed.

Additionally, consider setting thresholds for specific metrics relevant to your operations—for instance, average execution time or success rates of generated reports over time. Regularly analyzing these metrics can reveal trends that inform adjustments in processes or resource allocation.

This combination of structured logging and real-time alerts fosters a culture of accountability and foresight within automation initiatives. By equipping yourself with these tools, you enhance individual projects and set a standard across teams for quality assurance and reliability in automated workflows.

Emphasizing proactive strategies signifies a shift toward more responsible automation practices—where anticipation replaces reaction—transforming how professionals like Alex navigate tech-savvy environments.

Case studies in troubleshooting

In the world of Excel automation, troubleshooting can often feel like navigating a labyrinth. However, real-world case studies can illuminate pathways to resolution, offering insights that save time and help prevent future errors. Let's explore some examples that highlight common challenges faced during automation and the solutions implemented to overcome them.

Take, for instance, a finance department responsible for generating monthly revenue reports. Initially, their automation script functioned smoothly for several months until an unexpected error arose: a missing data file. The team relied on an external database that went offline for maintenance, leading to a sudden failure in the automation process. This setback resulted in delayed reports and disrupted decision-making.

To address this challenge, the team revamped their script to include a pre-check for data availability. Before attempting to generate reports, the automation now verifies that the necessary files are accessible. If any files are missing, it logs an error and alerts the appropriate team member. This proactive measure transformed their process from reactive to anticipatory, significantly reducing downtime.

In another scenario, a marketing team employed Python scripts to gather data from multiple sources for campaign analysis. They frequently encountered discrepancies in reporting figures due to inconsistent data formats across platforms. This inconsistency not only complicated data cleaning but also led to erroneous insights derived from flawed data.

To resolve this issue, they developed a robust data validation function within their automation workflow. This function checks for missing values, format mismatches, and outliers. By enforcing strict criteria on incoming data, the team could identify issues early in the process rather than after significant analysis had been conducted. That's why, the accuracy of their reports improved dramatically, enabling more reliable strategic decisions.

A different challenge arose in a logistics company where automated scripts were responsible for updating inventory levels based on daily sales data. These scripts occasionally hung or crashed due to excessive processing times when handling large datasets. The logistics manager recognized that these interruptions were not only inconvenient but also detrimental to inventory accuracy.

To tackle this problem, they implemented batch processing within their script. Rather than processing all sales transactions simultaneously, the automation was restructured to handle smaller chunks of data sequentially. This adjustment minimized memory usage and reduced the likelihood of crashes while ensuring timely updates of inventory levels. Additionally, they incorporated logging to track how long each batch took to process, providing valuable insights into system performance over time.

A compelling example of collaboration emerged from a healthcare organization grappling with patient data management. They faced frequent failures when automating report generation from Excel due to complex formulas embedded within their sheets. These formulas sometimes referenced outdated cells or invalid ranges, causing scripts to break unexpectedly.

The solution came through collaborative troubleshooting sessions involving both IT and healthcare staff. By documenting and analyzing error logs together, they identified specific formula patterns that triggered issues. Armed with this knowledge, they restructured the Excel templates used for report generation—simplifying formulas and ensuring compatibility with automated processes. This collaborative effort not only resolved immediate problems but also fostered a stronger partnership between departments.

These cases highlight the importance of robust troubleshooting mechanisms in automation workflows. By learning from setbacks and implementing proactive measures—such as validation checks, batch processing, and cross-departmental collaboration—organizations can create resilient systems that adapt effectively to challenges.

Essentially of these examples is the understanding that every error presents an opportunity for improvement. Embracing a culture of continuous learning and proactive monitoring enables teams not only to address current issues but also to anticipate future challenges in their automation efforts.

As professionals navigate their automation journeys, these case studies remind us that troubleshooting goes beyond merely fixing what's broken; it's about enhancing processes to foster greater efficiency and reliability across operations. Each successful resolution serves as a stepping stone toward mastering Excel automation with Python, paving the way for innovation even in the most complex tasks.

Building robust scripts with fail-safes

In the world of Excel automation, creating robust scripts equipped with fail-safes is not just advisable; it is essential. Fail-safes function as safety nets, ensuring that your automation processes maintain their integrity, even when faced with unexpected errors or system failures. To effectively integrate these safeguards into your scripts, careful planning and strategic coding practices are vital.

Consider a typical scenario involving data extraction from external sources. Picture a sales team that relies on automated scripts to retrieve daily sales figures from a third-party API. If that API becomes unavailable or returns data in an unexpected format, the entire automation process could break down, leading to inaccurate reports and poor decision-making. To mitigate this risk, it's crucial to implement a robust error handling mechanism within your script. Take this example, utilizing try-except blocks can help catch exceptions during API calls. Here's a simple Python example illustrating this approach:

```python
import requests

def fetch_sales_data(api_url):
try:
response = requests.get(api_url)
response.raise_for_status()    \# Raises an error for bad responses
return response.json()
except requests.exceptions.HTTPError as err:
print(f"HTTP error occurred: err")
return None \# Return None or a default value
except Exception as e:
print(f"An error occurred: e")
return None

\#\# Usage
data = fetch_sales_data("https://api.example.com/sales")
if data is not None:
\#\# Proceed with data processing
else:
```

\#\# Handle missing data scenario

` ` `

This code snippet ensures that if the API request fails, the script won't crash. Instead, it gracefully manages the situation by logging the error and allowing you to decide how to proceed —such as using cached data or notifying a team member for further action.

In addition to basic error handling, incorporating logging throughout your scripts can significantly bolster their reliability. Logging enables you to monitor execution events, providing insights into potential issues as they arise. For example, when processing large Excel files, it's beneficial to log key actions and milestones:

` ` `python

import logging

\#\# Configure logging

logging.basicConfig(filename='automation.log', level=logging.INFO)

def process_large_excel(file_path):

try:

logging.info(f"Starting processing for file_path")

\#\# Code to process the file...

logging.info("Processing completed successfully.")

except Exception as e:

logging.error(f"Error occurred while processing: e")

\#\# Usage

process_large_excel('sales_data.xlsx')

` ` `

In this example, every significant step within the script is logged, whether indicating success or detailing any errors encountered. This practice not only aids in troubleshooting but also provides an audit trail for compliance and accountability.

And, implementing validation checks at various stages of your automation process can protect against common pitfalls. Take this example, if user input drives your automation scripts, validating this input before proceeding can avert numerous errors from propagating through your workflow.

Take, for example, a script that accepts dates as input for report generation. By ensuring these dates are valid before executing any operations, you can prevent unnecessary complications:

` ` `python

from datetime import datetime

def validate_date(date_string):

try:

datetime.strptime(date_string, '%Y-%m-%d')

return True

except ValueError:

print(f"Invalid date format: date_string. Expected format is YYYY-MM-DD.")

```
return False

\#\# Example usage
date_input = "2023-10-32"  \# Invalid date
if validate_date(date_input):
\#\# Proceed with report generation
else:
\#\# Handle invalid date input scenario
` ` `
```

Finally, establishing fallback mechanisms can enhance your scripts' resilience. When automating reporting processes, consider how to respond if an expected output fails to generate. Take this example, if an email report cannot be sent due to connectivity issues, your script might be designed to automatically retry sending it after a delay or log an alert for manual follow-up later.

By integrating practices such as error handling, logging, validation checks, and fallback mechanisms, your scripts will not only withstand unforeseen challenges but also evolve into reliable tools for Excel automation. Each layer of protection you add reinforces your workflow against potential disruptions.

In summary, building robust scripts with fail-safes goes beyond merely preventing errors; it fosters confidence in your automation processes. Through iterative testing and feedback, you will find that these scripts operate more smoothly and create an environment where innovation can flourish without the fear of failure—a crucial aspect of any successful automation strategy in today's fast-paced data-driven landscape.

Continuous improvement strategies

In the world of Excel automation, the journey extends beyond the mere implementation of robust scripts; it evolves into a commitment to continuous improvement. This proactive mindset ensures that your automation solutions remain effective and relevant in a landscape that is always changing. By focusing on enhancing both processes and skills, you can achieve greater efficiency and increased productivity.

An important part of continuous improvement is regularly reviewing and iterating on your automation scripts. After deploying a solution, it's essential to step back and evaluate its performance over time. Are there recurring errors? Is the script executing as efficiently as anticipated? Engaging in this reflective practice helps identify areas for enhancement. Take this example, if a particular script takes longer than expected to run, investigating potential bottlenecks becomes crucial. You might discover that optimizing data retrieval methods or refining algorithms could yield significant performance gains.

Gathering feedback from users who interact with your automated processes is another vital strategy. By fostering open communication channels, you can collect insights that may not be apparent from a purely technical perspective. Team members might find certain reports challenging to interpret or specific tasks cumbersome. Their feedback can guide you in making user-centric adjustments, resulting in more intuitive workflows. Incorporating user experience into your development cycle cultivates a sense of ownership and encourages collaboration across teams.

Regular training sessions are also instrumental in keeping you and your team up-to-date with new technologies and techniques in Python and Excel automation. The field is rapidly evolving, with new libraries, tools, and best practices emerging frequently. Dedicating time to professional development—whether through workshops, online courses, or peer-led sessions—empowers you to leverage these advancements effectively. For example, learning about the latest features in libraries like Pandas or OpenPyXL can unlock new capabilities within your existing scripts.

Embracing metrics as part of your continuous improvement strategy provides tangible data for informed decision-making. Tracking key performance indicators (KPIs) related to your automation processes can reveal trends over time. Are your automated reports being generated on schedule? How often do errors occur during execution? Utilizing these metrics helps establish a baseline for performance and measure the impact of any changes you implement.

Adopting an agile mindset further encourages adaptability within your workflows. This approach allows for iterative development where small changes can be tested quickly without overhauling entire systems at once. Take this example, if you're considering integrating a new data source into an existing report generation script, testing this change on a smaller scale first can mitigate risks while providing immediate feedback on functionality.

Documentation is another critical component often overlooked in the pursuit of continuous improvement. Maintaining thorough documentation aids current users and provides clarity for future enhancements or troubleshooting efforts. Documenting not just what your scripts do but also why decisions were made along the way creates a valuable knowledge base that can guide future developers—or even yourself—when revisiting projects down the line.

A culture of experimentation fosters innovation within your organization as well. Encouraging team members to propose new ideas or alternative solutions without fear of failure nurtures creativity and often leads to discovering more efficient methods or tools for automation tasks. Whether trying out different libraries for data processing or exploring novel ways to visualize data in Excel, an open-minded approach invites fresh perspectives that significantly contribute to growth.

Lastly, actively engaging with the broader community—whether through forums or social media groups focused on Python or Excel automation—can provide insights into common challenges others face and how they overcome them. Participating in discussions about successful projects or pitfalls encountered by peers often reveals strategies you might not have considered otherwise.

At its core, embedding continuous improvement strategies into your workflow cultivates an environment where adaptation and learning become second nature. By regularly evaluating performance, incorporating user feedback, committing to ongoing education, leveraging metrics for informed decision-making, fostering agility in development practices, maintaining documentation, encouraging experimentation, and engaging with external communities, you'll establish a dynamic framework for innovation that enhances both individual competence and collective organizational capability.

By nurturing this culture of continuous improvement within yourself and across teams, you position yourself not just as a technology user but as an innovator capable of navigating the complexities of Excel automation with confidence and creativity—a vital asset in today's fast-paced business environment where adaptability is key to long-term success.

CHAPTER 13: SECURITY CONSIDERATIONS IN EXCEL AUTOMATION

Identifying security risks

For Excel automation using Python, recognizing and addressing security risks is crucial. As you automate tasks involving sensitive data, the likelihood of vulnerabilities increases. These vulnerabilities can arise from various factors, including insecure scripts, mishandling of confidential information, and accidental exposure due to misconfigured environments. The first step in safeguarding your automated processes is to acknowledge these risks.

Data handling practices represent a significant area of concern. When automating processes that deal with personal or confidential information—like financial records or customer data—it's essential to ensure secure storage and transmission. Take this example, managing credentials for database or API connections requires careful consideration. Hardcoding sensitive information into scripts can create serious vulnerabilities. Instead, opt for environment variables or configuration files with strict access controls to protect these credentials.

File access permissions also demand attention. When

automating the creation or manipulation of Excel files, it's vital to specify who can access these files and what actions they are permitted to take. A common mistake is neglecting to restrict access to sensitive reports generated by automation scripts, which can inadvertently allow unauthorized users to view or alter critical information. Establishing a clear permission structure within your file management process ensures that only authorized personnel can interact with sensitive data.

In addition to these practices, network security is essential for protecting automated workflows that involve external connections. When scripts communicate with remote databases or web services, securing these interactions is vital to prevent man-in-the-middle attacks or data breaches during transmission. Utilizing secure protocols like HTTPS for web scraping and ensuring encrypted database connections can significantly reduce these risks.

Cultivating a culture of security awareness within your team also bolsters resilience against potential threats. Regular training sessions on identifying phishing attempts and adhering to secure coding practices empower team members to recognize vulnerabilities before they escalate into issues. By engaging everyone in discussions about security best practices, you foster a proactive environment where security becomes an integral part of the automation process rather than an afterthought.

Staying informed about emerging threats and best practices is equally important for effective risk management. The cybersecurity landscape evolves rapidly; what was once considered secure may no longer hold true as new vulnerabilities are continuously discovered. Subscribing to industry news feeds or participating in relevant forums helps you keep pace with the latest developments and adapt your automation strategies accordingly.

Another often-overlooked aspect is the regular auditing of your automation processes and codebases. Periodic reviews help identify outdated libraries with known vulnerabilities and assess compliance with established security protocols. During these audits, consider employing static code analysis tools that automatically check for common security flaws in your Python scripts—this proactive approach can uncover issues before they lead to serious breaches.

Finally, incorporating incident response planning into your overall security strategy is essential. In the event of a data breach or other security incident related to your automated processes, having a clear action plan enables swift responses that minimize damage and expedite recovery. This plan should detail communication steps within your organization and any necessary notifications required by regulations concerning affected stakeholders.

By proactively identifying potential security risks associated with Excel automation using Python—from securing sensitive data during handling and storage to fostering awareness among team members—you establish a solid framework for secure automated workflows. This diligence not only protects valuable information but also enhances organizational integrity by demonstrating a commitment to responsible data management practices in an increasingly interconnected world where cyber threats are ever-present.

Securing Python scripts and data

When securing Python scripts and the data they manage, the primary objective is to establish a robust framework that minimizes vulnerabilities while maximizing operational efficiency. A foundational step in this process involves adopting code security practices, particularly focusing on how sensitive data is managed within your scripts.

Hardcoding sensitive information, such as API keys or database credentials, directly into your Python scripts can lead to significant risks. If these scripts are shared or stored in version control systems like Git, unauthorized individuals may gain access to this sensitive information. To mitigate this risk, consider using environment variables to store sensitive credentials. By utilizing libraries such as python-dotenv, you can create a .env file that securely holds these variables and loads them into your script at runtime, keeping them out of your codebase.

```python
from dotenv import load_dotenv

import os


load_dotenv()


api_key = os.getenv("API_KEY")
```

In this example, the load_dotenv() function reads environment variables from a .env file, allowing you to use secrets without exposing them in your code. This approach extends beyond API keys; any sensitive information—such as database connection strings—should be handled similarly.

In addition to managing secrets, careful consideration is necessary for how data is processed and stored. When dealing with Excel files containing confidential information, implementing encryption during transmission and at rest is essential. Take this example, when transferring files over networks, secure protocols like HTTPS or SFTP should be employed. And, encrypting Excel files before saving them adds an extra layer of protection against unauthorized access.

Using libraries like cryptography, you can easily encrypt data within your Python applications. Here's a brief example illustrating how to encrypt an Excel file:

```python
from cryptography.fernet import Fernet

# Generate a key for encryption
key = Fernet.generate_key()
cipher_suite = Fernet(key)

# Read your data from an Excel file
with open("sensitive_data.xlsx", "rb") as file:
    file_data = file.read()

# Encrypt the data
encrypted_data = cipher_suite.encrypt(file_data)

# Write encrypted data back to an Excel file
with open("sensitive_data_encrypted.xlsx", "wb") as encrypted_file:
    encrypted_file.write(encrypted_data)
```

Another critical aspect of securing Python scripts and associated data is implementing proper access controls. Limiting permissions based on roles within your organization ensures that only authorized users can execute automation tasks or access specific datasets. Establishing Role-Based Access Control (RBAC) systems clarifies who can interact with which resources.

Additionally, consider incorporating logging mechanisms into your automation scripts to track user actions and monitor access to sensitive information. Python's built-in logging library allows you to capture relevant events while ensuring that sensitive details remain obscured or excluded from log outputs.

```python
import logging

\#\# Configure logging

logging.basicConfig(level=logging.INFO)


def secure_action():

\#\# Log an action without exposing sensitive details

logging.info("User performed a secure action.")


secure_action()
```

Regular audits of both code and processes are essential for maintaining security over time. As software dependencies evolve, it becomes crucial to track known vulnerabilities; tools like pip-audit can help identify insecure packages within your project's environment.

Continuous integration/continuous deployment (CI/CD) pipelines also present opportunities for automated testing of security measures throughout development cycles. By integrating security checks into these pipelines, potential vulnerabilities can be detected early in the development process before deployment occurs.

Lastly, fostering an organization-wide culture that prioritizes secure coding and data handling through training is vital. Encourage discussions about potential threats and recent breaches to keep everyone vigilant about protecting not only their own work but also the broader organizational infrastructure.

By focusing on these strategies—using environment variables for secret management, employing encryption techniques for data protection, establishing robust access controls, implementing comprehensive logging systems, conducting regular audits, and providing team training—you can significantly enhance the security posture of your Python automation efforts with Excel. A proactive approach will empower you to mitigate risks effectively while building trust among stakeholders through a commitment to responsible data management practices in today's cyber landscape.

Handling sensitive data responsibly

When handling sensitive data in Python automation, responsible management is crucial. This process begins with identifying the types of sensitive information, such as financial records, personal details, or proprietary business insights. Recognizing the potential consequences of mishandling this data reinforces the importance of adhering to best practices.

A key principle to follow is data minimization. Collect only the information necessary for your specific tasks, thereby reducing exposure to sensitive data. Take this example, when automating a report that aggregates sales data, avoid including unnecessary personal details about employees or customers unless they are essential to the report's purpose. This approach not only mitigates risk but also helps ensure compliance with data protection regulations like GDPR and HIPAA.

After identifying and minimizing sensitive data, it's

important to focus on its entire lifecycle—from collection to storage, processing, and eventual deletion. During data collection, implement strict access controls to guarantee that only authorized personnel can input or access sensitive information within your Python scripts. Utilizing libraries such as pandas can aid in secure handling; for example, when loading data from Excel files, you can use read_excel() with parameters to limit visibility.

```python
import pandas as pd


\#\# Load sensitive data with limited visibility

sensitive_data        =        pd.read_excel('sensitive_data.xlsx', usecols=['Column1', 'Column2'])
```

In this code snippet, the usecols parameter allows you to specify which columns to load, preventing unnecessary exposure of sensitive information.

Storage is another critical aspect of managing sensitive data. When using databases or cloud storage solutions, always opt for encryption at rest. This guarantees that even if unauthorized access occurs, the information remains protected. Python libraries like sqlalchemy can be configured to encrypt connections, safeguarding all transactions.

Processing sensitive data requires careful consideration as well. Whenever possible, implement anonymization techniques. For example, if you're analyzing user behavior patterns without needing to identify individuals directly, replace identifiable information with pseudonyms or random identifiers during your analysis phase. This way, you can derive insights without compromising individual privacy.

When sharing reports or datasets that contain sensitive

information, use secure file-sharing protocols and always encrypt files before distribution. Employing strong password protections or digital rights management (DRM) features can further safeguard against unauthorized use.

Additionally, it's vital to be meticulous about data deletion. When sensitive information is no longer needed, ensure proper disposal methods are followed. For Excel files specifically, simply deleting them may not suffice; consider overwriting the file multiple times or using secure delete tools that comply with industry standards for data destruction.

Fostering a culture of security awareness within your organization is essential. Regular training sessions on data sensitivity and responsible handling practices will keep your team informed. Discussing real-world examples of breaches caused by negligence can reinforce the importance of diligent adherence to these practices.

Finally, maintaining thorough documentation of all processes involving sensitive data is crucial. Keeping track of who has access to what types of data and how it flows through your systems creates an invaluable audit trail for security assessments or compliance checks.

By embedding these practices into your automation workflows and instilling a sense of accountability among team members, you build a robust framework for responsibly managing sensitive data. The consequences of neglecting these responsibilities can be severe—both legally and reputationally—making it imperative for professionals engaged in Python automation with Excel to prioritize integrity in their operations.

Best practices for secure automation

For secure automation, implementing best practices is essential—not merely a recommendation. The landscape of data security is continually evolving, and as you use Python to automate tasks in Excel, it's crucial to take proactive steps to safeguard sensitive information. By combining Python's capabilities with robust security measures, you can ensure that your automated processes are both efficient and secure.

Start with secure coding practices. It's vital to validate inputs rigorously to prevent injection attacks, particularly when handling user-generated data or external sources. Take this example, if you're scraping information for Excel reports from a user-inputted URL, be sure to validate that the input adheres to expected formats and protocols. Using regular expressions is a practical approach for filtering acceptable URLs.

```python
import re

def is_valid_url(url):
    pattern = r'^(http|https)://'
    return re.match(pattern, url) is not None

user_input = "https://example.com
if not is_valid_url(user_input):
    raise ValueError("Invalid URL format.")
```

In addition to input validation, it's crucial to apply least privilege access principles. That means users and systems should have only the minimum level of access necessary to perform their tasks. In your scripts, ensure that credentials or API keys are not hardcoded; instead, use environment variables or secure vaults for storing sensitive information. For example, you can retrieve environment variables using Python's os module, keeping sensitive data out of your code.

```python
```

```python
import os

api_key = os.getenv('API_KEY')
```

Regular software updates are another critical best practice. Keeping your libraries and tools up-to-date helps prevent vulnerabilities from being exploited. Libraries like pandas, openpyxl, and XlsxWriter frequently release patches addressing security issues. Use package managers like pip to check for updates periodically:

```bash
pip list --outdated
```

Integrating logging and monitoring into your automation framework is also essential. Implement logging mechanisms within your Python scripts to track actions performed on sensitive data, including access attempts and modifications. By utilizing Python's built-in logging module, you can configure different logging levels—such as info, warning, and error—facilitating audits and troubleshooting later on:

```python
import logging

logging.basicConfig(level=logging.INFO)
logging.info("Sensitive data accessed by User XYZ.")
```

For effective monitoring, consider setting up alert systems that notify you of unusual activities—such as repeated failed access attempts—so you can respond swiftly.

Another key practice involves incorporating encryption into

your workflows to protect data at rest and in transit. When storing sensitive information in databases or Excel files, utilize established libraries such as cryptography for encryption. When transmitting data over networks or APIs, ensure you use SSL/TLS protocols for secure transmission.

```python
from cryptography.fernet import Fernet


\#\# Generate a key for encryption

key = Fernet.generate_key()

cipher_suite = Fernet(key)

cipher_text = cipher_suite.encrypt(b"Sensitive information")
```

When sharing automated reports containing sensitive details, always opt for encrypted files and transmit them via secure channels. Tools like PGP (Pretty Good Privacy) can provide an additional layer of security in these situations.

Finally, foster a culture of continuous learning regarding security practices within your team or organization. Regular workshops on emerging threats and trends can enhance awareness and promote vigilance among colleagues engaged in automation processes.

By implementing these best practices, you'll not only strengthen the security of your automated processes but also cultivate trust in the integrity of the systems you deploy within your organization. As automation increasingly plays a role in managing sensitive data through Python and Excel, establishing a solid foundation based on these principles will prepare you for future challenges while ensuring compliance with regulatory requirements.

Compliance with data protection regulations

In the world of Excel automation with Python, compliance with data protection regulations is essential—not just a legal obligation but a cornerstone of integrity and trust. In an era where data breaches frequently make headlines, organizations must prioritize compliance to protect personal information and avoid substantial fines. By understanding these regulations, you can design automation processes that align with established standards.

Start by familiarizing yourself with key regulations, such as the General Data Protection Regulation (GDPR) in the European Union and the California Consumer Privacy Act (CCPA) in the United States. The GDPR requires that personal data be processed lawfully, transparently, and for specific purposes. For example, if your automation scripts manage customer data for reporting, you must obtain explicit consent from users to process their information. Documenting this consent creates a clear audit trail.

Next, evaluate how your automated workflows manage personal data throughout its lifecycle—from collection to deletion. It's vital to establish clear protocols regarding data retention; under GDPR, data should not be held longer than necessary for its intended purpose. If your automation involves archiving old reports in Excel, implement mechanisms to regularly review and delete data that no longer serves a legitimate business need.

Another critical aspect of compliance is implementing data minimization principles. This means only collecting and processing the minimum amount of personal data necessary to achieve your automation goals. Take this example, if you are automating sales reports that require only email addresses for follow-up communications, refrain from gathering additional information such as phone numbers or mailing addresses unless absolutely essential.

Ensuring that your automated scripts support user rights

as outlined in various regulations is equally important. Users have the right to access their personal data, request corrections, or demand deletions. Your Python scripts can facilitate this by providing functionality for users to submit requests through a web interface or an automated email response system. For example, you might implement an endpoint that allows users to request their data:

```python
from flask import Flask, request

app = Flask(__name__)

@app.route('/request_data', methods=['POST'])
def request_data():
user_id = request.form['user_id']
\#\# Logic to retrieve user data
return "Data sent.

if __name__ == '__main__':
app.run()
```

And, establishing strong security protocols for handling sensitive information within your Excel automation processes is crucial. As previously mentioned, using encryption during both storage and transmission is essential. When dealing with APIs or database connections requiring sensitive credentials, utilize environment variables or configuration files with restricted access rights to protect this information from unauthorized access.

Training your team on data protection practices should not be overlooked. Regular workshops can ensure that everyone involved in automation understands their responsibilities regarding compliance. It's important to convey how non-compliance can lead to serious consequences—not just financial penalties but also reputational damage.

Finally, consider employing tools and frameworks designed for compliance monitoring and reporting. Libraries like pandas can automate audits by generating reports on data handling practices within your organization's workflows. Regularly reviewing these reports will help identify areas for improvement and ensure adherence to regulations.

Creating a culture of compliance within your organization goes beyond merely avoiding penalties; it fosters trust with customers and stakeholders alike. By integrating these principles into your automation processes using Python and Excel, you contribute significantly to cultivating an environment where data privacy is prioritized and respected. As automation continues to evolve, staying ahead of regulatory requirements will position you as a leader in secure and compliant data practices.

Case studies in data security breaches

In the rapidly evolving landscape of data security, case studies of breaches starkly illustrate the consequences of inadequate protection measures. One prominent example is the 2017 Equifax data breach, which affected approximately 147 million consumers. The breach resulted from a failure to patch a known vulnerability in their web application framework, highlighting how lapses in security protocols can lead to devastating outcomes for both organizations and individuals.

The fallout from the Equifax incident was profound—not only did it cost the company over 4 billion in total expenses, but it also severely damaged its reputation. Rebuilding trust after such an event is an uphill battle, emphasizing the need for proactive risk management and compliance strategies. Organizations must recognize that security breaches disrupt operations and can compromise customer loyalty while inviting legal scrutiny from affected individuals seeking recourse.

Another significant example is the 2020 SolarWinds cyberattack, which infiltrated various government agencies and corporations through a compromised software update. This breach exploited vulnerabilities within the supply chain, underscoring how interconnected systems amplify risks. The implications for Excel automation processes are substantial; if your automated workflows depend on external data sources or third-party applications, it is crucial to scrutinize their security practices.

These breaches serve as valuable lessons for your own Excel automation projects. If you leverage external APIs for data retrieval or interact with cloud services for reporting, ensuring robust authentication mechanisms is essential. Incorporating multi-factor authentication and API keys into your toolkit can help secure these integrations against unauthorized access.

The case of Marriott International further reinforces this point. In 2018, the hotel chain disclosed a breach affecting around 500 million guest records due to unauthorized access that began back in 2014. Weaknesses in legacy systems were largely to blame, illustrating how outdated technology can become a liability over time. As you develop Python automation scripts that interface with legacy Excel files or databases, regular audits and updates are vital for protecting sensitive information.

Additionally, it's important to learn from regulatory responses following these breaches. After incidents like those involving Equifax and SolarWinds, lawmakers have pushed for stricter regulations regarding data protection and breach notification requirements. Companies are now often mandated to inform affected users within specific timeframes after discovering a breach. Incorporating notification systems into your automation processes—perhaps using Python scripts that trigger alerts when anomalies are detected—can help ensure compliance while enhancing overall security vigilance.

An interesting aspect of these case studies is how companies reacted post-breach. Many organizations undertook comprehensive reviews of their cybersecurity policies and adopted advanced technologies such as artificial intelligence for threat detection and response capabilities. These actions highlight a shift towards prioritizing prevention over reactive remediation.

In the end, examining these breaches reveals critical lessons about safeguarding data within Excel automation initiatives using Python. Security cannot be an afterthought; it must be integrated into every layer of your processes—from design to implementation and ongoing maintenance.

By incorporating insights gained from real-world examples into your practices, you can build resilient systems that withstand potential threats. Embracing continuous improvement protocols ensures that your methods evolve alongside emerging risks—positioning you at the forefront of secure automation practices while reinforcing trust within your organization and among stakeholders alike.

Tools and techniques for enhancing security

Security in Excel automation presents a complex challenge, particularly when integrating Python scripts. To effectively bolster security, it's essential to grasp the available tools and techniques. A foundational element in this effort is the use of version control systems like Git. By implementing Git, you can track changes in your scripts, creating a reliable backup and an audit trail that proves invaluable for identifying how security vulnerabilities may have developed over time.

In addition to version control, employing environment management tools such as virtual environments or Docker containers can greatly enhance security. Virtual environments allow you to create isolated spaces for your Python projects, ensuring that dependencies are managed separately for each project. This isolation reduces the risk of cross-contamination, especially when handling sensitive data across different projects. Docker containers take this concept further by encapsulating your entire application—including code, runtime, libraries, and environment variables—into a single deployable unit. This not only enhances security through the enforcement of specific policies for each container but also maintains flexibility in deployment.

Encryption is another critical aspect of safeguarding sensitive information within Excel files. Libraries like cryptography in Python offer straightforward methods to encrypt data before writing it to Excel sheets. For example:

```python
from cryptography.fernet import Fernet

\#\# Generate a key for encryption

key = Fernet.generate_key()

cipher = Fernet(key)


\#\# Sample sensitive data

sensitive_data = "Sensitive Financial Data

encrypted_data = cipher.encrypt(sensitive_data.encode())


\#\# Save encrypted data to Excel
```

```python
import pandas as pd

df = pd.DataFrame('Encrypted Data': [encrypted_data])
df.to_excel('secure_data.xlsx', index=False)
```

By encrypting sensitive information prior to saving it in Excel, you significantly mitigate the risk of unauthorized access. Even if someone gains access to your Excel file, they would be unable to decipher the content without the appropriate decryption key.

Also, implementing user access controls can substantially enhance security. When sharing workbooks or scripts, it's crucial to limit access based on roles within your organization. Tools like Microsoft SharePoint or OneDrive provide granular permission settings that allow you to manage who can view or edit documents according to their job functions. By restricting edit permissions to those who truly need them, you reduce the risk of accidental changes or unauthorized access.

Regular audits of your automation processes are equally important. Utilizing logging libraries such as logging in Python enables you to monitor activities carried out by your scripts effectively. By logging critical actions and errors, you can track performance and identify issues:

```python
import logging

\#\# Set up logging configuration
logging.basicConfig(filename='automation.log',
level=logging.INFO)
```

```
def secure_script_action():

try:

\#\# Simulate an action

logging.info('Starting secure action.')

\#\# ... perform action ...

logging.info('Secure action completed successfully.')

except Exception as e:

logging.error(f'Error occurred: e')
```
` ` `

This strategy allows for real-time tracking and facilitates post-incident analysis should any irregularities arise. By regularly reviewing logs for anomalies, organizations can proactively address potential threats before they escalate into serious issues.

Another important layer of security involves adopting secure coding practices when developing automation scripts. Avoid hardcoding sensitive credentials directly into scripts; instead, use environment variables or secret management tools like AWS Secrets Manager or HashiCorp Vault. These methods allow you to manage sensitive information securely without exposing it in your source code.

Lastly, ongoing education and training are vital components of a robust security posture in Excel automation practices. Providing team members with up-to-date training on emerging threats and secure coding techniques fosters a culture of vigilance and accountability among staff involved in automation projects.

By combining these tools and techniques—version control

systems for change tracking, environment management for isolation, encryption for data protection, user access controls for safeguarding against unauthorized modifications, logging for monitoring activities, and secure coding practices to protect sensitive information—organizations can significantly enhance their security framework surrounding Python-Excel integrations. Security is not merely a one-time setup; it's an ongoing process that demands vigilance and adaptability as new threats emerge in the landscape of data automation and management.

CHAPTER 14: CASE STUDIES IN PYTHON-EXCEL AUTOMATION

Overview of diverse automation use cases

Automation in Excel using Python has emerged as a vital tool for enhancing workflows across various industries. The flexibility of Python enables professionals to streamline numerous tasks that were once labor-intensive and time-consuming. By exploring diverse automation use cases, we can uncover how these techniques can significantly improve daily operations and boost productivity.

Take the financial sector, for instance, where data accuracy is crucial. Financial analysts routinely handle extensive datasets to create reports, monitor market trends, and predict future performance. Python can transform the extraction and processing of financial data from multiple sources into a more efficient process. With libraries like Pandas, analysts can quickly aggregate and analyze data pulled from APIs or databases, allowing them to minimize manual data entry and dedicate more time to interpreting insights that inform decision-making.

Similarly, automation plays a critical role in supply chain management by enhancing efficiency and accuracy. Businesses must navigate the complexities of managing inventories, tracking shipments, and ensuring timely deliveries. A simple Python script can automate the updating of inventory levels in Excel by sourcing real-time data from suppliers or logistics partners. For example, integrating with shipping service APIs provides instant updates on shipment statuses, which are reflected in Excel dashboards. This real-time visibility empowers managers to make informed decisions swiftly, optimizing operations while reducing the risk of human error.

Marketing departments also stand to gain significantly from automating their reporting processes. Understanding campaign performance metrics is essential for gauging customer engagement and return on investment (ROI). Automating the collection and analysis of marketing data not only saves time but also enhances reporting accuracy. Python scripts can scrape web analytics data or social media metrics and consolidate this information into comprehensive Excel reports. By visualizing these metrics through Excel charts or dashboards, marketers can effortlessly communicate performance results to stakeholders without the tediousness of manual compilation.

The healthcare sector is another area ripe for automation through Python-Excel integration. Medical professionals often need to analyze patient data for both research and administrative purposes. Automating this process facilitates more efficient data handling while ensuring compliance with privacy regulations. Take this example, using Python to extract patient records from databases and generate reports in Excel can streamline tasks such as tracking patient outcomes or managing billing processes. This automation frees up valuable time for healthcare workers, allowing them to concentrate on patient care rather than administrative duties.

In education, there is a growing interest in automation tools that enhance the teaching experience. Educators can leverage Python to automate grading systems by analyzing student submissions and providing instant feedback through Excel reports. By developing scripts that grade assignments based on predefined criteria stored in an Excel sheet, teachers can save hours typically spent on manual grading. This not only increases efficiency but also enriches the learning experience for students by providing quicker responses.

Across these examples—finance, supply chain management, marketing, healthcare, and education—the common theme is transforming repetitive tasks into automated processes that deliver accurate results while saving time. As you embark on your journey into automation with Python and Excel, it's important to identify specific challenges within your organization where these techniques can be applied effectively.

Automation is not merely about replacing human effort; it's about enhancing capabilities and enabling professionals to focus on higher-level tasks that demand creativity and critical thinking. As you explore various use cases throughout this guide, reflect on how each example may relate to your unique challenges or aspirations within your field.

The potential applications extend far beyond those discussed here. As we delve deeper into specific strategies for leveraging Python in Excel automation, remain open to how these tools can adapt to meet your needs and ultimately transform your workflow. Embracing this innovative approach will not only boost productivity but may also position you as a leader in your industry's technological evolution.

Financial modeling and automation

In financial modeling, precision and efficiency are crucial. Financial analysts often navigate complex calculations, projections, and extensive datasets to extract insights that guide strategic decisions. Automation through Python can significantly enhance this process, revolutionizing the construction, maintenance, and analysis of financial models.

Updating financial models with new data inputs is a prime example of where automation can make a difference. Traditionally, analysts manually entered data from various sources into spreadsheets—a task that is both tedious and prone to errors. However, Python offers a solution by automating this routine. Take this example, using libraries like Pandas allows analysts to pull data directly from APIs or databases, refreshing their models in real-time. A simple script can extract current market prices or company financials and automatically update an Excel model, ensuring that data is always accurate without the burden of manual entry.

For forecasting revenue based on historical trends and other variables, automation can streamline the process even further. Rather than adjusting cells in an Excel workbook every time new data becomes available, you can create a forecasting model in Python. Utilizing libraries such as NumPy for numerical calculations and Scikit-learn for machine learning algorithms enables you to develop predictive models that improve in accuracy as they process more data. Once generated in Python, these forecasts can be easily exported back into Excel for reporting and visualization.

Another significant advantage of automation is its ability to facilitate scenario analysis with ease. Financial analysts often need to evaluate various "what-if" scenarios influenced by changes in key variables like interest rates or market conditions. Instead of maintaining multiple versions of an Excel model with different assumptions, a Python script can streamline this analysis. By defining a range of input parameters and running simulations, you can efficiently generate outcomes for each scenario. The results can then be compiled into a single Excel report, presenting the various forecasts side by side for straightforward comparison.

Visualization also plays an important role in financial modeling. While Excel provides basic charting capabilities, Python's Matplotlib and Seaborn libraries offer advanced options for creating insightful visual representations of financial data. Imagine automating the creation of charts that display trends in your forecasts alongside historical performance metrics. Once established, this process ensures that updated visuals are automatically generated with each analysis run, ready for presentation to stakeholders.

Beyond speed and accuracy, automation fosters better collaboration within teams. In many finance departments, shared spreadsheets can become cumbersome as multiple users make simultaneous updates. Transitioning to a Python-based workflow—where all data manipulations are handled programmatically—can help avoid common pitfalls such as version control issues and inconsistencies between user inputs. This shift not only creates a more reliable environment but also allows team members to concentrate on analysis rather than data entry.

As you consider integrating automation into your financial modeling practices, think about how these techniques might fit your specific context. Reflecting on past experiences with manual data handling can help identify areas where automation could save time or significantly reduce errors.

In the end, enhancing financial modeling through Python automation is not just about acquiring technical skills; it's about empowering yourself to deliver insights more effectively and strategically influence business outcomes. As we delve deeper into specific methodologies for integrating Python into Excel workflows throughout this guide, remain attentive to opportunities for innovation within your own modeling practices. Embracing automation will not only transform your current projects but also position you as a forward-thinking leader in your organization's financial strategy.

Supply chain management and reporting

Supply chain management hinges on the accuracy and timeliness of data. In today's fast-paced business environment, where the movement of goods can significantly impact success, precise reporting has become essential. Automation using Python presents powerful solutions for navigating the complexities of supply chains, enabling businesses to respond swiftly to market demands and operational challenges.

Consider a company sourcing components from diverse suppliers around the globe. Each supplier has varying lead times, price fluctuations, and delivery schedules. Tracking these variables manually in Excel can quickly become overwhelming, leading to errors and inefficiencies. By leveraging Python, companies can automate data collection from suppliers' APIs or spreadsheets, creating a centralized dashboard that provides real-time updates on inventory levels, order fulfillment rates, and shipping delays. This approach not only saves time but also enhances visibility across the entire supply chain.

Analyzing performance metrics is another critical aspect of supply chain reporting. Traditional reporting methods often rely on static reports generated at fixed intervals, which may fail to capture real-time insights effectively. With Python libraries like Pandas, analysts can automate the extraction and transformation of data into actionable reports. Take this example, a script can aggregate monthly sales data along with associated costs from multiple sources. Once processed, this data can be visualized using libraries such as Matplotlib, allowing teams to track trends over time and pinpoint areas for improvement.

Demand forecasting is yet another vital component of effective supply chain management. Accurate predictions enable businesses to maintain optimal inventory levels, minimizing excess stock while ensuring product availability. Python's machine learning capabilities facilitate the development of sophisticated models that analyze historical sales patterns in conjunction with current market trends. By utilizing Scikit-learn, you can create a predictive model that accounts for seasonal variations and promotional impacts, providing accurate forecasts for future demand. The results can be seamlessly integrated into an Excel dashboard, helping stakeholders visualize expected trends and make informed purchasing decisions.

Collaboration among departments is crucial for effective supply chain management. When teams across procurement, logistics, and sales operate in silos, efficiency can suffer. Automating data sharing through Python scripts fosters better communication and transparency among these teams. For example, a script could automatically update a shared Excel sheet whenever stock levels or supplier statuses change, ensuring everyone has access to the most current data. This alignment reduces miscommunication and facilitates quicker decision-making.

One significant advantage of automation is its ability to simplify reporting processes. Instead of manually generating weekly or monthly reports, a well-structured Python script can automate this task based on predefined parameters—such as inventory levels dropping below a certain threshold or delivery delays exceeding specified limits. With just a few clicks, stakeholders receive comprehensive insights into supply chain performance without the delays associated with traditional reporting methods.

To implement these automation strategies effectively, it's essential to understand your specific reporting needs and challenges within your supply chain processes. Reflecting on areas where manual reporting consumes excessive time or leads to inconsistencies will guide you in designing tailored Python solutions that integrate smoothly into your existing workflows.

In summary, enhancing supply chain management through automation not only streamlines operations but also empowers organizations to make confident, data-driven decisions. By harnessing Python's capabilities for real-time tracking and predictive analytics, companies can adapt swiftly to changing market conditions while driving efficiency across their operations. As we explore practical methodologies for incorporating Python into reporting practices throughout this guide, be on the lookout for innovative ways to transform your supply chain processes into a competitive advantage.

Sales data analysis and visualization

Sales data analysis and visualization are crucial for driving business success. As the volume of sales transactions continues to grow, companies must adopt effective strategies to navigate this data, derive actionable insights, and communicate findings clearly. By automating these processes with Python, organizations not only enhance efficiency but also empower their teams to make swift, data-driven decisions.

The journey of analyzing sales data typically begins with aggregating information from various sources, such as regional sales reports, product performance metrics, and customer feedback. Rather than manually compiling these datasets in Excel, Python scripts can streamline the extraction and consolidation process. Take this example, using the Pandas library, you can read multiple CSV files representing different sales territories, merge them into a single DataFrame, and perform essential data cleaning tasks, such as addressing missing values or correcting data types. This efficient approach saves time and minimizes the risk of human error.

After consolidating the data, the next step is to extract meaningful insights. Identifying sales trends can be challenging when viewing raw figures in isolation. This is where visualization comes into play. Leveraging libraries like Matplotlib or Seaborn in Python allows you to create visual representations that highlight key trends over time. For example, a line chart illustrating monthly sales growth across various products or regions enables stakeholders to quickly understand performance dynamics and pinpoint areas that may need further investigation.

Imagine your organization has launched a new product line; analyzing its performance alongside existing products can yield valuable insights into market reception. With Python, you can develop a dynamic dashboard that updates in real-time with sales data. Utilizing Plotly for interactive visualizations allows stakeholders to hover over data points for detailed metrics like revenue generated or units sold per region. This interactivity transforms static reports into engaging tools for exploration and analysis.

Sales forecasting is another vital component of data analysis that greatly benefits from automation. Historical sales data often reveals patterns that can inform future projections. Python's machine learning libraries, such as Scikit-learn, provide powerful tools for creating predictive models based on historical trends. By incorporating past sales figures along with relevant factors like seasonality or marketing campaigns, you can predict future sales volumes with greater accuracy. These forecasts can be visualized within an Excel dashboard for easy sharing across teams.

Effective communication of insights is equally important as the analysis itself. Generating insights is just the first step; they must be communicated clearly to influence decision-making. A well-crafted report can succinctly summarize findings and recommendations. Python allows you to automate report generation by integrating libraries like XlsxWriter or OpenPyXL to write directly to Excel files. For example, you could set up a script that compiles visualizations and key metrics into a polished report format at regular intervals—weekly or monthly—ensuring consistency while freeing up valuable time for your team.

Also, automation creates opportunities for continuous monitoring of sales performance metrics without the need for constant manual input. Setting up alerts based on predefined thresholds—such as when sales drop below a certain percentage compared to previous months—enables teams to respond proactively rather than reactively. A simple Python script running in the background can ensure stakeholders receive timely email alerts whenever significant changes occur.

To integrate these techniques effectively, it's essential to consider your organization's specific needs and the reporting challenges within the sales process. Engaging with team members across departments will help identify their pain points related to current reporting methods. This collaboration will guide you in designing tailored automation solutions that enhance efficiency without disrupting established workflows.

To wrap things up, leveraging Python for sales data analysis and visualization not only streamlines operations but also equips teams with powerful tools for making informed decisions based on real-time insights. By automating data collection, applying advanced analytics techniques, and improving communication through compelling visualizations, organizations position themselves advantageously in competitive landscapes while fostering an environment conducive to proactive decision-making. Embracing these capabilities lays the groundwork for improved business performance and sets the stage for ongoing success in an ever-evolving market landscape.

Marketing insights and dashboards

Marketing insights and dashboards are essential in shaping strategies that resonate with consumers. In today's hyper-competitive landscape, businesses must go beyond merely collecting data; they need to transform it into meaningful insights that inform decision-making. By leveraging Python for marketing analytics, organizations can automate data processing and enhance visualization, ultimately leading to more effective campaigns.

Effective marketing analysis begins with gathering data from a variety of sources, including social media metrics, website traffic, email campaigns, and customer feedback surveys. Instead of grappling with spreadsheets or manual calculations, marketers can streamline these processes with Python. Utilizing libraries like Requests and Beautiful Soup simplifies the collection of data from web APIs or enables the scraping of relevant statistics directly from platforms like Google Analytics or social media sites. For example, a straightforward script can extract daily engagement metrics and consolidate them into a single dataset for further analysis.

Once the necessary data is compiled, the focus shifts to deriving actionable insights. This is where advanced analytics come into play. By segmenting customers based on demographics, behavior patterns, or purchase history, businesses can gain clarity on how different groups respond to various marketing tactics. Using Pandas for grouping and aggregation allows marketers to identify high-value segments that deserve targeted campaigns. Take this example, a retail brand analyzing customer purchase patterns could apply a clustering algorithm like K-Means through Scikit-learn to uncover distinct groups such as "frequent buyers" or "seasonal shoppers," guiding tailored marketing efforts.

Communicating these insights effectively is crucial for engaging stakeholders. Python libraries like Matplotlib and Seaborn enable marketers to create compelling visual narratives that highlight key trends and performance indicators. A well-designed dashboard displaying campaign performance metrics—such as click-through rates (CTR) or conversion rates—allows teams to quickly assess effectiveness. Picture a bar chart comparing various ad channels over time; this visual representation not only identifies thriving strategies but also underscores underperforming areas that may require immediate attention.

Creating a dashboard goes beyond simple visualization; it involves integrating diverse data sources into an interactive platform that updates in real-time. Consider using Plotly Dash —a powerful library designed for building interactive web applications—to develop an intuitive dashboard showcasing marketing KPIs dynamically. By connecting this dashboard to your databases or live data streams, marketing teams can access up-to-date campaign performance without manual intervention. This real-time perspective fosters agility in decision-making, enabling teams to adjust strategies swiftly based on current data.

Additionally, automated reporting capabilities significantly enhance how insights are disseminated across departments. Rather than manually creating static reports each month, marketers can implement scripts that compile key findings and visualizations into professional presentations formatted for Excel or PDF using libraries like XlsxWriter or ReportLab. By setting parameters for automatic report generation at regular intervals, organizations ensure that all team members remain informed of progress without unnecessary delays.

An important aspect of effective marketing analytics is the continuous improvement facilitated by A/B testing strategies. Controlled experiments can reveal the impact of different elements—such as email subject lines or landing page designs —on consumer behavior. Python's statistical libraries, such as StatsModels, allow for rigorous analysis of test results, helping determine the optimal approach moving forward.

Collaboration among team members is vital when establishing these systems and developing insightful dashboards tailored to specific organizational needs. Engaging closely with colleagues from sales and product development can uncover critical questions about customer engagement patterns that warrant attention. Incorporating their insights helps refine the focus of your dashboards—transforming them from mere reporting tools into instruments that shape strategy.

In summary, harnessing Python for marketing insights and dashboard creation significantly enhances analytical capabilities, empowering teams to make informed decisions based on real-time data trends rather than outdated information. This seamless integration optimizes workflow and positions organizations strategically in their markets, ensuring responsiveness and proactivity—key elements for success in today's fast-paced business environment where adaptation is crucial.

Real-world applications in healthcare

The real-world applications of Python in healthcare highlight the transformative potential of automation and data analysis in a field where timely and accurate information is essential. The healthcare sector generates vast amounts of data, from patient records to clinical trials, and utilizing Python to harness this data can lead to improved patient outcomes and streamlined operations.

A particularly compelling application is the analysis of electronic health records (EHRs). By leveraging libraries like Pandas, healthcare professionals can efficiently process and analyze patient data. Take this example, consider a hospital aiming to identify patterns in patient admissions. A Python script can extract relevant data from EHR systems, filter it based on specific criteria such as diagnosis or treatment received, and aggregate the information to reveal trends over time. This capability enables healthcare providers to better anticipate patient needs and allocate resources more effectively.

Beyond EHR analysis, Python plays a crucial role in predictive analytics within the healthcare domain. Using libraries like Scikit-learn, machine learning models can be developed to forecast patient outcomes based on historical data. For example, a hospital could implement logistic regression to predict the likelihood of readmission for patients with chronic conditions. By analyzing past admissions alongside various factors—such as age, treatment plans, and socio-economic status—healthcare providers can devise targeted interventions aimed at reducing readmission rates. Insights derived from these models can significantly influence care strategies and improve overall patient health.

Python also excels in clinical trial management, where coordinating trials demands meticulous tracking of numerous variables—from participant recruitment to data collection and analysis. Automating these processes with Python not only boosts efficiency but also minimizes human error. Researchers can utilize tools like Jupyter Notebook for documentation and code execution, creating comprehensive workflows that seamlessly integrate data collection and analysis. Take this example, a clinical trial might employ web scraping techniques to gather real-time data from clinical trial registries or relevant literature databases, ensuring researchers have access to the most current information.

Data visualization is another vital aspect of effectively conveying complex healthcare findings. Libraries such as Matplotlib and Seaborn enable professionals to create clear visual representations of their analyses, making it easier for stakeholders—from clinicians to executive teams—to grasp essential insights. A graphical depiction of trial results, for example, can highlight differences between treatment groups, facilitating quick assessments that guide decision-making.

Also, integrating Python with other tools enhances its utility in healthcare settings. Connecting Python scripts with databases like SQL or NoSQL allows for robust data retrieval methods that support comprehensive analyses across different systems. A hospital's patient management system could collaborate with Python scripts to automate reporting on key metrics, such as average length of stay or treatment efficacy across various departments.

As telemedicine continues to grow in popularity, Python's capabilities extend into monitoring remote patients through wearable technology. Scripts can analyze real-time health data transmitted from devices—tracking metrics such as heart rate or glucose levels—and alert medical personnel when intervention is necessary. This proactive approach not only improves patient safety but also empowers individuals by providing immediate feedback on their health status.

Collaboration among multidisciplinary teams is essential when implementing these applications in healthcare settings. Involving professionals from IT, clinical research, and administration fosters a holistic understanding of how automated processes can enhance care delivery while ensuring compliance with regulatory standards related to patient privacy and data security.

The potential for Python in healthcare is vast and rapidly evolving. By embracing automation and advanced analytics through Python, healthcare organizations can enhance operational efficiencies while improving the quality of care provided to patients. These applications exemplify how technology serves as a catalyst for innovation within the industry, ensuring that care remains responsive and informed by the best available evidence.

Learning from failures and successes

Failures and successes in Python-Excel automation offer invaluable lessons that can drive professionals toward greater innovation and efficiency. Understanding that missteps often pave the way for breakthroughs is essential. For example, consider a financial analyst who set out to automate quarterly earnings reporting. Initially, the scripts encountered errors due to mismatched data types in Excel sheets. Rather than seeing this as a setback, the analyst embraced it as an opportunity to enhance their knowledge of data types and error handling in Python. By refining the code to incorporate thorough checks for data consistency, they not only resolved the immediate issue but also established a more robust reporting framework.

This mindset of embracing failure cultivates a growth perspective, encouraging professionals to seek creative solutions when automation processes stumble. A notable case from a healthcare organization illustrates this point. When they launched a Python script to process electronic health records, they faced performance bottlenecks with large datasets. Instead of abandoning their efforts, the team collaborated to implement more efficient algorithms and leveraged libraries like Dask for parallel processing. This strategic pivot not only significantly improved performance but also equipped the team with new skills in scalable computing practices, applicable to future projects.

On the flip side, successes serve as powerful validation of the strategies employed during automation initiatives. Take this example, a marketing department that successfully integrated Python into their data analysis workflow experienced immediate benefits in campaign tracking and customer insights. Utilizing Pandas for data manipulation and Matplotlib for visualization enabled them to present findings clearly and effectively to stakeholders. This achievement became a benchmark within the organization, inspiring other departments to explore similar automation solutions. The takeaway here is that celebrating small wins can amplify enthusiasm across teams, fostering further adoption of innovative practices.

Additionally, documenting both failures and successes is vital for creating a knowledge repository that others can learn from. For example, a team might maintain a shared document logging issues encountered during automation attempts along with the resolutions discovered. This practice promotes open communication and nurtures an environment where learning from experience takes precedence over the fear of failure. Such documentation becomes an invaluable resource for onboarding new team members and helps prevent the repetition of past mistakes.

Beyond personal reflections, organizations can benefit from conducting regular reviews or retrospectives after completing major automation projects. These sessions should center on what went well, what didn't, and what could be improved moving forward. Engaging in honest discussions about challenges encountered during implementation fosters transparency and encourages a culture of continuous improvement. This approach not only solidifies lessons learned but also strengthens team dynamics as members collaborate toward shared objectives.

In the end, learning from both failures and successes enriches one's approach to Python-Excel automation by nurturing resilience and adaptability. Professionals who embrace these experiences become adept at troubleshooting and pioneering innovative solutions within their organizations. The journey through automation is rarely linear; it resembles a winding path filled with obstacles that lead to deeper insights and enhanced capabilities.

Harnessing these lessons lays a solid foundation for future endeavors—whether it involves tackling larger datasets or integrating more complex functionalities into existing workflows. Each experience contributes to a broader narrative of growth that informs decision-making and shapes strategies moving forward. As you reflect on your own experiences with Python-Excel automation, consider how both triumphs and setbacks have uniquely influenced your professional journey. This perspective will empower you as you continue to explore advanced techniques in this dynamic field.

CHAPTER 15: THE FUTURE OF EXCEL AUTOMATION WITH PYTHON

Emerging trends in automation

Emerging trends in automation are fundamentally reshaping business operations and innovation. At the forefront of this transformation is the integration of artificial intelligence (AI) with traditional automation tools, which is turning routine tasks into smarter, more intuitive processes. Take this example, machine learning algorithms can analyze data patterns far more efficiently than manual methods, enabling companies to make quicker, informed decisions. Organizations that embrace these advancements not only save time but also gain insights that would be nearly impossible to extract manually.

In addition to AI, low-code and no-code platforms are gaining traction, democratizing automation capabilities across the workforce. These user-friendly interfaces allow professionals without extensive programming skills to design workflows and automate processes. So, employees from various departments—such as marketing, finance, and operations— are empowered to create customized solutions that boost productivity. This shift fosters a culture of innovation, encouraging teams to experiment with their own ideas rather than relying solely on IT departments.

Cloud computing plays a crucial role in this evolution by hosting automation tools and data storage online. This approach offers organizations scalability and flexibility, allowing teams to deploy automation solutions swiftly without the limitations of local hardware. For example, a finance team could set up an automated reporting system that aggregates real-time data from multiple sources directly into cloud-based Excel dashboards, leading to more timely and accurate financial insights.

The significance of real-time data access cannot be overstated. With the ever-increasing volume of data generated each second, businesses need systems capable of processing information instantaneously for effective decision-making. Automation tools equipped with real-time analytics enable organizations to respond quickly to shifts in market conditions or customer behavior. Retailers, for example, are employing automated inventory management systems that monitor stock levels in real time and automatically trigger reorder alerts when thresholds are reached.

And, the Internet of Things (IoT) is revolutionizing how automation interacts with physical processes. Smart devices now communicate autonomously, optimizing production lines in industries like manufacturing. Sensors embedded in machinery can gather performance data and trigger automated responses—such as scheduling maintenance or adjusting operational parameters—thereby enhancing efficiency and minimizing downtime. This interconnectedness is redefining traditional business models by allowing real-time adjustments based on data collected from physical environments.

As organizations increasingly rely on automation, security considerations also come to the forefront. Protecting systems against cyber threats is essential. Emerging technologies like blockchain are being explored for their potential to create secure transaction records and enhance transparency within automated processes. Take this example, a supply chain management system could leverage blockchain to trace product provenance while integrating automated tracking features for improved visibility and accountability.

Lastly, ethical considerations surrounding automation are gaining importance as businesses strive to balance efficiency with responsibility. Concerns about job displacement due to increased automation are prompting organizations to rethink their workforce strategies. Reskilling programs designed to equip employees with relevant skills for emerging technologies will be vital in addressing these challenges. Companies committed to ethical practices recognize that fostering a culture of continuous learning is essential for adapting to an ever-evolving landscape.

These emerging trends signal a transformative era for businesses willing to embrace innovation through automation. By integrating advanced technologies into their workflows, companies not only streamline operations but also create pathways for future growth opportunities. As you reflect on how these trends may impact your organization or professional development, consider how adopting these innovations can position you ahead of the curve in an increasingly competitive environment.

Impact of AI and machine learning

The impact of AI and machine learning on automation is profound, fundamentally transforming the way businesses operate. These technologies enable organizations to quickly analyze vast datasets, providing insights that drive real-time decision-making. For example, a financial institution utilizing machine learning algorithms to assess credit risk can predict loan defaults more accurately than traditional methods by examining historical data patterns. This capability enhances risk management and improves customer experiences by streamlining approval processes.

As businesses harness these advanced analytics, they can uncover trends and anomalies that might be difficult to detect manually. In the retail sector, for instance, machine learning models can analyze customer purchasing behaviors and forecast demand for specific products. This information allows retailers to optimize inventory levels—ensuring popular items are well-stocked while minimizing overstock of less popular ones. So, companies achieve greater operational efficiency and heightened customer satisfaction.

The integration of AI in automation goes beyond data analysis; it also promotes intelligent decision-making processes. AI systems can recommend actions based on predictive analytics, guiding employees toward optimal choices. In manufacturing, AI-driven systems monitor equipment performance and automatically suggest maintenance schedules based on usage patterns. This proactive approach reduces downtime and extends the lifespan of machinery, ultimately leading to cost savings.

And, the emergence of intelligent chatbots illustrates how AI enhances customer service capabilities. These bots can autonomously handle common inquiries, allowing human agents to focus on more complex issues. When customers interact with these systems through websites or messaging platforms, they receive instant responses to their queries, resulting in higher satisfaction rates. For organizations, this means reduced operational costs while maintaining high service quality.

However, the deployment of AI and machine learning also presents challenges that organizations must address thoughtfully. Data privacy concerns are significant since these systems require access to large amounts of personal information for training purposes. Companies must implement robust data protection measures to safeguard user information and comply with regulations such as GDPR or CCPA. Striking a balance between innovation and ethical considerations is essential as businesses adopt these technologies.

In addition to privacy issues, there's the risk of algorithmic bias in machine learning models. If the training data reflects existing biases—whether racial, gender-based, or socioeconomic—the outcomes produced by these models may perpetuate discrimination. Take this example, an AI tool used for hiring decisions could inadvertently favor candidates from certain demographics over others due to skewed underlying data. Addressing these biases necessitates continuous evaluation and refinement of algorithms to ensure fairness and equity in decision-making.

To maximize the potential benefits while mitigating risks associated with AI adoption, organizations should cultivate a culture of innovation coupled with responsibility. Emphasizing transparency in AI operations fosters trust among stakeholders and consumers alike. Additionally, companies should invest in ongoing training for their workforce to ensure employees understand how to use these technologies effectively while recognizing their limitations.

As we delve deeper into the intersection of automation and advanced technology within Excel workflows, it's crucial to consider how integrating AI can elevate your automation efforts beyond mere scripting and task management. The potential for increased efficiency and enhanced insights is substantial when leveraged appropriately, positioning you at the forefront of industry innovation.

Looking ahead, developing a comprehensive understanding of how these tools interact with traditional applications like Excel is vital while remaining aware of the ethical implications they introduce into everyday business practices. Embracing this knowledge will not only enhance your proficiency but also prepare you for a future where automation increasingly relies on intelligent technologies.

Innovations in data connectivity

The landscape of data connectivity is undergoing a rapid transformation, fueled by innovations that enhance how we interact with and analyze data. A key development in recent years has been the emergence of cloud-based platforms, which enable real-time access to data and foster collaboration across geographical boundaries. Tools like Microsoft Azure and Google Cloud Platform allow users to link their Excel spreadsheets directly to expansive databases, facilitating dynamic updates and comprehensive analysis without the need for manual input. Take this example, consider a financial analyst who can seamlessly integrate real-time stock market data into their Excel spreadsheets, generating up-to-the-minute reports that accurately reflect current market conditions.

Another significant advancement reshaping our approach to data connectivity is API (Application Programming Interface) integration. APIs facilitate seamless communication between different software applications, allowing users to automate workflows that were once labor-intensive. For example, a marketing team can utilize APIs to automatically retrieve customer insights from social media platforms directly into Excel for analysis. This not only improves the quality of the insights generated but also conserves countless hours that would have otherwise been spent on data extraction. The combination of Python scripts with APIs further streamlines these processes, enabling automated data pulls at designated intervals or triggered by specific events.

In addition to cloud services and APIs, the integration of machine learning models for predictive analytics within Excel represents another exciting trend. Python libraries such as Scikit-learn and TensorFlow are increasingly being incorporated into Excel workflows, empowering users to develop complex models without leaving their familiar environment. Take this example, a sales manager can analyze historical sales data in Excel to forecast future performance using machine learning techniques, thereby enabling proactive decision-making. This evolution transforms Excel from a simple spreadsheet application into a robust analytical tool capable of delivering actionable insights.

Equally noteworthy is the rise of low-code and no-code tools that democratize access to advanced analytics capabilities. Platforms like Microsoft Power Automate allow non-technical users to create automated workflows with minimal coding knowledge. Such innovations empower professionals across various departments—finance, marketing, operations—to leverage data without relying on IT support or requiring extensive training in programming languages.

And, advancements in real-time data processing technologies significantly enhance our ability to analyze streaming data feeds within Excel. Tools such as Apache Kafka or AWS Kinesis enable businesses to ingest large volumes of streaming data and employ Python scripts for near-instantaneous trend analysis. This capability proves particularly valuable in industries like finance or e-commerce, where timely insights can profoundly influence strategy and operations.

Finally, as we integrate diverse sources of data connectivity, prioritizing security innovations is essential. As organizations increasingly depend on external databases and APIs for business intelligence, implementing robust security measures becomes critical. Encryption methods and secure authentication protocols protect sensitive information during transmission and storage. Data governance frameworks also play a vital role in ensuring compliance with regulations like GDPR or CCPA while maintaining accessibility for authorized users.

Collectively, these innovations signify a paradigm shift in how professionals leverage Excel alongside Python for advanced automation tasks. The ability to connect diverse datasets through cutting-edge technologies not only enhances efficiency but also enriches decision-making processes across industries. Embracing these advancements is crucial for any professional striving to remain competitive in today's fast-paced landscape.

The evolving role of Excel in business

The evolving role of Excel in business signifies a profound transformation in how organizations manage, analyze, and extract insights from their data. Once regarded merely as a basic spreadsheet tool for record-keeping and simple calculations, Excel has surpassed its original purpose to become a crucial element within sophisticated data ecosystems. Today, it integrates seamlessly with Python and other advanced technologies, empowering professionals across various sectors.

This transformation is largely driven by Excel's remarkable versatility. Beyond serving as a platform for data storage and manipulation, it acts as a springboard for complex analyses that inform strategic decision-making. The integration with Python enables users to automate repetitive tasks, leverage advanced algorithms, and conduct intricate analyses without needing to switch between different software environments. Take this example, financial analysts can utilize Python libraries to run Monte Carlo simulations directly within Excel, streamlining risk assessments that would have been laborious to perform manually.

And, Excel's capabilities in facilitating real-time data collaboration have further enhanced its relevance in today's fast-paced business environment. With cloud-based services like Microsoft 365, teams can work simultaneously on spreadsheets from various locations, sharing insights and updates instantaneously. Consider a project team dispersed across continents; they can monitor progress and update financial forecasts in real time, avoiding the delays often associated with traditional email exchanges or file versioning issues. This functionality fosters a culture of agility and responsiveness that is essential for success in contemporary business landscapes.

Additionally, the emergence of integrated data visualization tools within Excel has revolutionized how organizations communicate insights. Users can now create dynamic dashboards that incorporate live data streams into visually engaging formats. This capability allows stakeholders to quickly grasp complex information and make informed decisions based on real-time metrics rather than static reports. For example, marketing teams can visualize customer engagement data alongside sales figures in an interactive dashboard that highlights trends and correlations—insights that can drive timely adjustments to campaigns.

However, as Excel's role continues to expand, professionals must navigate several challenges. One significant concern is ensuring data accuracy amid increasing operational complexity and the sheer volume of available information. As organizations integrate multiple data sources—whether through APIs or direct connections to databases—maintaining data integrity becomes paramount. Employing data validation techniques using Python scripts within Excel can help mitigate errors by automating checks against predefined criteria before analysis begins.

The demand for continuous learning has also intensified due to these advancements. Professionals are now expected to combine traditional Excel skills with programming knowledge to fully leverage the synergies between these tools. Training initiatives focused on enhancing Python proficiency among staff will not only improve efficiency but also position them as key players in harnessing data-driven insights for competitive advantage.

As businesses increasingly embrace digital transformation, Excel's evolving role is likely to expand further beyond its current capabilities. Organizations must remain proactive in adopting innovative practices that enhance productivity while fostering a culture of data literacy across all operational levels. By leveraging the full range of features available within Excel alongside powerful programming tools like Python, professionals can transform their datasets into actionable strategies that drive success.

In this landscape of modern business, merely being familiar with software is insufficient; it requires an understanding of how these tools interact within broader technological frameworks. Embracing these changes will not only equip you with essential technical skills but also provide the strategic insight necessary to thrive in an increasingly competitive marketplace.

Preparing for future advancements

Preparing for the future of Excel automation and Python integration requires a proactive approach to anticipating emerging trends and adapting your skills. The data management landscape is constantly evolving, influenced by technological advancements and shifting business needs. To stay competitive, professionals must embrace these changes.

One of the most notable trends on the horizon is the growing integration of artificial intelligence (AI) and machine learning (ML) into Excel workflows. As these technologies become more accessible, the ability to analyze large datasets and extract predictive insights will become increasingly crucial. For example, consider the potential of using Python's powerful libraries, such as Scikit-learn or TensorFlow, directly within Excel to run predictive models. This capability could enable a marketing analyst to forecast customer behavior based on historical data without requiring extensive programming expertise. The implications are significant, as this integration has the power to transform decision-making across various sectors.

Simultaneously, the rise of cloud computing is reshaping collaboration in data analytics. Tools like Microsoft 365 allow for real-time updates and seamless sharing, making teamwork more effective than ever. However, this increased connectivity also presents challenges, particularly regarding data privacy and security, as multiple users access information from different locations. Understanding cloud infrastructure and its impact on data governance is essential for anyone looking to responsibly leverage these advancements.

And, organizations are increasingly prioritizing automation to streamline operations and boost productivity. The trend towards no-code and low-code platforms supports this effort by enabling users with limited technical skills to create custom applications or automate tasks easily. Take this example, integrating Python scripts with platforms like Microsoft Power Automate allows non-programmers to set up workflows that automate repetitive tasks in Excel, such as generating monthly reports or synchronizing data across systems.

To navigate this rapidly changing environment successfully, continuous learning is vital. Engaging in professional development opportunities—such as workshops, online courses, or certifications—not only keeps you updated on new tools but also nurtures an adaptive mindset that embraces innovation. Exploring resources focused on advanced data analytics techniques or AI applications in business can provide you with practical insights that can be directly applied in your organization.

Building a strong professional network can further enhance your readiness for future advancements. Connecting with peers who are exploring similar tools can foster shared learning experiences and collaborative opportunities that keep you ahead of industry trends. Participating in forums or local meetups centered on Python and Excel automation can stimulate discussions about best practices and innovative technology uses that you may not have previously considered.

Lastly, cultivating a mindset of experimentation is crucial for encouraging creativity in problem-solving. Embrace the opportunity to test new techniques or explore unconventional solutions using Python scripts within Excel. Even experimenting with seemingly marginally relevant code snippets can lead to unexpected discoveries about efficiency improvements or features you have yet to utilize.

By thoughtfully preparing for these advancements and strategically embracing change within your skill set, you position yourself at the forefront of an increasingly sophisticated business landscape. The convergence of technologies—such as AI integrations and collaborative cloud-based tools—offers tremendous potential for enhancing productivity and decision-making across industries.

Understanding this dynamic environment equips you not only with essential technical skills but also with the strategic foresight necessary to thrive in an era defined by rapid technological progress. As Python and Excel capabilities continue to expand into previously unimagined realms, those who adapt swiftly will lead the charge toward innovative solutions that shape the future of our data-driven world.

Skills for the next generation of professionals

To thrive in the rapidly evolving landscape of Excel automation and Python integration, professionals must cultivate a broad array of skills that extend beyond mere technical expertise. While mastering Python and its libraries is essential, developing an adaptable mindset focused on continuous learning is equally crucial.

Data literacy stands out as a key skill for the next generation of professionals. Effectively interpreting and analyzing data can distinguish you in a field saturated with technical specialists. This competency transcends simple data manipulation; it involves extracting insights from visualizations and communicating those findings clearly to stakeholders. Take this example, the ability to translate complex analyses into actionable recommendations can significantly enhance your contributions during team discussions or project presentations.

In addition to data literacy, strong collaboration and communication skills are paramount. In our interconnected world, working effectively with diverse roles—such as data analysts, software developers, and business leaders— can spur innovation. Emphasizing cross-functional teamwork helps dismantle silos that often hinder progress. Engaging in projects that involve various perspectives enriches your understanding of how automation affects different departments, empowering you to propose solutions that benefit the entire organization.

Critical thinking is another vital area of development. With the rise of automation, professionals must cultivate the ability to question existing processes and identify opportunities for enhancement. An analytical mindset enables you to evaluate whether current methodologies are efficient or if alternative approaches could conserve time and resources. For example, by comparing a manual reporting process with an automated solution, you can critically assess both options and advocate effectively for adopting new technologies.

Beyond Python and Excel, expanding your technical repertoire is essential. Familiarity with related technologies such as SQL for database management or APIs for software integration can equip you with a comprehensive toolkit. Understanding how these systems interact not only enhances your versatility but also bolsters your capacity to implement end-to-end solutions that streamline workflows across various platforms.

Proficiency in project management principles can also be incredibly advantageous. Automation projects often involve multiple stakeholders and complex timelines; thus, effectively managing these components is key to successful implementation. Familiarizing yourself with methodologies like Agile or Scrum will provide you with the necessary tools to lead projects from conception through execution while remaining flexible enough to adapt as challenges arise.

Perhaps the most significant skill of all is the capacity for lifelong learning. Embracing new technologies and methodologies as they emerge will help you stay relevant in this fast-paced environment. Regularly engaging with online courses, webinars, or industry conferences allows you to keep pace with advancements in both Python programming and Excel automation techniques. Take this example, participating in a workshop on advanced machine learning applications may open avenues for incorporating predictive analytics into your Excel reports.

Finally, fostering creativity will empower you to think outside conventional boundaries when developing automation solutions. Whether brainstorming unique ways to visualize data or experimenting with innovative coding techniques, a creative approach nurtures innovation. Consider exploring open-source projects where collaboration with like-minded individuals can spark fresh ideas and inspire breakthroughs in your own work.

As demand for integrated technological solutions grows, positioning yourself as a well-rounded professional who navigates both technical challenges and interpersonal dynamics will prove invaluable. By investing time in developing these complementary skills alongside your technical knowledge of Python and Excel, you'll be well-prepared not only for current opportunities but also for the uncharted territories that lie ahead in automation. The future looks bright for those who embrace a holistic approach to professional development—one that seamlessly integrates technical acumen with robust communication skills, critical thinking, and an ever-evolving thirst for knowledge.

A vision for seamless integration of Python and Excel

A vision for the seamless integration of Python and Excel starts with an appreciation for the unique strengths each tool offers. Excel is renowned for its data visualization capabilities, valued for its accessibility and widespread adoption in business settings. However, it often faces challenges when managing large datasets and automating complex processes efficiently. In contrast, Python excels at data manipulation, automation, and scalability. By combining the two tools, organizations can transform tedious tasks into efficient operations.

Take, for instance, a finance team responsible for generating monthly reports from various data sources. Traditionally, this task might require hours of manual effort, involving data consolidation, analysis, and presentation. By incorporating Python into their workflow, these professionals can automate repetitive tasks effectively. Utilizing libraries such as Pandas for data manipulation and OpenPyXL for interacting with Excel simplifies the process considerably. A single script can extract data from different formats—like CSV files, databases, or APIs—process it according to predefined rules, and generate an Excel report ready for distribution.

As we delve deeper into this integration, it's crucial to emphasize that collaboration is at its core. The effectiveness of automation increases when stakeholders across departments understand how Python and Excel can work together. For example, a marketing analyst might use Python scripts to automatically pull social media metrics into an Excel dashboard. This not only requires technical knowledge but also effective communication with IT teams that provide access to essential APIs or data pipelines.

Taking a holistic approach involves creating user-friendly interfaces that enable non-technical users to benefit from automation without needing extensive programming skills. Tools like Jupyter Notebooks can serve as interactive platforms where users can execute scripts with minimal input while still leveraging Python's capabilities behind the scenes. This layer of abstraction empowers individuals across various skill levels to engage with their data meaningfully without feeling overwhelmed by underlying complexities.

Looking forward, organizations that prioritize this integration are likely to experience enhanced productivity and improved decision-making capabilities. With real-time data access made possible through automated workflows, teams can concentrate on interpreting insights rather than spending excessive time on data entry or formatting tasks. Additionally, automated reporting reduces the likelihood of human error— an invaluable advantage when accuracy is critical in business operations.

Consider another scenario involving sales forecasting: By developing a machine learning model using Python libraries like Scikit-learn alongside historical sales data stored in Excel, businesses can significantly refine their forecasts. The model could analyze trends based on various factors such as seasonality or market shifts while outputting results directly into an Excel spreadsheet for easy access by sales teams.

However, successful integration of these technologies necessitates careful planning. Ensuring compatibility between Python and Excel data structures is essential; inconsistencies can create barriers that impede productivity instead of enhancing it. Leveraging Python's robust error handling features allows teams to proactively address potential issues before they disrupt workflow.

This vision goes beyond individual projects; it seeks to

foster an organizational culture that embraces automation through training initiatives designed to demystify both Python programming and advanced Excel functions for employees at all levels. By instilling confidence in staff members to utilize these tools collaboratively, organizations cultivate an environment ripe for innovation and continuous improvement.

In the end, envisioning a future where Python and Excel coexist seamlessly requires a commitment—not just to technology but also to nurturing skills that facilitate collaboration across disciplines. As professionals increasingly recognize the potential within these integrated tools, they unlock new avenues for exploration and growth within their roles while contributing to organizational success.

This comprehensive vision inspires not only efficiency but also creativity in problem-solving—encouraging individuals to challenge boundaries and discover innovative ways to enhance operational workflows through technology integration. In doing so, they position themselves as catalysts for change within their fields—an essential role in today's rapidly evolving business landscape where adaptability is crucial for thriving amid constant shifts and advancements.

CONCLUSION

Your journey through "Using Python for Advanced Excel Automation" has provided you with a powerful skill set that goes beyond traditional data management. You now possess a deep understanding of the technical aspects of Python and Excel, along with the ability to apply these tools in practical, real-world situations. As you reflect on your progress, consider the transformative potential you've harnessed to enhance your workflow and make a meaningful impact within your organization.

You've gained the ability to set up your environment, install essential libraries like Pandas and OpenPyXL, and manipulate datasets with confidence. Your knowledge of advanced data manipulation techniques, such as cleaning and merging datasets, empowers you to extract valuable insights from even the most complex data structures. This skill set is more than just technical; it enables you to make informed decisions based on data rather than intuition alone.

Throughout this exploration, automation has been a central theme. You've learned how to streamline repetitive tasks, significantly cutting down on the time spent on manual data entry and analysis. Each automated process you implement brings you closer to greater efficiency, allowing you to concentrate on high-level strategic thinking instead of getting caught up in routine operations. For example, automating reports not only boosts productivity but also reduces the risk of errors that can occur with manual handling.

Integrating Python with Excel elevates your reporting

capabilities to a new level of sophistication. By utilizing libraries like XlsxWriter and mastering dynamic dashboards, you can create comprehensive visualizations that resonate with stakeholders across various departments. These insights not only enhance collaboration but also support informed decision-making—qualities that are invaluable in any business setting.

As you've explored concepts such as database connectivity and web scraping, you've broadened your skill set to gather and analyze data from diverse sources. The combination of Python's flexibility and Excel's user-friendly interface empowers you to tackle challenges ranging from sales forecasting to financial modeling with ease. This versatility is essential in today's data-driven landscape, where organizations must adapt quickly to changing conditions.

Your learning journey doesn't end here; consider this guide a foundation for further growth. Embrace continuous improvement by seeking out new challenges that push your boundaries. Explore additional libraries, delve into machine learning applications, or investigate how AI can be integrated into your workflows. The skills you've developed here are stepping stones toward mastering even more advanced techniques.

As you navigate your professional landscape equipped with these tools, remember the importance of collaboration. Share your knowledge with peers and teach them how Python can simplify their tasks as well. By fostering a culture of learning within your organization, you are not only enhancing your career but also paving the way for collective growth and innovation.

In this rapidly evolving field where technology continually reshapes roles and responsibilities, staying curious will serve you well. Keep an eye on emerging trends in automation technologies and be ready to embrace them as they arise.

Your proactive approach will position you as a leader in transforming workflows within your team or organization.

In the end, the future is bright for those willing to integrate these powerful tools into their daily practices. You have not only acquired practical skills but also developed a mindset focused on leveraging technology for operational excellence. Embrace this momentum and let it propel you toward new opportunities where creativity meets efficiency.

As you close this book, let it serve as a constant reminder of the possibilities that arise when ambition meets action. You are equipped not just with knowledge but also with a vision—one where automation transforms tedious tasks into streamlined processes that drive success forward. Embrace this vision wholeheartedly as you advance in your career; it is yours for the taking.

- **Recap of key learnings**

As you reflect on your journey through "Using Python for Advanced Excel Automation," you've cultivated a wealth of knowledge that empowers you to tackle complex data tasks with confidence. Each chapter has uniquely contributed to your understanding, starting from the foundational aspects of Python and Excel and advancing toward sophisticated automation techniques.

Your exploration began by establishing a strong foundation, where you set up your Python environment and became acquainted with essential libraries such as Pandas, OpenPyXL, and XlsxWriter. These tools are crucial not only for managing data but also for automating repetitive tasks, enabling you to manipulate Excel files programmatically and handle large datasets with ease.

From there, you ventured into advanced data manipulation. You immersed yourself in DataFrames, mastering the skills of cleaning and transforming data until they became second nature. Techniques for filtering, sorting, and aggregating data have enriched your analytical capabilities, allowing you to extract actionable insights that inform decision-making processes.

The introduction of XlsxWriter further refined your skill set by allowing you to create visually appealing charts and implement conditional formatting techniques. With these new skills, you're equipped to present data in ways that resonate with stakeholders, significantly enhancing the clarity and impact of your findings.

Your exploration extended beyond Excel's boundaries when you integrated Python with Excel VBA. This hybrid approach showcased how both languages can complement one another's strengths. By understanding how to call Python scripts from VBA, you've broadened your ability to automate workflows seamlessly. This interoperability enables you to leverage existing VBA projects while harnessing Python's powerful data manipulation capabilities.

You also delved into database connectivity, which illuminated the process of accessing external data sources directly from your Python scripts. Learning how to retrieve and write back data from SQL databases is crucial for automating reports based on real-time updates. This capability allows you to create comprehensive reporting solutions that can quickly adapt to changing business needs.

And, mastering web scraping techniques has equipped you with the tools needed to extract valuable information from online sources. In today's data-driven world, the ability to gather timely information can significantly influence strategic decision-making. Your newfound skills ensure that the data collected is clean and ready for analysis.

Data visualization is another critical area where you've made significant strides. By learning how to utilize libraries like Matplotlib and Seaborn alongside Excel, you've enhanced your capacity to communicate insights visually. Focusing on storytelling through data transforms raw numbers into compelling narratives that engage stakeholders effectively.

As you consider the array of skills you've acquired— from scripting and automation to advanced analytics— this journey transcends mere technical mastery. It's about fostering a mindset geared toward continuous improvement and innovation within your organization. The practical applications of these concepts encourage collaboration, enabling you not only to boost your productivity but also to inspire those around you.

In summary, this book has provided a comprehensive framework for integrating Python into your daily workflow with Excel, unlocking efficiencies previously thought unattainable. You've gained the ability to automate complex tasks, visualize data effectively, and present information in compelling ways—all essential skills in today's fast-paced work environment.

Armed with this knowledge, you're now positioned not merely as a user but as a thought leader within your organization— someone who leverages technology for operational excellence and drives change through innovation. Continue this journey of learning and experimentation; the powerful tools at your disposal are invaluable allies in achieving even greater heights in your professional endeavors.

- **Looking beyond Excel: expanding automation skills**

Your journey through "Using Python for Advanced Excel Automation" has equipped you with a powerful set of skills aimed at boosting efficiency and fostering innovation in your work. However, as data management and analysis continue to evolve, it's essential to adapt your approach to automation. While Excel remains a robust tool, the pursuit of greater efficiency and sophistication encourages you to explore additional avenues for automation beyond its familiar boundaries.

Consider expanding your toolkit to include a broader ecosystem of data manipulation, which encompasses powerful programming languages and frameworks. For example, learning R can significantly enhance your statistical capabilities. While Python excels in general-purpose programming and automation tasks, R is particularly effective for specialized statistical analysis and visualizations. By combining these two languages, you can harness their respective strengths based on the requirements of each project. Imagine a seamless workflow where Python scripts automate data extraction from databases, while R scripts conduct complex statistical analyses—resulting in a comprehensive approach to data handling.

Next, delve into SQL (Structured Query Language). Mastering SQL not only complements your Python skills but also enables you to manipulate large datasets directly within databases. Gaining proficiency in querying, updating, and managing database records can dramatically reduce the time spent on data retrieval. This expertise allows you to automate tasks that previously relied on manual data entry or manipulation in Excel, minimizing errors and freeing up your time for more in-depth analysis.

Additionally, consider exploring cloud computing platforms like AWS or Google Cloud. These platforms offer a range of tools designed for scalability and efficiency. By learning how to leverage cloud services such as AWS Lambda or Google Cloud Functions, you can automate workflows that integrate various services beyond Excel. Take this example, imagine automating the retrieval of daily sales data from an online database and generating reports that are sent directly via email—all executed without manual intervention.

Incorporating machine learning techniques into your skill set can further expand your analytical capabilities. Python libraries like Scikit-learn provide user-friendly interfaces for implementing machine learning algorithms that predict trends based on historical data. By automating these predictions as part of your reporting process, you enhance the insights you provide and position yourself as a forward-thinking professional who leverages advanced analytics to drive decision-making.

Exploring tools specifically designed for task automation —such as Apache Airflow or Zapier—can also streamline repetitive processes across various applications beyond Excel. These tools enable you to create workflows that trigger actions based on specific events or conditions, integrating multiple platforms seamlessly. For example, envision a workflow that automatically pulls data from an API every week, processes it with Python scripts, and updates your Excel reports—all without daily oversight.

As you look beyond Excel, don't overlook the importance of soft skills in driving change within any organization. Effective communication about these advanced automation solutions will empower you to advocate for their adoption among colleagues and leadership. Consider developing presentations that highlight success stories from your automation projects —demonstrating not only what was achieved but also how it positively impacted productivity and accuracy within your team.

Engaging with communities focused on automation can also provide inspiration and insight into new methodologies or tools. Online forums, webinars, and local meetups are excellent venues for exchanging ideas and learning about emerging trends in automation technology. Building a network of peers who share similar interests fosters collaboration while keeping you informed about innovations that could further enhance your work.

Finally, maintain a curious and experimental mindset when

it comes to automation. The technological landscape is constantly evolving, with new tools emerging regularly that can offer even more streamlined ways to handle tasks. Embrace continuous learning—whether through online courses, tutorials, or hands-on projects—to stay ahead in this dynamic field.

By expanding your automation skills beyond Excel, you transition from being merely an efficient user to becoming a versatile problem-solver capable of navigating diverse challenges across different domains. As you embark on this broader journey of possibilities, remember that every step taken toward mastering new tools is an investment not just in personal growth but also in enhancing operational excellence within your organization. Your adventure has only just begun; countless opportunities await as you strive to become an innovator in automation.

- **Final thoughts and resources for further learning**

The journey through "Using Python for Advanced Excel Automation" has been transformative, equipping you with valuable skills that significantly enhance your data analysis capabilities. As you reflect on the concepts explored and the tools mastered, it's important to recognize that this learning experience marks just the beginning. The realm of automation is vast, and embracing continuous improvement is essential for maintaining relevance and efficiency.

To further enrich your understanding, consider exploring online platforms such as Coursera or edX. These sites offer specialized courses focused on both Python programming and advanced Excel techniques. Often led by expert instructors with real-world experience, these courses bridge the gap between theory and practical application. Engaging with these resources allows you to deepen your knowledge in specific areas—like data visualization or machine learning—while also exposing you to contemporary practices that can enhance your skill set.

Books also serve as invaluable resources for expanding your expertise. Titles like "Python for Data Analysis" by Wes McKinney and "Automate the Boring Stuff with Python" by Al Sweigart provide practical insights into effectively using Python for data tasks. These books not only cover foundational concepts but also include real-life scenarios and projects that reinforce learning through hands-on experience. The practical examples presented can inspire you to undertake similar initiatives in your own work environment.

Engaging with online communities can significantly accelerate your learning process. Platforms like Stack Overflow and GitHub provide forums where you can ask questions, share solutions, and collaborate with others who share your passion for automation and programming. Participating in these discussions fosters a sense of belonging while exposing you to diverse perspectives on tackling challenges. You might discover new methodologies or best practices that could enhance your automation strategies.

Attending workshops or conferences dedicated to data analytics and automation offers valuable networking opportunities that can lead to professional growth. These events often feature talks from industry leaders who share insights into emerging trends, tools, and case studies demonstrating successful automation implementations. Interacting with peers facing similar challenges not only fosters collaboration but also sparks innovative ideas you may not have previously considered.

Incorporating project-based learning into your routine can solidify your understanding of advanced Excel automation concepts. Identify a project within your workplace where automation could save time or reduce errors; use it as a testing ground for the skills you've acquired. Documenting this process will reinforce what you've learned while positioning you as an innovator within your organization.

Finally, adopting a mindset of lifelong learning will serve you well as technology continues to evolve at an unprecedented pace. Stay curious about new tools, techniques, and languages emerging in the fields of automation and data analysis. Engaging in continuous education—whether through formal courses or self-directed study—will equip you with the adaptability needed to thrive in an ever-changing landscape.

By integrating these resources into your ongoing education plan, you're not just reinforcing what you've learned; you're actively expanding upon it. This proactive approach transforms you from a user of Python for Excel automation into a knowledgeable professional capable of leading initiatives within your organization. Embrace the complexity of this field; each new skill gained is a step toward becoming an authoritative figure in data-driven decision-making processes.

Your future endeavors will be shaped by how effectively you leverage these tools, resources, and connections cultivated throughout this journey. Keep pushing boundaries and exploring innovative solutions; every challenge presents an opportunity for growth—a pathway to becoming an expert not only in Excel automation but also across the broader spectrum of data analytics.

- **Encouragement to experiment and innovate**

Reflect on the skills you've developed throughout this book and consider how you can apply them creatively in your own projects. Is there a part of your current workflow that feels cumbersome or outdated? Identify that pain point and brainstorm how Python could streamline or enhance it. By addressing real-world challenges using the solutions you've learned, you're not just practicing automation; you're transforming the way you work.

Imagine leveraging libraries like Pandas or OpenPyXL in

innovative ways. Take this example, think about creating a unique dashboard that visualizes key performance indicators in real-time using data from multiple Excel files. Projects like this push the boundaries of what you can achieve with Python while deepening your understanding of both Excel and programming concepts. The more ambitious your projects become, the richer your learning experience will be.

Don't hesitate to share your experiments with peers or online communities. Engaging with others fosters a vibrant exchange of ideas that can lead to unexpected insights and improvements. You might discover a technique someone else used to solve a challenge similar to yours or even find collaborators who share your passion for advancing automation skills.

Innovation often springs from a playful exploration of possibilities without the fear of failure. Reflect on Alex's journey—there were moments of uncertainty alongside instances of serendipity, where unexpected solutions emerged through trial and error. Give yourself permission to tinker with different approaches in your scripts or explore new libraries outside your usual toolkit. Even if an idea doesn't pan out initially, you'll gain valuable insights into what works and what doesn't fit within your workflow.

As you delve further into experimentation, remember that documentation is crucial. Keep track of what succeeds and what falls short; these notes will be invaluable as you refine your techniques over time. Creating a repository of code snippets, functions, and scripts can serve as a personal knowledge base for future reference—acting both as an archive of progress and a source of inspiration when facing new challenges.

Finally, maintain an adaptable mindset. The landscape of technology and data management is ever-changing, so being open to learning about emerging tools or methodologies will keep you at the forefront of advancements in automation—a vital trait for anyone looking to drive efficiency within their organization.

Experimentation and innovation are not just buzzwords; they embody the essence of growth in any technical field. As you step into this dynamic world armed with newfound skills, continue pushing boundaries—question assumptions, seek creative solutions, and embrace challenges as they arise. Each experience will deepen your understanding and empower you to forge unique pathways within Excel automation that align with both personal aspirations and professional goals.

Your journey doesn't end here; it's only just begun! Embrace every opportunity to innovate as another stepping stone toward becoming an expert capable of effectively navigating complexities in data-driven decision-making processes.

www.ingramcontent.com/pod-product-compliance
Lightning Source LLC
LaVergne TN
LVHW051220050326
832903LV00028B/2173